Chronology of
The Political Broadcast Act of 1970

FLOW CHART NUMBER	EVENT	DATE(S)
1a	Introduction of H.R. 13721	Sept. 10, 1969
1b	Introduction of S.2876	Sept. 10, 1969
2	Hearings before the Communications Subcommittee of the Senate Commerce Committee	Oct. 21–23, 1969
3	A "clean" bill, S.3637, is reported out of committee	March 25, 1970
4	Debate, amendment and vote (50–35) on S.3637	April 13–14, 1970
5	S.3637 is sent to the House, where it is referred to the Interstate and Foreign Commerce Committee	April 15, 1970
6	Hearings before the Communications and Power Subcommittee	June 2–4, 1970
7	A "clean" bill, H.R.18434, is reported out of committee	July 29, 1970
8	A hearing for a special order is held before the House Rules Committee	August 4, 1970
9	The special order, H.Res.1177, is reported out of committee	August 10, 1970
10	Debate and vote (273–98) on H.R.18434	August 11, 1970
11	Conference committee meets	August 12–13, 1970
12	Conference committee compromise is reached	August 13, 1970
13	Conference report is filed	August 13, 1970
14	The House debates and approves the conference report (247–112)	Sept. 16, 1970
15	The Senate debates and approves the conference report (60–19)	Sept. 23, 1970
16	The enrolled copy of S.3637 is signed by the Speaker of the House and the President Pro Tempore of the Senate	Sept. 24–29, 1970
17	The enrolled copy of S.3637 is received at the White House	Sept. 30, 1970
18	Formal executive review of S.3637 begins	Sept. 30–Oct. 1, 1970
19	The President vetoes	Oct. 12, 1970
20	The Senate debates and fails to override the President's veto by the necessary two-thirds vote (58–34)	Nov. 23, 1970

"What Do You Think You're Gonna Do, Shorty?"

TO ENACT A LAW: CONGRESS AND CAMPAIGN FINANCING

Robert L. Peabody, Jeffrey M. Berry,
William G. Frasure, and Jerry Goldman

PRAEGER PUBLISHERS
New York • Washington • London

PRAEGER PUBLISHERS
111 Fourth Avenue, New York, N.Y. 10003, U.S.A.
5, Cromwell Place, London SW7 2JL, England

Published in the United States of America in 1972
by Praeger Publishers, Inc.

Dee. 12, 1972

Library of Congress Catalog Card Number: 73–160477

Printed in the United States of America

To
Judy, Lori, Bonnie, and Eve

CONTENTS

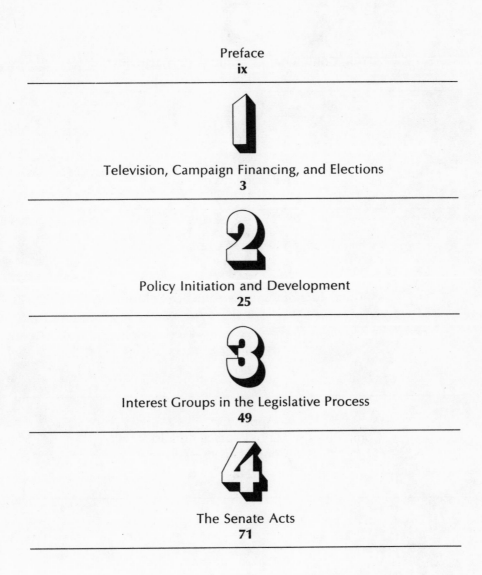

Preface

Writing a preface to a book is both difficult and satisfying. It is difficult because the main purpose of a preface is to present the book's underlying rationale. It is satisfying because this portion is almost always the last part of the book to be written. The long travail—one part creativity, four or five parts plain hard work—is about to end. Indebtedness to the many others who make a book possible can also be acknowledged, and this too is satisfying.

This collaborative effort began with a legislative-process class at The Johns Hopkins University during the academic year 1970–71. When the time came to cover the routine procedures by which a bill becomes a law, an attempt was made to simulate the process through role playing. One student became a congressman; another, his legislative assistant; still a third, a subcommittee chairman; and so on. While a good time was had by almost all (including the instructor relieved of formal lectures), later critiques pointed out one glaring shortcoming—lack of a substantive content to make the role playing truly meaningful and instructive.

Several course participants suggested an alternative. Why not write a short, introductory text, replete with copies of actual documents, that would both illustrate the process and provide the substance? After we had considered several other policy areas and specific bills, the subject of campaign finance reforms and the Political Broadcast Act of 1970 seemed most appropriate to the requirements of such a book.

The process of lawmaking in the United States Congress possesses a number of features that an introductory approach to that process ought to illuminate. Some familiarity with formal procedural rules of Congress is necessary simply in order to make sense of events as they transpire on the floors of the two chambers. Most observers of Congress would agree, however, that an understanding of the formalized aspects of the legislative process does not provide an understanding of how the House and Senate "really" work. Thus, a broader explanation of the legislative process requires a knowledge of the role of party leadership and congressional committees, of the relations between Congress and the executive branch, of the activities of interest groups and the degree of constituency pressures, and, not least, of the impact of personalities on the congressmen themselves. Finally, and perhaps most essentially, the various features of the legislative process should be understood within the context of American electoral politics, interparty competition, and intraparty rivalry.

To explain these characteristics of the legislative process and to illustrate the interplay among them, we have chosen the medium of a case study of a single bill—the Political Broadcast Act of 1970. This legislation's history had a rich measure of committee activities, parliamentary maneuvering, bargaining, and compromise. Interest group involvement, while not as great as is sometimes the case, was substantial and relatively easy to identify. Particularly advantageous, for purposes of explaining relations between Congress and the executive, is the fact that the bill was vetoed. And most important, the issues that the bill confronts are current, are critical for the American political system, and can be appreciated with only a modicum of special knowledge. Indeed, as will soon become apparent, a particular feature of campaign finance reform is that every member of Congress considers himself an expert. After all, each member has run for national office, financed his own campaign, and *won*.

First and foremost, this book was written to explain how a bill becomes or fails to become a law. The reader is taken step by step through the legislative process. What is the genesis of a bill? Who sponsors and who opposes it? What happens to the legislation in subcommittee, in committee, and on the floor? If a bill secures majorities in both the House and the Senate, will they hold up in conference committee? Finally, what role do the President and his executive branch confidants play in the success or defeat of legislation? At every state of the legislative process, we have tried to portray the complexities without getting excessively bogged down in parliamentary technicalities. We have attempted to capture the subtleties without losing sight of the end purposes behind campaign reform.

Each chapter includes a number of documents—copies of the bill, letters from interest groups, committee reports, excerpts from the *Congressional Record*, the President's veto message—which attempt to capture some of the reality of a legislative struggle. Students (and even instructors) are urged to read these documents carefully. A single provision in a bill can sometimes make, more often break, the bill's chances of becoming a law. In the Political Broadcast Act of 1970, a great deal of controversy centered upon the effective date of the legislation. Would it go into effect before or after the November, 1970, midterm elections?

This bill did not become a law. But the forces agitating for change, both inside and outside of Congress, are still active. Indeed, the drives for major campaign finance reform have escalated exponentially in the 92d Congress. These developments are discussed at some length in the Epilogue.

This book could not have been written without the assistance of many people. A number of Congressmen gave willingly of their time and special insights, among them, John B. Anderson, James T. Broyhill, Robert F. Drinan, Thomas S. Foley, Wayne L. Hays, Dan Rostenkowski, William L. Springer, Morris K. Udall, and Lionel Van Deerlin. Senators Phillip A. Hart, Charles McC. Mathias, Jr., John O. Pastore, and Hugh Scott were especially cooperative.

Among the many congressional staff members who gave us the benefit of their competence and understanding we would like to single out Richard J. Agnich, Robert G. Allett, Emory S. Arrington, John E. Barriere, Lewis E. Berry, Jr., Terry Bracy, Margaret Culhane, Ken Davis, Edythe Edwards, Mary Spencer Forrest, Leslie E. Gerwin, Robert F. Guthrie, James C. Healey, Jr., Gary G. Hymel, Robert D. Hynes, Jr., John H. McLaren, Paul Malloy, Linda Melconian, Robert R. Nordhaus, Darrell St. Claire, Harry M. Shooshan, David Stockman, Nicholas Zapple, and, last but not least, several House and Senate aides who prefer to remain anonymous.

Our greatest debt is to Susan Bennett King and Russell D. Hemenway, the Washington and national directors of the National Committee for an Effective Congress. Very early in our research, they provided us with abundant access both to NCEC files and to their strategic thinking. In an attempt to make our case study as objective as possible, we may have sometimes erred on the side of minimizing the substantial and continuing contribution NCEC has made to the fight for campaign finance reform.

Many other participants and observers also contributed a great deal to our understanding. Among media experts we would especially like to thank Jon Bednarik, Josh Kane, Charles Kinsolving, and Robert Squier. Without the comprehensive coverage of such reporters as Neal Gregory, Jerry Landauer, Don Oberdorfer, Robert Walters, and Warren Weaver, the full story of the Political Broadcast Act of 1970 would have been much more difficult to piece together. In addition, we would like to express our appreciation to William L. Gifford and Richard P. Nathan for shared insights on congressional liaison activities, as well as for their arrangement of several White House "background" interviews.

Several of our colleagues, especially Milton C. Cummings, Jr., and

J. Woodford Howard, offered inspiration and critical guidance at key junctures in the book's development.

Evelyn Scheulen helped with the prospectus and initial outlines of the book. Kate Madison not only typed the first and revised drafts, she also aided in making the manuscript more readable. In Marian Wood, we realized even more than our initially high expectations—an editor who combined high intellect, substantive competence, and charm.

No doubt we have made some errors of omission or commission. For these we accept full blame. May we have the opportunity to correct them in a second edition.

R.L.P.
J.M.B.
W.G.F.
J.G.

Baltimore, Maryland
December, 1971

TO ENACT A LAW: CONGRESS AND CAMPAIGN FINANCING

Television,
Campaign Financing,
and Elections

On October 12, 1970, President Richard M. Nixon overturned two years of Congressional activity on campaign finance reform by vetoing S.3637, the Political Broadcast Act of 1970. The primary purpose of this legislation was to reduce the costs of major American election campaigns by setting limits on how much individual candidates could spend on radio and television broadcasting. Initially, the bill would have applied only to candidates for the Presidency, the Vice-Presidency, the Senate, and the House of Representatives, and, on the state level, to Governors and Lieutenant Governors. S.3637 would also have relieved broadcasters of the requirement that they offer equal time to every Presidential candidate, no matter how insignificant his candidacy or how remote his chance of winning. Unless the President's veto could be overridden by a two-thirds vote of both the Senate and the House of Representatives, the Political Broadcast Act would not become a law.

For President Nixon, S.3637 was a "good aim, gone amiss."

Nearly everyone who is active or interested in the political process wants to find some way to limit the crushing and growing cost of political campaigning. But this legislation is worse than no answer to the problem—it is a wrong answer.[1]

Critics both within and outside Congress were quick to label the President's action, if not his rhetoric, crassly partisan. His opponents charged that he favored no bill at all rather than partial legislation because he preferred the status quo to campaign finance reform, and they found support for such charges in the fact that, in 1968 and 1970, Republicans were raising and spending about twice as much campaign money as Democrats. Whatever the President's reasons, some six weeks after his veto, following the November, 1970, midterm election recess, the Senate was to fall four votes short of the necessary two-thirds needed to override. For the time being, the President's view had prevailed.

This book has two major objectives: first, to introduce the student to the process of how a bill becomes or fails to become a law and, second, to shed light on the thorny, complex, and vital problem of campaign finance reform. Why is it, if "nearly everyone," in President Nixon's words, "wants to find some way to limit the crushing and growing cost of political campaigning," that no solution was found in the 1960's and prospects are only moderately bright in the 1970's? Our primary vehicle for accomplishing both objectives is

[1] President Richard Nixon, Veto Message accompanying S.3637 (see Document 7–3, Chap. 7), Oct. 12, 1970.

a stage-by-stage analysis of how the Political Broadcast Act of 1970 was introduced, passed in both Houses, survived a stormy conference committee, but succumbed to the Presidential veto.

TELEVISION AND POLITICAL CAMPAIGNING

Attempts to pass the Political Broadcast Act of 1970 were the outgrowth of a growing concern among American public officials, interest groups, the mass media, and private citizens over the use and possible abuse of television for political campaign purposes. The issue is not simply one of uneasiness about the spiraling costs of running for elective office, costs closely associated with the expanding use of television "spot" commercials. Critics are also worried about the impact and quality of campaign presentation. If democracies are dependent upon an informed and balanced electorate, then the practice of "selling a candidate like a bar of soap" and the danger of voters reacting to the image of a candidate rather than to the soundness of his proposals are further reasons for apprehension. Finally, campaign finance reform must take into account the old saw "he who pays the piper calls the tune." Money and politics have always been inextricably interrelated, but the restrictive cost of television campaigning threatens to make politics even more of a rich man's game.

The costs of running for public office have more than doubled in the past decade. Almost 75 per cent of the members of the U.S. Senate spent over $100,000 in their last campaign; more than 40 per cent spent over $200,000. In the largest, most populous states like New York and California, it can cost more than a million dollars *just to lose* a Senate primary. Don Oberdorfer, a *Washington Post* staff writer, details some of the finance problems and strategic decisions confronting would-be Senators; in this case, his subject is the controversial 1970 Tennessee senatorial campaign. [*Doc. 1-1*]

Television: Increasing Use, Spiraling Costs

In 1952, television figured for the first time as a significant factor in a Presidential election. Since that year, it has become by far the most important means by which candidates for high office seek to reach and influence voters. A study on political spending, issued by the Citizens' Research Foundation, reveals that for all political contests in 1968, $58.9 million was spent on radio and television as against only about $20 million for newspapers.[2] A Federal Communications Commission study has shown that the real costs of radio and television time for the 1968 Presidential election were about 50 per cent higher than the official totals reported by the two major-party candidates. The Republican Presidential ticket of Nixon-Agnew reported over $9 million, but the FCC report shows that the local stations and networks billed the GOP $12.6 million in 1968. The Democratic ticket of Humphrey-Muskie reported spending $4.2 million, but the total billings as reported by the FCC were closer to $6.1 million.

The differences between reported spendings and actual billings are not necessarily due to dishonesty or a failure to account for actual broadcasting costs. Rather, they point up still another tricky problem in campaign finance reform: *The differences reflect money spent by independent supporters of the two major candidates for broadcasts that were not under major-party sponsorship or control.* In other words, these were individual or local groups either acting on their own initiative or purposely set up to avoid reporting limitations. Fully one-third of all money spent on political broadcast advertising is spent not by the candidates themselves but by independent committees and individuals. Often they operate with the knowledge and consent of the national party candidates. Legislation to limit expenditures must somehow incorporate this "outside spending" without denying these individuals their right of free expression.

The total costs of general election campaigns for federal office (President, Senate, and House of Representatives) have more than tripled since 1952. From about $23 million in that year, the amount spent in general election campaigns for all federal offices increased steadily until, in 1968, it was more than $70 million. Of this increase, the greatest part is accounted for by broadcast spending, which amounted to over $40 million in 1968. In 1960, when total campaign costs for federal offices were about $33 million, the amount spent on broadcasting in the general election was a little more than $14 million. By 1968, spending for broadcasting in the general elections exceeded the 1960 figure by an amount greater than the *total costs* of the 1952 general elections. In terms of *reported* expenditures, broadcasting amounted to 57 per cent of the general election campaign costs in 1968, compared with 42 per cent in 1960.

The figures just cited reflect only the reported amounts spent in general elections; hence, they do not fully represent the true costs of election campaigning in America. The laws governing the reporting of

[2] Data on campaign costs are taken from Herbert E. Alexander, *Financing the 1968 Election* (Lexington, Mass.: Heath Lexington Books, 1971); *Congressional Quarterly Weekly Report*, vol. 27, no. 49 (Dec. 5, 1969); and Federal Communications Commission, *Survey of Political Broadcasting* (1969).

DOCUMENT **1-1**: A Rich Man's Game

Rival Image Makers Clash in Tennessee

By Don Oberdorfer
Washington Post Staff Writer

NASHVILLE, Tenn.— In April, 1969, a young man from Oshkosh, Wis., who never before had set foot in this state, arrived to plan the election of a United States Senator from Tennessee.

Acting as a paid campaign consultant, Kenneth C. Rietz, 27, traveled the state for two weeks and drew up a 64-page election plan for his client, Rep. William E. Brock of Chattanooga. The plan included details of campaign strategy and organization, and a schedule of events from June, 1969, to the final television-radio-newspaper media blitz in the last 12 days before the November, 1970, election.

Brock approved the plan and hired Rietz for a fee "close to" $40,000. During the next 19 months, the candidate took the advice and advertising spots and layouts he was given by Rietz and his senior partner, image-maker Harry Treleaven. Their campaign succeeded. Brock won.

The senatorial race this year was between incumbent Democrat Albert Gore and Republican William Brock. But it was also a race between rival image-makers, media coordinators and advertising agencies, all working for big money in by far the costliest senatorial race in the state's history.

Gore forces collected and spent over $500,000 in this year's primary and general elections—more than five times as much as in either of Gore's 1958 or 1964 campaigns for re-election. Of this year's spending, about $235,000 went for television and radio time, including advertising agency and image-maker's commissions, and $83,000 more went as a fee to Charles Guggenheim of Washington, D.C., who created the Gore electronic commercials.

According to data collected by The Washington Post from major TV stations, Gore slightly outspent Brock, $53,089 to $50,260, on Nashville television in the general election. However, Gore spent less than Brock, $31,-010 to $42,943, in general election television in Memphis, the state's other big market. Brock was the top spender in East Tennessee, his home area.

Gore declined to be interviewed about details of his 1970 campaign. Aides said, however, that more than $100,000 in campaign contributions came from labor unions. According to union political reports, the United Auto Workers paid $5,-252 for Gore bumper stickers and the AFL-CIO's Committee on Political Education spent $3,014 for Gore leaflets. Major money contributions came from political funds associated with 19 national unions ranging from carpenters to retail clerks.

Gore also received $70,000 from the anti-war "1970 Campaign Fund," $25,000 from the National Committee for an Effective Congress and $20,625 from the Senate Democratic Campaign Committee.

Gore campaign workers say they were strapped for funds throughout.

Brock's spending of $1 million to $1.25 million is at least three to

Doc. 1-1 *(cont.)*

four times the largest sum previously spent by a Republican candidate in the history of the state.

Brock aides admit to $250,000 for television time and agency fees, $75,000 on radio, $50,-000 to Treleaven for TV-radio production, $150,000 for billboards, $75,000 for newspaper ads, $50,000 for leaflets, bumper stickers and such, $100,000 to $150,000 in paid workers and headquarters overhead, and $200,000 in other expenses.

Senatorial candidates are not required by Tennessee law to report the sources of their campaign funds.

Brock, the heir to a candy company fortune, said he did not spend any of his personal money on the race. "I have no idea where the money came from and I don't want to know," he said. Nashville insurance executive David K. Wilson, the Brock finance chairman, said, "There was very little in the way of records, and I imagine most of them have already been flushed."

Capitol Hill filings by money-giving committees provide only a few details of Brock's finances. Contributions which show up there include $10,000 from "Committee for Action —South," a group of general contractors; $10,000 from "Volunteers for Better Government," executives and officials of the big Eastman Kodak chemical works at Kingsport, Tenn.; $5,000 from Trust for Special Political Agricultural Community Education of Louisville, Ky. (milk producers); $35,000 from the Republican Booster Fund and $12,-770 from the Senate Republican Campaign Committee.

Brock said in an interview that the quantum jump in campaign spending poses "a danger" to the political system and declared that "we desperately need a revision of laws about campaign fund reporting." However, he described the attempt to limit campaign broadcast spending as "garbage" and said that "a guy who is inordinately wealthy or who is getting contributions from unfortunate sources might simply shift to other types of spending" if a TV-radio limit is enacted.

---

campaign expenditures are replete with loopholes and are poorly enforced. For example, the Federal Corrupt Practices Act of 1925 established a requirement that candidates and political committees file reports to Congress on their contributions and expenditures. No report was required, however, of committees operating within a single state. Thus, through the use of multiple committees, candidates could easily avoid disclosing their campaign costs and the names of those who helped to pay them. Indeed, in recent Congressional elections, more than one-fourth of House incumbents did not even bother to file a report. The weakness of the reporting laws means that it simply is not possible to know how much money is actually spent on political campaigning.

Equally important, these figures do not include spending in the primaries. The laws do not require that expenditures for primary election campaigns be reported at all. In states so completely dominated by one party that candidates of that party are virtually certain to be elected, the primary elections are the most important part of the election process. Even in two-party states and in campaigns for the Presidential nomination, vast amounts of money are spent on primaries. In contrast to general elections, Democrats have outspent Republicans in recent primary campaigns by better than two to one.

Television's use in primary campaigns, particularly Presidential primaries, is almost as significant as its use in general elections. More than twenty states now sponsor such contests. In most Presidential primaries, the candidates are running in states where they may not be well known. Thus, given the relatively short campaign period, television presents the quickest and most effective means for a Presidential aspirant to make his name familiar to a wide audience. In 1968, when more than $14.5 million was spent on television time in the general Presidential election, more than $6 million was spent on television time in the Presidential primaries.[3]

Finally, the television expenditures we have been quoting are merely "time costs." They do not include expenditures for the services and advice of specialists in film technology and televised image-building. The inclusion of the expense of hiring specialists and the costs of producing the spot advertisements and other presentations used on the airwaves would increase by a third or more the total reported costs of television campaigning.

The skyrocketing of campaign costs since 1952 is most strikingly illustrated in a chart prepared for the Twentieth Century Fund by its Commission on Campaign Costs in the Electronic Era. While covering all costs, the precipitous rise since 1952 is mainly attributable to media expenditures, especially those for television. [Doc. 1-2]

Television: Is the Medium the Message?

Television's impact as a campaign medium can be as powerful as it is expensive. Senator John F. Kennedy's bid for the Presidency in 1960 received a major impetus from his showing in the first Kennedy-Nixon television debate. Senator Edmund Muskie's poll ratings as the leading contender for the 1972 Democratic nomination leaped 7 percentage points after his eve-of-the-election television response to President Nixon in November, 1970. Concern over television's use, for better or for worse, is directly related to some basic

[3] FCC, *Survey of Political Broadcasting.*

DOCUMENT **1-2**: The Spiraling Costs

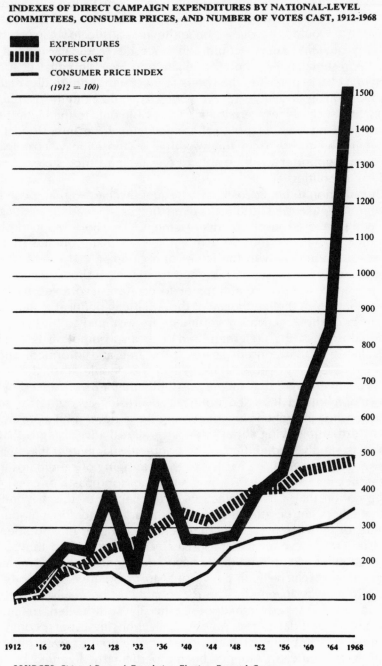

INDEXES OF DIRECT CAMPAIGN EXPENDITURES BY NATIONAL-LEVEL COMMITTEES, CONSUMER PRICES, AND NUMBER OF VOTES CAST, 1912-1968

■ EXPENDITURES
|||||| VOTES CAST
— CONSUMER PRICE INDEX
(1912 = 100)

SOURCES: Citizens' Research Foundation, Elections Research Center, Bureau of Labor Statistics.

considerations about the responsiveness and quality of the American political system.

The problem of television in politics is fundamentally one of fairness. The high cost of television time results in a substantial advantage to the candidate who is in a position to buy more time than his opponents. It would, of course, be quite unrealistic to believe that any legally qualified citizen could announce his candidacy for the House of Representatives or the U.S. Senate and have an equal chance with anyone else to persuade the voters to elect him. Admittedly, high office is not equally available to everyone. It would nonetheless be unfortunate if such offices were in effect available only to the highest bidder. The growing costs of political campaigning have intensified the fear that in the future only the wealthy, or those heavily obligated to wealthy supporters, will be able to engage in district, state, or national elective politics.

In addition to being costly, it is frequently charged that much of contemporary televised political advertising is misleading. Critics argue that the favored kind of advertisement, the short "spot" lasting no more than ten seconds to a minute, is an inappropriate method of confronting voters with the issues of a campaign. The spot, in fact, is intended not to present a reasoned treatment of the issues but, rather, to engage the voters' emotions or to create a favorable *image* of the candidate. Yet, the legitimacy of the American political system and the powers of the American government are assumed to be derived from the consent of the governed, and such an assumption becomes less justifiable as that consent ceases to be free and informed. Though it may not yet be possible to fool all of the people all of the time, the distressing thought that such a possibility might be enhanced by recent developments in televised political advertising accounts for some of the growing apprehension concerning those developments. [*Doc. 1-3*]

A further misgiving about televised political advertising is that much of it is simply undignified. It is frequently lamented that the trend toward spot advertising has led to the *packaging* of candidates in order that they may be sold like so many tubes of toothpaste or cans of soup. The notion that a man's election to the Senate or the mayoralty of a large city might be attributable to his "star" image, the glamour of his smile, or the way he casually drapes his jacket over his shoulder would be ludicrous, save for its all-too-close approximation to the truth.

It should be kept in mind, however, that none of these problems can be blamed exclusively on television. Most of these existed long before television was invented. There probably is no realistic method of neutralizing the advantage of financially well-heeled or physically attractive candidates; few American elections have been contested on the basis of important issues alone; and seldom, if ever, has running for elective office in America been a particularly dignified business. If

DOCUMENT **1-3**: The Selling of the Candidates

The Selling of the Candidates 1970

The picture on the TV screen is more than vaguely reminiscent of Mark Shaw's famous photographs of John F. Kennedy. Down a deserted beach strolls another tall, handsome young man, accompanied by his pretty wife and tow-headed children. Finally, the camera moves in for a flattering view of California Congressman John Tunney, son of the man who beat Jack Dempsey and a Kennedy family friend. Tunney, who is running for a seat in the U.S. Senate, looks into the camera from under a Kennedy-style mop of hair. "We can fly to the moon, we can split the atom, we can build great cities. But we cannot build the ocean or the sky," he tells his unseen audience earnestly. "These are gifts . . . my vote and voice will be with the protection of this great state of ours." It all takes a trifle less than 30 seconds. Then the slogan flashes across the screen: "You need a fighter in your corner. John Tunney is a fighter."

His coat is off, his sleeves rolled up, his collar open. Silver-haired Howard Metzenbaum, the millionaire liberal, is commiserating with a crew of construction workers. Metzenbaum, who is running for the Senate in Ohio, agrees that things are tough these days and he talks about the spiraling inflation and unemployment figures. Within seconds one of the hard hats is weeping over his family's plight. A credit notes that this dramatic slice of life was presented by the Citizens for Metzenbaum Committee.

The face is that of Adlai Stevenson III, the Democratic Senate candidate in Illinois, looking owlish and a bit bemused. But the voice is something else again. "Why doesn't he speak out against busing?" it demands. The camera zooms in closer on Adlai's face. "Why doesn't he denounce those students who try to force our universities to close?" the voice persists. The camera comes closer still. "What has Ad-a-lay got against the FBI and the Chicago police?" The screen is now entirely filled by Stevenson's nose and glassy eyeballs. "Why doesn't he admit he's a liberal and put an end to all the pretense?" A question mark flickers briefly onscreen, then the camera goes back to staring into Stevenson's myopic eyes. "Why doesn't he?" insists the voice. Before the picture fades, a tiny message across the bottom of the screen reveals that the instant inquisition was paid for by supporters of Sen. Ralph Smith, Stevenson's Republican opponent.

Used by permission of *Newsweek magazine.* Copyright © Newsweek, Inc., October 19, 1970.

television is to be faulted, its error lies in having added powerful new dimensions to these problems, in having enlarged their impact rather than having helped to control or diminish them.

Section 315: The Equal Time Provision

Currently, the use of radio and television by candidates for public office is primarily subject to the provisions of Section 315 of the Communications Act of 1934. This law, amended by Congress in 1952 and 1959, establishes the frequently discussed *equal-time* requirement. Strictly speaking, "equal time" is a misnomer; the statute speaks not of equal *time*, but of equal *opportunities*. Thus, when a candidate makes use of radio or television in his election campaign, the stations that broadcast his advertisements must provide an equal opportunity to gain exposure to all other candidates for the same office. A station can neither *give* free time to one candidate without offering equal free time to all his opponents nor *sell* time to one candidate without affording his opponents the opportunity to purchase equal time at the same price. When, in 1959, the Federal Communications Commission ruled that this requirement applied to appearances by candidates on news programs, the uproar of protest on the part of broadcasters and politicians was sudden and sonorous. Congress reacted quickly by amending Section 315 to exclude appearances on various types of news programs from the equal-opportunities requirement.[4] [*Doc. 1-4*]

One result of the equal-time requirement is a reluctance on the part of broadcasters to provide free time to candidates for any offices. Broadcasters argue that local radio and television stations and national networks would be willing to provide free time, as a public service, to the major-party candidates for important offices. However, if free time were provided to the major-party candidates, Section 315 would require that it also be provided to other candidates. Very often, in addition to the Republican and Democratic candidates, there will be several legally qualified candidates for important offices. Sometimes such candidates are serious contenders for office, and, even when a candidate has no chance of winning, he may be playing a significant role in the public discussion of important issues. There are several recent examples of significant candidates who were not running as the nominees of either major party. In 1970 in New York, James Buckley ran

---

[4] The equal-opportunities requirement of Section 315 should be distinguished from the more general "fairness doctrine," which requires that, when a broadcaster presents one point of view with reference to a controversial issue of public importance, he has a public responsibility to offer a contrasting view. This doctrine, promulgated by the Federal Communications Commission, would probably remain in effect even if the equal-opportunities requirement were repealed.

for—and won—the office of U.S. Senator in a three-way race; he ran on the Conservative Party ticket. John Lindsay, the Mayor of New York City, won re-election in 1969 after having lost Republican Party endorsement in the primary. And in 1968, George Wallace's third-party candi-

---

DOCUMENT 1-4: Section 315 of the Communications Act of 1934
(47 U.S.C. §315)

The Communications Act of 1934 has been amended several times to take into consideration the enlarged impact of television, as compared to radio, broadcasting. The reference to 47 U.S.C. §315 directs the reader to Title 47 of the United States Code, Section 315. The Code, consisting of a total of fifty titles, is a codification of all the statutes that have been passed by Congress since 1787. Title 47 includes all laws treating of "Telegraphs, Telephones, and Radiotelegraphs," in addition to television.

As used in Section 315, "licensee" means the owners of the 700-odd television and over 6,800 radio stations currently operating in the United States. The "Commission" referred to in Section 315(a)(4) is the Federal Communications Commission (FCC), which is charged with overseeing this and other laws covering communications.

---

§ 315. Candidates for public office; facilities; rules.

(a) If any licensee shall permit any person who is a legally qualified candidate for any public office to use a broadcasting station, he shall afford equal opportunities to all other such candidates for that office in the use of such broadcasting station: *Provided,* That such licensee shall have no power of censorship over the material broadcast under the provisions of this section. No obligation is imposed upon any licensee to allow the use of its station by any such candidate. Appearance by a legally qualified candidate on any—

(1) bona fide newscast,

(2) bona fide news interview,

(3) bona fide news documentary (if the appearance of the candidate is incidental to the presentation of the subject or subjects covered by the news documentary), or

(4) on-the-spot coverage of bona fide news events (including but not limited to political conventions and activities incidental thereto),

shall not be deemed to be use of a broadcasting station within the meaning of this subsection. Nothing in the foregoing sentence shall be construed as relieving broadcasters, in connection with the presentation of newscasts, news interviews, news documentaries, and on-the-spot coverage of news events, from the obligation imposed upon them under this chapter to operate in the public interest and to afford reasonable opportunity for the discussion of conflicting views on issues of public importance.

(b) The charges made for the use of any broadcasting station for any of the purposes set forth in this section shall not exceed the charges made for comparable use of such station for other purposes.

(c) The Commission shall prescribe appropriate rules and regulations to carry out the provisions of this section.

dacy was a critical element in the Presidential election. It is improbable, even without the equal-time requirement of Section 315, that many broadcasters would deal unfairly with a Buckley, a Lindsay, or a Wallace. But what of uninspiring yet serious candidates for lower offices? Should it be up to the broadcaster to make such determinations?

For their part, broadcasters are reluctant to provide free time to office-seeking politicians because of the presence in many elections of several legally qualified candidates whose candidacies nevertheless must appear as insignificant, if not ridiculous. A pig farmer from Secaucus, New Jersey, ran for President three times as the candidate of the Poor Man's Party. With a pig as his symbol, he declared in his first race, in 1952, "The Democrats have been hogging the Administration at Washington for twenty years, and it's about time the people began to squeal." The equal-time requirement of Section 315 fails to distinguish among candidates of the major parties, a George Wallace or John Lindsay, and a pig farmer from Secaucus.

Congress suspended the equal-time requirement for the 1960 Presidential election in order to make possible the "great debates" between candidates Richard M. Nixon and John F. Kennedy. It has been suggested frequently that those debates were the crucial factor in Kennedy's victory. Theodore H. White observed:

> When they [the debates] began, Nixon was generally viewed as being the probable winner of the election contest and Kennedy as fighting an uphill battle; when they were over, the positions of the two contestants were reversed. . . .
>
> Any reporter who followed the Kennedy compaign remembers still the quantum jump in the size of crowds that greeted the campaigning Senator from the morrow of the first debate, the morning of Tuesday, September 27th, when he began to campaign in northern Ohio. His crowds had been growing for a full seven days before the debates, but now, overnight, they seethed with enthusiasm and multiplied in numbers, as if the sight of him, in their homes on the video box, had given him a "star quality" reserved only for television and movie idols.[5]

While it is difficult in any election, particularly one as close as that of 1960, to point to any single factor as being decisive, the emphasis on the debates in most analyses of that election illustrates another characteristic of Section 315: *The reluctance of broadcasters, as a result of the equal-time requirement, to provide free time to candidates generally operates to the advantage of the candidate who is best known to the voters at the outset of a campaign.* An incumbent officeholder running for re-election is usually better known to the voters than are

[5] Theodore H. White, *The Making of the President 1960* (New York: Atheneum, 1961), pp. 318–19.

his opponents. He has many more opportunities to generate news and, hence, to reap the benefits of bona fide news coverage, which is exempted from the equal-time provisions of Section 315. The equal-time requirement thus generally works to the benefit of existing office-holders. It is hardly surprising that Congress—which, after all, is made up of incumbents, most of whom plan to run for re-election—has been hesitant to tamper with the equal-time requirement. [*Doc. 1-5*]

DOCUMENT **1-5**: The Advantage of Being an Incumbent

In the Senate debate on the Political Broadcast bill, Senator Charles Percy (R., Ill.) recalls his uphill struggle against former Senator Paul Douglas, who had represented Illinois for three terms before his 1966 defeat. The Senator's remarks can be found in the Congressional Record, *April 13, 1970, p. S.5636.*

Mr. PERCY. Will the Senator yield for another question?

Mr. PASTORE. I yield.

Mr. PERCY. I keep thinking of the built-in advantages that an incumbent has, and I feel comfortable about it, being an incumbent; but I can also remember the problems I had as a challenger, looking from the outside in. I can remember the built-in advantages that a challenger is working against, the franking privilege and the post office privilege. A challenger is working against the advantages that an incumbent has in the way of television studios downstairs, with films being ground out at cost. A challenger is constantly working against the income-tax laws.

I can remember working against Paul Douglas, and I can remember seeing the public service telecasts coming on Sunday morning or Saturday night for 15 minutes, black and white at that time. Thinking about how much it would cost a challenging candidate to get 15 minutes of sometimes prime time, trying to get name identification, when I was not known from a barn door, and when Paul Douglas, the incumbent, had been known for 18 years. I remember the amount of money it took in my State. It took $1 million in my State to wage a losing campaign, just to try to pull name identification up from zero to somewhere into 50 or 60 percent, and still be battling a name recognition of 80 or 90 percent.

I wonder if it is not unfair to a challenger to put an arbitrary limitation on the most dramatic way he has of getting his name and story across, even though I realize it would be a tremendous advantage to me? The incumbent does not declare until he has to. The equal time provision does not apply until he becomes a candidate. So all the incumbent has to do is withhold his candidacy, trying to get as much of the free time as is available to him as so-called public service. Yet he thinks of it not so much as public service as utilizing it for running for his next candidacy. I wonder if the challenger should be so limited in view of the built-in advantages that an incumbent has.

Attempts were made in 1964 and, again, in 1968 to suspend the equal-time requirement for the Presidential elections so that debates between the major candidates would be possible. Each time, partisan considerations seemed to motivate the actions of both supporters and opponents of the proposals. In 1964, Congressional Republicans attempted to suspend the equal-time requirement in the hopes of making televised debates possible between Senator Barry Goldwater, their underdog nominee, and Lyndon Johnson, the incumbent Democratic President. President Johnson, who was riding the crest of his personal popularity at that time, would have had almost nothing to gain by engaging in such debates. Senate Democrats had little difficulty killing the Republican proposal, thus ensuring that there would be no "great debates" in 1964.

By 1968, the tides of political favor had turned. With the Republican candidate, Richard Nixon, running far ahead in the polls, it was the Democratic Congressmen who were pressing for televised debates, which they hoped would benefit their financially hard-pressed candidate, Senator Hubert Humphrey. A bill to suspend the equal-time requirement was passed in the House, although outnumbered Republicans, in an attempt to forestall passage, forced the House to stay in session for twenty-seven consecutive hours. When the bill was finally passed, it was in a form different from that of the Senate version; it then had to be returned to the Senate. There, the Republicans' determination to engage in delaying tactics to prevent the bill's passage forced the Democratic leadership to give up the fight. Once again, hopes for televised debates between the major Presidential contenders had to be abandoned.

WHAT IS TO BE DONE?

The mounting costs of American elections, the difficulties encountered in trying to enforce existing campaign finance legislation, and some of the more unfortunate uses to which television has been put have raised once again the issue of what, if anything, can or should be done. Most proffered solutions revolve around one or more of five main proposals: (1) increasing the amount of free time available to legally qualified candidates through repeal of Section 315; (2) restricting campaign expenditures, especially the amounts that can be spent on television broadcasting; (3) controlling the incoming contributions, both in individual and over-all amounts; (4) requiring open disclosure of expenditures or contributions, or both; and (5) establishing federal subsidies for election costs, including television, direct mail-ings, and even staff allowances. The second and third proposals would establish ceilings for various offices beyond which a candidate could not spend or receive; the last proposal envisions a "floor" of support, such that all candidates would get under way more or less evenly.

The Political Broadcast Act of 1970 was a limited proposal, based primarily upon the first two propositions: more free time and an over-all expenditure ceiling. Through a *limited repeal* of the equal-time provision, it took advantage of the simplest way to increase the amount of free radio and television time. Doing away with all of Section 315 would have meant that networks and broadcasters could make free prime time available to the major candidates at all federal office levels and that televised debates between significant contenders for office might become a regular feature of American elections. Nonetheless, to abolish the equal-time requirement entirely would also put an enormous amount of power in the hands of local broadcasters and would probably spell a kind of practical doom for all but the regular candidates of the major parties. It would increase the difficulty of bringing to the voters' attention dissenting views on issues and unorthodox policy proposals, which has been one of the traditionally important functions of minor parties and schismatic candidates in American politics. Because it would probably be interpreted as an attempt to further institutionalize the entrenched parties and would generally reek of intended unfairness, the outright abolition of the equal-time requirement beyond the Presidential level is not likely to occur. [*Doc. 1-6*]

Another form of limited repeal calls for the rescinding of Section 315 only as it applies to the general election for the offices of President and Vice-President. This is what was done in 1960 and attempted in 1964, 1968, and 1970. The main problem with this kind of approach is one that pervades the whole issue of campaign financing: as was seen earlier in the chapter and as will come up again in this book, when genuine attempts are made by incumbent politicians to deal with televised political campaigning, the issue can quickly degenerate into one of partisan cause. Only the underdog party will seek repeal in order to bring about debates; the party of the sitting incumbent or odds-on favorite will generally drag its feet, and perhaps even veto the bill.

Between entirely abolishing the equal-time requirement and suspending it sporadically for Presidential elections lies a third possibility: revising the law to the extent that minor candidates would be entitled to *some* television time but not time *equal* to that offered the major candidates. A proposal along these lines was made in 1969 by the Twentieth Century Fund's Commission on Campaign Costs in the Electronic Era. Their suggested solution to the campaign spending problem was something they called "Voters' Time." Beginning in Presiden-

DOCUMENT **1-6**: The Enrolled Bill

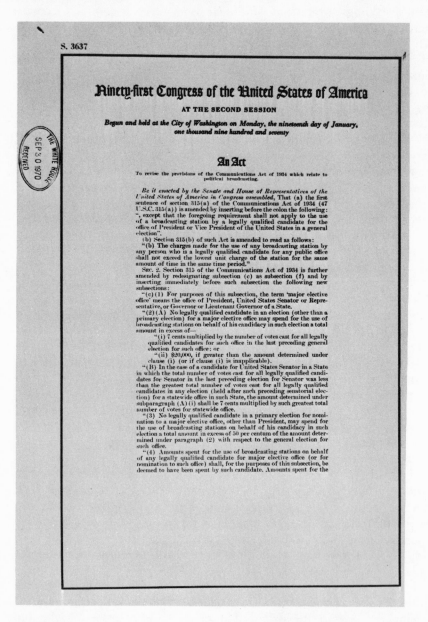

S. 3637

Ninety-first Congress of the United States of America

AT THE SECOND SESSION

Begun and held at the City of Washington on Monday, the nineteenth day of January, one thousand nine hundred and seventy

An Act

To revise the provisions of the Communications Act of 1934 which relate to political broadcasting.

Be it enacted by the Senate and House of Representatives of the United States of America in Congress assembled, That (a) the first sentence of section 315(a) of the Communications Act of 1934 (47 U.S.C. 315(a)) is amended by inserting before the colon the following: ", except that the foregoing requirement shall not apply to the use of a broadcasting station by a legally qualified candidate for the office of President or Vice President of the United States in a general election".

(b) Section 315(b) of such Act is amended to read as follows:

"(b) The charges made for the use of any broadcasting station by any person who is a legally qualified candidate for any public office shall not exceed the lowest unit charge of the station for the same amount of time in the same time period."

SEC. 2. Section 315 of the Communications Act of 1934 is further amended by redesignating subsection (c) as subsection (f) and by inserting immediately before such subsection the following new subsections:

"(c)(1) For purposes of this subsection, the term 'major elective office' means the office of President, United States Senator or Representative, or Governor or Lieutenant Governor of a State.

"(2)(A) No legally qualified candidate in an election (other than a primary election) for a major elective office may spend for the use of broadcasting stations on behalf of his candidacy in such election a total amount in excess of—

"(i) 7 cents multiplied by the number of votes cast for all legally qualified candidates for such office in the last preceding general election for such office; or

"(ii) $20,000, if greater than the amount determined under clause (i) (or if clause (i) is inapplicable).

"(B) In the case of a candidate for United States Senator in a State in which the total number of votes cast for all legally qualified candidates for Senator in the last preceding election for Senator was less than the greatest total number of votes cast for all legally qualified candidates in any election (held after such preceding senatorial election) for a statewide office in such State, the amount determined under subparagraph (A)(i) shall be 7 cents multiplied by such greatest total number of votes for statewide office.

"(3) No legally qualified candidate in a primary election for nomination to a major elective office, other than President, may spend for the use of broadcasting stations on behalf of his candidacy in such election a total amount in excess of 50 per centum of the amount determined under paragraph (2) with respect to the general election for such office.

"(4) Amounts spent for the use of broadcasting stations on behalf of any legally qualified candidate for major elective office (or for nomination to such office) shall, for the purposes of this subsection, be deemed to have been spent by such candidate. Amounts spent for the

tial elections, perhaps to be expanded to other elections at a later time, the federal government would purchase television time at a reduced rate; this would then be made available free to significant candidates. The Commission divided what it considered to be significant candidates into three ordered categories, generally according to the support

Doc. 1-6 *(cont.)*

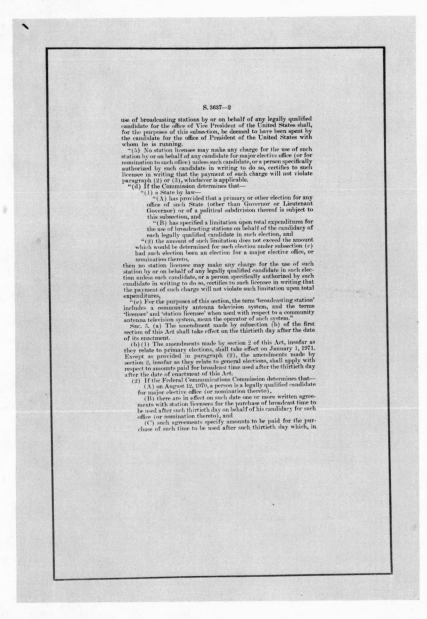

S. 3637—2

use of broadcasting stations by or on behalf of any legally qualified candidate for the office of Vice President of the United States shall, for the purposes of this subsection, be deemed to have been spent by the candidate for the office of President of the United States with whom he is running.

"(5) No station licensee may make any charge for the use of such station by or on behalf of any candidate for major elective office (or for nomination to such office) unless such candidate, or a person specifically authorized by such candidate in writing to do so, certifies to such licensee in writing that the payment of such charge will not violate paragraph (2) or (3), whichever is applicable.

"(d) If the Commission determines that—

"(1) a State by law—

"(A) has provided that a primary or other election for any office of such State (other than Governor or Lieutenant Governor) or of a political subdivision thereof is subject to this subsection, and

"(B) has specified a limitation upon total expenditures for the use of broadcasting stations on behalf of the candidacy of each legally qualified candidate in such election, and

"(2) the amount of such limitation does not exceed the amount which would be determined for such election under subsection (c) had such election been an election for a major elective office, or nomination thereto,

then no station licensee may make any charge for the use of such station by or on behalf of any legally qualified candidate in such election unless such candidate, or a person specifically authorized by such candidate in writing to do so, certifies to such licensee in writing that the payment of such charge will not violate such limitation upon total expenditures.

"(e) For the purposes of this section, the term 'broadcasting station' includes a community antenna television system, and the terms 'licensee' and 'station licensee' when used with respect to a community antenna television system, mean the operator of such system."

Sec. 3. (a) The amendment made by subsection (b) of the first section of this Act shall take effect on the thirtieth day after the date of its enactment.

(b)(1) The amendments made by section 2 of this Act, insofar as they relate to primary elections, shall take effect on January 1, 1971. Except as provided in paragraph (2), the amendments made by section 2, insofar as they relate to general elections, shall apply with respect to amounts paid for broadcast time used after the thirtieth day after the date of enactment of this Act.

(2) If the Federal Communications Commission determines that—

(A) on August 12, 1970, a person is a legally qualified candidate for major elective office (or nomination thereto),

(B) there are in effect on such date one or more written agreements with station licensees for the purchase of broadcast time to be used after such thirtieth day on behalf of his candidacy for such office (or nomination thereto), and

(C) such agreements specify amounts to be paid for the purchase of such time to be used after such thirtieth day which, in

their party received in past elections. The higher a candidate's category, the more time would be made available to him. The highest category, and thus the most time, is for all practical purposes limited to the candidates of the major parties. New parties and minor parties would continue to be at a disadvantage. Still, it seems probable that any

Doc. 1-6 (*cont.*)

S. 3637—3

the aggregate, exceed the limitation imposed by section 315(c)(2)
of the Communications Act of 1934 with respect to the general
election for such office,
then such amendments shall not apply to any of the candidates for
election to such office in an election held before January 1, 1971.

Speaker of the House of Representatives.

President of the Senate pro Tempore.

I certify that this Act originated in the Senate.

Secretary.

eventual solution to the equal-time dilemma will resemble this proposal in its attempt to balance the realistic need for voters to hear the
major candidates against the more obscure, but no less real, need for
voters to be exposed to candidates other than Republicans and Democrats.

Suggestions for dealing with the problem of campaign costs have
taken other forms than mere manipulation of the equal-time requirement. One extreme solution would be to prohibit completely the use

of television in election campaigns. Whatever the merits of that solution, its chances of becoming a reality are less than minuscule. Other proposals resemble the Political Broadcast Act of 1970 in seeking to restrict either the amount of money a candidate may spend on broadcasting or the amount of total television time available to any one candidate. The standard formula that seems likely to become law is based upon so many cents—in the case of the Political Broadcast Act, seven cents—per total vote cast in the last general election, or a set figure, say $20,000, if that amount is higher. (The base amount appears to be needed for those Congressional races, generally in the South, where past voter turnout has been light.)

Still another basic approach is largely to overlook expenditure limitations and concentrate instead on controlling contributions. Such control may take the form of limiting to a set amount what any one individual or committee can contribute—for example, $5,000 under the existing Federal Corrupt Practices Act. From experience thus far, the grave shortcoming of this approach has been "proliferating committees" on behalf of the same candidate and a general inability to enforce limitations.

A major modification would be to abandon all limitations on the amounts that may be contributed by any one individual, and instead place the emphasis on full disclosure. The assumption underlying this approach is that the public, aware of where the money came from, would then be in a position to judge their officeholders accordingly.

By and large, Democratic incumbents have favored expenditure limitations. Republicans have tended to support disclosure provisions. Not surprisingly, these basic stances are in close accord with the perennial shortage of campaign contributions faced by many Democrats, especially Presidential aspirants, and the relative surfeit of money available to most GOP contenders for higher office.

A final approach—federal subsidization of elections—has met with increasing enthusiasm on the part of Democrats, but general opposition from Republicans. Funding would be made available either as a result of tax deductions or in the form of a tax credit of perhaps one dollar per voter. The resulting $70 million or more might be redistributed to the parties on the basis of their votes in the last Presidential election, or to individual candidates on the basis of eligible voters in their districts. The strongest argument for federal support would be its relative fairness, although the question of what to do about new or minor-party candidates is not easy to resolve. In addition to genuine concern about federal encroachment, the prospects for this approach to campaign finance reform are dimmed by a general reluctance on the part of most Congressional incumbents to yield part of their inherent advantage under the present system.

Should any limitations at all be placed on the use of money and television in political campaigns? It seems clear that limits on campaign expenditures and free access to television do work to the advantage of established officeholders. It is almost a standard tactic of opponents of such legislation to charge that it is an "incumbents' bill." Spending limits, it is argued, impair a challenger's ability to overcome an incumbent's built-in access to publicity, staff, and franking privileges, to say nothing of his name's usually greater familiarity among the voters. Television is so deeply imbedded in American life that individuals or groups, particularly those outside the highest leadership circles of government, seeking to alter the political status quo must find some means of bringing their case to the people through the medium of television. To the extent that such is the case, attempts to set ceilings upon efforts to oust incumbents or attempts to limit access to television may be regarded as efforts to protect the status quo.

We have considered, in brief form, some of the issues involved in the use of television in American election campaigns. Partly out of concern for the quality of our political processes, partly out of partisan motivation, but, above all, because of a genuine fear about rising campaign costs, Congress turned its attention to these issues and attempted to enact a law: the Political Broadcast Act of 1970.

FURTHER READING

The seminal work on the subject of campaign financing is Alexander Heard's *The Costs of Democracy* (Chapel Hill: University of North Carolina Press, 1960).

Publications of the Citizens' Research Foundation, Princeton, N.J., are numerous and generally focus upon problems of election reform and campaign financing. Particularly useful are Herbert E. Alexander's *Financing the 1960 Election, Financing the 1964 Election,* and the most recent comprehensive summation of election expenditures and contributions, *Financing the 1968 Election,* the last named published in 1971 (Lexington, Mass.: D. C. Heath).

An example of a broad proposal for campaign reform that has found its way into proposed legislation (H.R.19904, 91st Congress, 2d session, introduced December 2, 1970) is N. N. Minow *et al., Voters' Time: Report of the Twentieth Century Fund Commission on Campaign Costs in the Electronic Era* (New York: The Twentieth Century Fund, 1969).

On the impact of television upon politics, the best general work so far is *Polls, Television and the New Politics* by Harold Mendelsohn and Irving Crespi (Scranton: Chandler Publishing, 1970). *The Selling of the President 1968* by Joe McGinnis (New York: Trident Press, 1969) presents a revealing "insider's" glimpse into the workings of a modern political campaign that relied heavily on television.

Policy
Initiation
and
Development

Public policy, almost by definition, is whatever evolves from decisions made by government officials. It is difficult to understand the content of a particular policy without analyzing, on the one hand, who the decision-makers are and what viewpoints they hold and, on the other, the nature of the institutions that help to shape, if not determine, the outcome. Any given public policy is a synthesis of the many competing and cooperating forces interacting with one another from the time it is first proposed until its adoption as a government program. For most policies, of course, the enactment of legislation is only a midpoint in their evolution. Administrators may interpret key sections differently than Congressmen. Litigants may institute suits that result in constraining court orders. Modifying amendments will frequently be introduced in subsequent Congresses. And so, public policy undergoes almost continual change.

SOURCES OF PUBLIC POLICY

To begin an examination of a specific policy one must first look at its origins. When and where was it proposed? Who were the initial forces behind it? Public policy may originate from a number of sources: A constituent has an idea about solving a pressing problem and writes his Congressman. Or the *New York Times* decides to publish secret documents on the Vietnam war obtained from a former Pentagon researcher. The Department of Justice enjoins the *Times* and other newspapers to cease publication of the leaked documents, and the resulting Supreme Court decision in favor of the newspapers sheds new light on freedom of the press under the First Amendment. Or the President commissions a special task force to look into an issue and suggest solutions. Sometimes the courts or the regulatory agencies promulgate important public policy. The Supreme Court, for example, established a far-reaching national policy in the mid-1950's when it ruled that separate schools for Negroes were not equal and required that segregated schools be integrated with "all deliberate speed." Independent government agencies like the Federal Communications Commission (FCC) or the Interstate Commerce Commission (ICC), which have an adjudicative as well as administrative function, sometimes set public policy, although usually they operate within fairly narrow boundaries set by Congress.

In our governmental system, the President and Congress—and, more rarely, the courts—are the most basic propagators of national policy. The President may use a variety of means to originate policy. As Commander-in-Chief of the armed forces and as director of the

27

country's worldwide diplomacy, he has great latitude in forming foreign policy. In theory, only Congress has the power to declare war; in fact, the President's ability to respond rapidly to crisis means that for all practical purposes it is primarily his decision as to how the country reacts to external aggression. And, of course, the past decade has witnessed the tragic consequences of an "undeclared war" in Southeast Asia. But the President also has great latitude in the domestic arena. Under executive powers granted by the Constitution or by specific legislation, he implements the major economic and fiscal policies of the land. One has only to recall that the wage-price freeze of 1971 was the result of unilateral action by President Nixon, having been granted by a 1970 act of Congress the power to declare an emergency and determine any appropriate action.

When the President is unable to develop and execute policy on his own, he frequently turns to Congress for the necessary authorization. Increasingly in the twentieth century, the President has come to play an important role as legislative initiator. Presidents Theodore Roosevelt, Woodrow Wilson, and Franklin D. Roosevelt have been instrumental in shaping the modern conception of the President as one who suggests legislative solutions, sends drafts of bills to Congress, supervises their disposition, and, finally, signs them into law. President John F. Kennedy continued in this tradition by initiating many imaginative proposals that were submitted to Congress. Close observers differ as to how many would have passed had the youthful leader not been assassinated. His successor, Lyndon B. Johnson, played a key role in getting Congress to enact most of them, plus some of his own proposals, especially in the landmark 89th Congress (1965–66).

Policy may be initiated from outside the institution that enacts it. The English economist John Maynard Keynes probably had a greater impact on our current economic and fiscal policies than any other individual. But, it required a series of Presidents, Congresses, and agency officials to institutionalize Keynesian economics as government policy. Individual citizens and interest groups cannot make national policy by themselves, but they can act as initiators through court litigation and the petitioning of regulatory agencies and by persuading Congressmen to introduce legislation for them.

Policy-making in Congress is a cumulative process. Each bill must survive a number of stages if it is to become the law of the land. At each stage, external and internal forces will impinge upon it, frequently necessitating compromise and bargaining if legislation is to be forthcoming. To understand the policy-making process in Congress, one must view it in the larger context of the legislative milieu, which includes the rules and strategies, as well as the dispersion of power, within both the House and the Senate.

Conditions Affecting Congressional Policy Initiation and Development

What factors help determine whether or not a specific piece of legislation is enacted? Whichever factors apply in particular instances, it is important to keep in mind that many of them influence not only whether a bill passes but also what form the bill takes during its consideration by the House and Senate.

External Factors. Congressmen are the elected representatives of the people, and consequently they are responsive, in some imprecise measure, to the "will of the people." Unfortunately, it is extremely difficult to ascertain at any given time what public opinion is on a specific issue in a single district, let alone in 435 districts or 50 states. Still, public opinion is a major external factor influencing Representatives and Senators, and it continues to play an important part in any analysis of Congressional behavior.

Public opinion is hard to define on a given issue, because it is usually so ambiguous. The public may be very aware of, and concerned about, an issue but have little idea of what it would like done in terms of particular policy alternatives. For example, when Congress created the Department of Transportation in October, 1966, it could reasonably be claimed that most Americans desired a better nationwide system of transportation. It is doubtful, however, that there was widespread public opinion specifically in favor of a new Department of Transportation as a means of solving the nation's transportation problems. It is probably a safe bet that most Americans didn't really care whether a new Cabinet-level department was established, as opposed to some other alternative the government might have chosen in an attempt to improve the country's highway, rail, water, and air networks. It is the task of legislators to convert just such vague general opinions on the part of the public into appropriate, operating government programs.

On other issues where there is a great deal of concern in all sectors of society relating to a particular problem, the pattern may be just the opposite. The Civil Rights Act of 1964 presents an obvious example because intense public opinion, both pro and con, developed prior to, as well as after, the passage of the legislation.

The factor that seems to be most crucial in assessing public opinion is its "intensity." Having an opinion and feeling strongly about it are two quite different things. As V. O. Key pointed out, "Verbal self-appraisals may have no relation to the way people behave."[1] Many

---

[1] V. O. Key, Jr., *Public Opinion and American Democracy* (New York: Alfred A. Knopf, 1964), p. 211.

people, for example, though they claim to feel strongly about ecology, will never take any action that demonstrates a concern for the environment. The intensity of feeling, a motivation to action, is much more difficult to measure than actual opinion. Thus, Congressmen are frequently thrown back on their own judgment in assessing just how strongly their constituents feel about a certain issue.

Pressure groups gain much of their influence precisely because of this ambiguity of general public opinion. They are able to express and direct the opinion of their membership on specific issues of substantial importance to them. Pressure groups are most effective on specialized legislation where there is little or no public opinion or awareness. The gas and oil industries have been successful for many years in getting Congress to block tax-reform legislation that would have lowered the depletion allowance. Other pressure groups that claim to represent the public at large or the "public interest" and concern themselves with broad and well-publicized issues have a more difficult task. For example, Common Cause, a public-interest group formed in the summer of 1970 and headed by John Gardner, former Health, Education, and Welfare Secretary, has made its top-priority issues reform of the Congressional seniority system and ending the war in Vietnam. A year later, it had demonstrated little, if any, positive legislative effect on either of these issues.

Public opinion may also be manifested through national elections. In electing Congress as well as the President, the electorate may express a broad endorsement of, or unhappiness with, a particular Administration's programs. When there is an election in which one of the parties is strongly favored, such as the 1964 Johnson landslide, which pulled many Democrats into Congress, one can anticipate significant movement in that Congress under the leadership of the majority party. Such was the case with the 89th Congress, which produced one of the most successful legislative performances in the twentieth century.

Internal Factors. In both the Senate and the House, there are many institutional characteristics that affect the shape and outcome of legislation. The manner in which the two houses are organized and the way in which power is distributed and focused may make the difference between life and death for any given piece of legislation.

The seniority system in both houses is a crucial determinant in the allocation of Congressional power. Those members of the majority party who serve continuously for the longest number of years on a given committee are awarded chairmanships. If a member is defeated but returns to Congress at a later election, he begins all over again at the bottom of the seniority ladder. The Senate now has seventeen standing (or permanent) committees, while the House has twenty-one.

Each committee, in turn, decides how many subcommittees it will have, typically six or eight. Committees range in size from the fifty-five members of the House Appropriations Committee to the seven-member Senate District of Columbia Committee. From time to time, each chamber will form select committees to undertake specific tasks, often investigative in nature, on a temporary basis. In addition, some ten joint committees operate with members from both houses—for example, the Joint Committee on Atomic Energy.

The ratio of majority members to minority members on each committee generally reflects the over-all ratio of Democrats to Republicans within each house. The party in the majority—it must have at least 50 of the 100 Senate seats, 218 of the 435 House seats—controls the major leadership positions, determines committee ratios, and selects the committee and subcommittee chairmen.

Over eighty years ago, a student of our national legislature remarked that "Congress in session is Congress on public exhibition, whilst Congress in its committee-rooms is Congress at work."[2] Woodrow Wilson may be forgiven for some oversimplification—after all, he had yet to journey to Washington to observe Congress firsthand—but it is true that the committees of Congress do most of the problem-solving and bill-drafting that occur there. Major revisions sometimes occur on the floor of the Senate; they happen less frequently in the House. If a bill undergoes major surgery through a series of amendments, it runs the grave risk of being recommitted to committee for further study, if not death.

Major power in the committees and subcommittees of Congress rests in the hands of the chairmen and, to a lesser extent, the ranking minority members (those members of the opposition who have the most seniority on the committee). Committee chairmen in large part determine which bills will be taken up, when hearings will be held and who will testify, and how soon the legislation will reach the floor, if at all. The more marginal the bill, the greater the control over its fate wielded by the chairman. His powers are not absolute, of course. If he becomes too arbitrary, a majority of the committee can revolt against him, force him to hold meetings, or report out legislation over his objections. The Legislative Reorganization Act of 1970 adds further procedural checks. In the main, however, power accrues to the senior members, especially the chairman. Other members must defer to him; they must bargain with him to get their favored legislation moving. In the words of the late Representative Clem Miller: "To catch the attention of Congress is a neat trick in itself."[3]

[2] Woodrow Wilson, *Congressional Government* (Boston: Houghton Mifflin, 1885), p. 79.

[3] Clem Miller, *Member of the House,* John W. Barker, ed. (New York: Charles Scribner's Sons, 1962), p. 5.

The seniority system fosters a built-in conservative bias, which in turn has a significant impact on legislation. Because it takes a good number of years before a Congressman has enough seniority to become a committee chairman, those who do serve as chairmen tend to be far older than the average Congressman and much older than the average American.[4] Although from time to time more liberally minded leaders such as Emanuel Celler of New York will head powerful committees like the House Judiciary, the more general pattern is often resistance to change. Perhaps more important, to accrue enough seniority to become a committee chairman, a Congressman must be re-elected over and over again. Thus, those who finally become committee chairmen usually come from "safe" districts or states where there is negligible competition from the opposing party. Too often, Congressmen from such districts are not as responsive to changing interests or demands as are members who represent so-called swing, or marginal, districts and states.

Party leadership is also important in affecting the substance, timing, and ultimate fate of legislation. In the House of Representatives, the Speaker of the House plays a crucial role in controlling the flow of legislation through that chamber. The Speaker's influence is vital in deciding whether a bill is to be speeded up or delayed, or whether it is to be scheduled at all. In the Senate, the President Pro Tempore is selected by the majority party to preside over the chamber in the absence of the Vice-President of the United States, but he is essentially a figurehead with minimal formal power.[5] The Majority Leader in the Senate has major control over the timing of floor action, though he lacks the over-all power of the Speaker of the House. In sum, party leaders play critical roles in facilitating the bargaining processes that help to build and maintain the coalitions necessary to pass legislation.

American parties seldom operate under a caucus system.[6] Therefore, on controversial legislation it is usually necessary to build a bipartisan coalition (one that includes both Democrats and Republicans). The

---

[4] In the 91st Congress, twelve of the sixteen Senate committee chairmen were sixty-five or over, with five of them in their seventies and one who was eighty. In the House, fourteen of the twenty-one chairmen were sixty-five or over, including seven in their seventies and two in their eighties. See Gerald Clarke, "Congress: The Heavy Hand of Seniority," *Time*, Dec. 14, 1970, pp. 22–23.

[5] Although the Constitution designates the Vice-President of the United States as the presiding officer of the Senate, he rarely attends unless there is a possibility of a tie vote on an important issue, in which case he may cast the deciding vote. As the Constitution states, he "shall have no vote, unless they be equally divided."

[6] A caucus system is one in which the parties, meeting separately off the floor of the chamber, vote for their party's policy positions. Once the party decision is reached, all members of that party, whether they agree or disagree, are bound to vote for that position on the floor of the legislature.

passage of laws is generally a product of both parties, different factions of which coalesce behind particular bills. Sometimes the winning coalition is made up of moderate-to-liberal Democrats from northern and western states who are joined by a handful of urban and northeastern Republicans. At other times, it will take the form of a majority of Republicans aligned with most of the more conservative southern Democrats.

Compromise and bargaining between the parties, as well as within them, characterize the nature of policy development in Congress. When the House and Senate pass different versions of the same bill, compromise between the two houses is institutionalized through the conference committee. The Speaker of the House and the presiding officer in the Senate appoint senior members from those committees having jurisdiction, and these members then meet and attempt to work out the differences between the two bills. The compromised version must still be ratified by both houses before it is sent on for Presidential approval.

From Problem to Policy. For almost all major issues and for most issues in general, there is a considerable lag between the time when a proposal for dealing with a problem is introduced and when, if at all, it becomes the law of the land. Some types of legislation bring significant departures from past policy; others simply continue or modify what has been done in the past. An increase in the minimum wage or social security benefits would be characteristic of the latter. The Medicare bill, which took fifteen years from the time it was first introduced until the time it was passed into law, is an example of legislation that brought about a major change in government policy. But, in either case, the external and internal factors mentioned above will affect the initiation and development of policy in Congress.

Methods of Policy Initiation in Congress

Congressional Action. Once interest in a problem has been stimulated, whether it be by a pressure group, public opinion, a crusading Congressman, or the President as "chief legislator," the actual process must begin of transforming a desire to deal with an issue into legislation. The first stage is the gathering of information and data that will enable the Congress to approach the problem intelligently. The great portion of a Congressman's time is spent not in original research but in receiving, synthesizing, and transmitting information that is presented to him from other sources. Principally, Congressmen receive their information from constituents, their personal staff, committee staff and committee hearings, the executive branch, the popular media, and pressure groups.

Most people have never written, nor will they consider writing, a letter to their Congressman. Other constituents, perhaps as many as a third, will write their official representatives in Washington to obtain help on a veteran's claim, information about federal programs and jobs, or just to blow off steam. Few Congressmen read every letter that comes into their office, perhaps as many as a hundred a day for the average Representative, three to five times that many for the typical Senator. Most, however, make a practice of trying to sample their mail and almost all, save the Senators from large industrial states, where the mail is heaviest, try to sign their outgoing responses.

The amount of legislation directly instigated by constituency mail is quite limited. Still, a letter coming in on University of Michigan station-ery or a large scientific laboratory letterhead may start a staff member or Congressman thinking about a problem, which in turn may lead to further exploration and research.

Congressmen's personal staffs are, of course, a vital asset in advanc-ing their legislative interests. The staffs are necessarily limited in what they can do, because much of their time is taken up answering mail, intervening with administrative agencies, and generally coping with constituency problems. The typical House office may have one or possibly two people working on legislation; Senators generally have much larger legislative staffs. Much of the staff assistant's time is given over to keeping the Congressman informed on pending legislation. It is the rare and valuable staff assistant who can carve out the time to help draft new legislation. In gathering information, many Congres-sional staffs depend extensively on the Congressional Reference Ser-vice of the Library of Congress. The office staff is further complemented by committee and subcommittee staff. Junior Congressmen—those with little seniority—have less access to these staffs than do chairmen and high-ranking members, who frequently appoint them and use them extensively. Sometimes the staff will be "professional," or non-partisan. Staffs appointed on partisan grounds are unequally distrib-uted between the majority and minority parties. The majority party generally has the support of more than two-thirds of the staff, and these are most responsive to the committee or subcommittee chair-men who appoint them.

Pressure groups provide a welcome service by giving both technical and political information to Representatives and Senators. Congress-men do not have the staff or resources to do research on more than a few issues at any one time. Hence, interest groups become a conve-nient source of information in their specialized areas. In addition, a competent lobbyist is a storehouse of information on the men and issues preoccupying Capitol Hill, although, as Milbraith points out in

The Washington Lobbyists, "Staff members evaluate all information from lobbyists and lobby groups with the knowledge that it might be slanted."[7] Sometimes Congressmen will play one lobby off against another.

The actual drafting of a bill can be done by personal or committee staff, by the executive branch, or by pressure groups. Staff members receive invaluable assistance in the drafting of legislation from the Office of Legislative Counsel, which has staffs serving in both the House and the Senate. These small staffs of about a dozen lawyers each act as nonpartisan clearinghouses for all types of legislation. Each office performs the function of taking the nascent forms of bills, or even ideas sent to them, and redrafting them to ensure that the legislation is substantively sound and couched in the proper legal terminology. The Office of Legislative Counsel cannot, of course, act independently; rather, it must follow the specific instructions given by a Congressman's office on those bills sent to it.

Presidential Action. The President, in addition to using his many methods of initiating policy outside the purview of Congress, may also formally present legislation for the consideration of the House and Senate. The Chief Executive may send Congress a Presidential message in which he communicates the Administration's position on certain issues. He may go further and include a specific draft of a bill together with his message. Both the draft and his Presidential message will have been cleared with the relevant executive departments and the Legislative Reference Service in the Office of Management and Budget (formerly the Bureau of the Budget). Of course, the President cannot introduce legislation directly. He must persuade a friendly Congressman to sponsor his legislation. A Congressman must affix his name to the bill before it can be placed in the hopper near the Speaker's rostrum and be referred to committee. On a more informal basis, a bill that ostensibly contains the Administration's position, although no specific Presidential message is sent to Congress, can be introduced by a sympathetic member.

This brings up the question of who speaks for the President in Congress. In areas of broad policy, the elected leaders of the President's party in Congress are usually his chief spokesmen. On specific pieces of legislation, however, the party spokesman will vary from bill to bill. Usually, the Administration will try to secure the chairman or ranking minority member of the committee having jurisdiction over the bill as its principal sponsor. Due to both the vast quantities of legislation being handled by Congress at any one time and the specialization of individual interests (nurtured by the committee and seniority systems),

[7] Lester Milbraith, *The Washington Lobbyists* (Chicago: Rand McNally, 1963), p. 307.

most Congressmen must concentrate their expertise on a relatively narrow number of issues. When such issues come before Congress, these
various rank-and-file Senators or Representatives may act as spokesmen for the Administration.

In gathering information and drafting legislation, the President has
not only White House staff to draw upon but also personnel from the
Cabinet departments and other executive agencies. Submitting a bill to
Congress is only the beginning of executive involvement in the legislation introduced. As a bill progresses through Congress and is modified
in the process, the executive branch must monitor each stage—subcommittee, committee, and floor activity. The President will have on
his staff aides for Congressional liaison who work closely with Congressional leaders, especially of his own party, so that they may be kept
informed of the Administration position at every juncture in the development of legislation. In this manner, a two-way flow of information
enables the President to move to press wavering Congressmen, should
a favored bill be in danger. At the same time, Congressional leaders
have the weight of Presidential authority behind them in their own
maneuvers to gather support for the legislation.

THE ORIGINS OF CAMPAIGN-REFORM LEGISLATION

The Initiators

The Political Broadcast Act of 1970 exemplifies the
hybrid nature of Congressional policy initiation. The prime innovator
was neither an enterprising Congressman nor the President, but a
public-oriented interest group, the National Committee for an Effective
Congress (NCEC). Russell D. Hemenway, the NCEC's executive director,
and Susan Bennett King, its principal Washington representative, were
the chief movers behind the introduction of the initial version of the
campaign-spending reform bill in September, 1969. Hemenway, a
former Foreign Service Officer who had been long active in New York
and national Democratic politics, has headed the organization since
1966. Mrs. King, a tall, attractive former Senate staff employee, has
coordinated NCEC Washington activities since 1967.

Founded in 1948, the NCEC has as its primary purpose the election
of those it regards as exceptional candidates to the Senate and the
House of Representatives. Its main office is in New York City, and the
Washington operation is run out of the basement apartment of a
townhouse about three blocks from the Capitol. Its core membership
is composed of some thirty prominent citizens who sit on its board

DOCUMENT **2-1**: Who Is NCEC?

Who is NCEC?

The distinguished philosopher Karl Jaspers describes NCEC as "an independent group of eminent individuals," which "does not support any party, but before an election it scrutinizes the candidates of both parties and endorses the best, no matter to which party they belong. The committee's integrity has given it great prestige; its endorsements are admitted to carry weight." For 22 years — under the chairmanship of Sidney H. Scheuer and his predecessor, the late Robert E. Sherwood — NCEC has brought together community leaders, historians, publishers, clergymen, educators and industrialists to evaluate candidate qualifications, make endorsements, allocate campaign assistance and deliberate national policy. The contributions of over 70,000 public spirited citizens make possible this political talent search and these efforts in the national interest.

Sidney H. Scheuer, *Chairman*

Henry Steele Commager   George R. Donahue
Vice Chairmen

S. Jay Levy   Thibaut de Saint Phalle
Secretary   *Treasurer*

Russell D. Hemenway, *National Director*

Members

Harry Ashmore	James Michener
George Backer	Francis P. Miller
George Biddle	Hans J. Morgenthau
Stimson Bullitt	Stewart R. Mott
Robert B. Choate	George E. Outland
George H. Combs	Laughlin Phillips
Fairleigh Dickinson Jr.	George D. Pratt Jr.
Thomas K. Finletter	Charles Rose
Paul Foley	Francis B. Sayre Jr.
Robert B. Gimbel	David E. Scoll
Alan Green	Telford Taylor
Alvin H. Hansen	David B. Truman
Orin Lehman	Barbara Tuchman
Isidore Lipschutz	Gerhard P. Van Arkel
Joseph P. McMurray	George Wald

National Committee for an Effective Congress
10 East 39 Street, New York, New York 10016.
MUrrayhill 3-2286

435 New Jersey Avenue, S.E.
Washington, D.C.
LIncoln 7-1151

The
National
Committee
for an
Effective
Congress

of directors. [*Doc. 2-1*] The NCEC is supported by private contributions from individuals who share the group's liberal political ideology. These contributors—upward of 70,000 to 80,000 people over a two-year Congressional period—are not normally consulted on the decisions made by the organization.[8] Thus the NCEC may be considered a

[8] A thorough study of the NCEC details the group's formation and analyzes the role of ideology in the development and operation of the organization. See Harry M. Scoble, *Ideology and Electoral Action* (San Francisco: Chandler Publishing, 1967).

mass-membership organization only in the broadest sense of the term.

The NCEC is primarily occupied with raising campaign funds, which it then distributes to Congressional candidates of its choosing. It considers itself to be a nonpartisan organization in that contributions are given to candidates of both parties. Over the years, however, NCEC has heavily favored Democratic candidates. It carefully screens those it is considering endorsing to see if their political ideology is compatible with the NCEC's moderate-to-liberal orientation. Contributions are allocated mainly to candidates competing in marginal states or districts.

Much of the fund-raising activity consists of acting as a middleman between wealthy contributors and needy candidates who represent an antiwar stance in Southeast Asia and hold positive views on such domestic issues as federally aided housing, civil rights, and consumer and environmental protection. To obtain an NCEC endorsement, "a candidate must demonstrate a clear choice over his opponent in philosophy, ability and personal history, he must need financial assistance, and his race must be close."[9] In 1970, NCEC raised and contributed approximately $830,000 to Congressional candidates; almost two-thirds of this money went to Senate candidates. For the first time in NCEC history, not a single GOP Senate candidate and only six Republican House candidates were backed in 1970. All told, the NCEC endorsed twenty-one Senate and fifty-eight House candidates during the 1970 primary and general election campaigns. Two-thirds of these were victorious.

Although the NCEC had entered the legislative arena from time to time—spearheading the fight against Senator Joseph R. McCarthy in the early 1950's, helping to found the Democratic Study Group in the late 1950's, acting as a liaison between members of both parties who authored the Civil Rights Act of 1964—the group's involvement in campaign finance reform was a turning point of sorts. For the first time, the NCEC took the leading role in drafting and sponsoring legislation rather than merely endorsing and working in behalf of legislative causes favored by its staff or board.

Ideas for campaign finance reform had been kicking around the Hill for years. Repeal of Section 315, in whole or in part, had also been freely discussed, especially after 1968, as Democrats began to lick their wounds and point toward the Presidential election of 1972. But it was probably the lessening return for each campaign dollar raised, more than the unfortunate quality of most television broadcast campaigning, that led Hemenway and King to try to put through an NCEC bill in the 91st Congress (1969–70). Mrs. King was quick to point out the plight of the candidate with only moderate means: "Without legislation,

[9] The National Committee for an Effective Congress, Fund-raising Brochure, 1971.

soon he wouldn't be able to run at all." Television broadcast control seemed the appropriate place to start. In Hemenway's words, "We decided control of television broadcast expenditures was the place to begin. The broadcast industry was already vulnerable, already down— they had had a lot of bad publicity. But most important, that is where most money is spent. And where most of the abuses occur."

Once the decision was made and informally cleared with leading members of the NCEC board, the NCEC staff turned to researching the problem. Anne Brooks, a former research associate for the American Broadcasting Company (ABC), had been hired in January, 1969. While she discussed the problem with her New York media contacts, Hemenway and Mrs. King were sounding out members of Congress, Federal Communications Commissioner Nicholas Johnson, an outspoken critic of the television industry, and a number of former FCC lawyers and broadcast personnel in Washington. Chief among the latter was Robert D. Squier, a bright young television consultant who had worked with the National Educational Television (NET) network and had been Director of Television for the Democratic National Committee during the 1968 Presidential campaign.[10] Working through a mutual friend, Wally Toner, who served on the staff of Representative Brock Adams (D., Wash.), they were able to draw upon the Office of the Legislative Counsel in developing the initial legislative draft. Of course, no draft springs full blown out of thin air. The Legislative Counsel lawyers had access to earlier versions of campaign-reform legislation introduced in previous Congresses for parts of the detailed language.

Once the NCEC had developed a draft, it launched a campaign for wider legislative support. It began by talking and writing to Congressmen—over a hundred by their own estimate—seeking support, hoping to generate a momentum behind the bill, but, above all, aligning sponsors. In the main, it focused on the members of the House and Senate commerce committees, the legislative committees with pertinent jurisdiction, on other members known to have a strong interest in campaign finance reform, and on its previous associates and friends, many of whom had received campaign contributions from the NCEC in the past. Out of its initial contacts came invitations to follow up. Personal visits gradually led to a core of key staff people in both houses, plus a few Senators and Representatives who were to carry on the fight during the balance of 1969 and 1970. [*Doc. 2-2*]

[10] Squier had come to the attention of the NCEC staff because of a speech he had given before the Federal City Bar Association emphasizing the need for political broadcast reform. The president of his own corporation, The Communications Company, Inc., Squier assumed responsibility for Senator Edmund Muskie's media campaign in 1970. (He engineered Muskie's 1970 election-eve broadcast from Maine, the effectiveness of which was coincidentally increased by proximity to a poorly produced televised speech by President Nixon.)

DOCUMENT **2-2**: Marshaling Support

NCEC

NATIONAL COMMITTEE for an EFFECTIVE CONGRESS
10 EAST 39th STREET   NEW YORK, N. Y. 10016   MURRAY HILL 3-2286

September 5, 1969

The Honorable John Melcher
U. S. House of Representatives
Washington, D. C.

Dear Congressman:

The NCEC would like to draw your attention to proposed
legislation to reduce the cost of television for Congressional
candidates in general election campaigns.

This measure will be introduced by Representative
Macdonald, Chairman of the Communications Subcommittee, on
Wednesday, September 10. A companion bill will be introduced
in the Senate on the same day by Senators Hart and Pearson and
a number of bipartisan cosponsors.

As you know, the NCEC has been involved in Congressional
elections and the raising of campaign funds for more than 20
years. Our Committee has become increasingly concerned over
the spiraling cost of running for public office. Particularly
as the use of television has increased, and broadcast costs
have risen, campaign expenses have jumped dramatically. For
this reason, the NCEC devoted much of the past 16 months to
examining this particular aspect of the problem. The bill to
be introduced on Wednesday contains many of the recommendations
developed by the Committee in this long study.

No single measure can solve all problems of financing
campaigns. Nonetheless, the voluntary rate reductions instituted
by several broadcasters in recent elections demonstrate that
this approach can provide a practical, effective first step
toward reducing the overall cost of campaigns.

We urge that you carefully consider this bill as
described by Representative Macdonald in his recent letter to
you, and we hope that you will lend your support and cosponsorship next Wednesday.

All best regards.

Sincerely yours,

Russ Hemenway

Russell D. Hemenway
National Director

The NCEC bill was introduced on September 10, 1969. Among its
leading sponsors were Torbert Macdonald (D., Mass.), chairman of the
Communications and Power Subcommittee in the House, and Senators
Philip A. Hart (D., Mich.) and James B. Pearson (R., Kan.), two influential members of the Senate Commerce Committee. Altogether, some
thirty-eight Senators and thirty-nine Representatives introduced the bill
as cosponsors. [*Doc. 2-3*]

DOCUMENT **2-3**: An Affirmative Response

United States Senate

COMMITTEE ON THE JUDICIARY

WASHINGTON, D.C. 20510

August 14, 1969

Mr. Russell D. Hemenway
National Director
National Committee for an Effective Congress
435 New Jersey Avenue, S.E.
Washington, D.C. 20003

Dear Russ:

    Many thanks for your recent letter about the Pearson-Hart legislation to provide reduced television rates for Congressional candidates.

    I will be glad to cosponsor the bill on my return to Washington in September, and would welcome your help in drafting a supporting statement. Please feel free to be in touch with my Legislative Assistant, Carrie Johnson, during the recess.

    With best wishes.

                Sincerely,

                Mac

                Charles McC. Mathias, Jr.
                United States Senator

CM/c
CC: Hon. James Pearson

    The final product, assigned the numbers S.2876 in the Senate and H.R.13721 in the House, had two basic provisions. First, it guaranteed "each legally qualified candidate" for Congress an opportunity to purchase a definite minimum amount of television broadcast time in his district or state. Second, it regulated the amount that could be charged by television stations for the time bought by candidates. The bill proposed to prevent stations from charging more than 30 per cent of what they would normally charge for a comparable spot advertisement and 20 per cent of what they would normally charge for a comparable half-hour broadcast. In other words, Congressional candidates in a general election would receive a 70 and 80 per cent discount for a fixed number of spot commercials and half-hour programs, respectively. As Documents 2-4 and 2-5 clearly illustrate, the NCEC draft largely prevailed in the initial House and Senate versions. This language was not to survive. [*Doc. 2-4*]

DOCUMENT **2-4**: An Excerpt from the NCEC Draft

" (B) Each legally qualified candidate for the office of United States Senator shall, with respect to each general election in which he is running, be entitled to purchase—

" (i) 120 one-minute segments of broadcast time or the equivalent (as determined under regulations of the Commission), and

" (ii) A 30-minute program-length broadcast or the equivalent (as determined under regulations of the Commission) from each television broadcasting station required under subsection (c) to provide opportunities to such candidate to purchase broadcast time.

" (C) If more than one television broadcasting station is required under subsection (c) to provide a candidate with opportunities to purchase broadcast time, all the television broadcast stations so required to provide such candidate with such opportunities shall divide equally among themselves (in accordance with regulations of the Commission) the responsibility to provide to the candidate the opportunity to purchase broadcast time described in clause (i) of subparagraph (A) or (B) of this paragraph, as the case may be.

Once the bill was formally submitted, it became subject to a variety of other forces over which the NCEC had less and less influence. The content of the legislation was to be changed many times during the next twelve months. The legislation that finally passed both houses of Congress in late 1970 and was sent to President Nixon was to bear but faint resemblance to the original NCEC bill. [*Doc. 2-5*]

External and Internal Factors

There were a number of external and internal factors that were important in the development and passage of this legislation by the Congress. The Political Broadcast Act of 1970 is typical of the

DOCUMENT **2-5**: An Excerpt from S.2876

The following is excerpted from this bill as it was introduced in the Senate. Notice the near identity of this and the NCEC version of the same copy.

5   " (B) Each legally qualified candidate for the office

6   of United States Senator shall, with respect to each general

7   election in which he is running, be entitled to purchase—

8   " (i) one hundred and twenty one-minute segments

9   of broadcast time (or the equivalent as determined under

10   regulations of the Commission) ; and

11   " (ii) a thirty-minute program-length broadcast or

12   the equivalent not to be used in segments shorter than

13   five minutes in length (as determined under regulations

14   of the Commission) from each television broadcasting

15   station required under subsection (c) to provide oppor-

16   tunities to such candidate to purchase broadcast time.

17   " (C) If more than one television broadcasting station is

18   required under subsection (c) to provide a candidate with

19   opportunities to purchase broadcast time, all the television

20   broadcast stations so required to provide such candidate with

21   such opportunities shall divide equally among themselves (in

22   accordance with regulations of the Commission) the responsi-

23   bility to provide to the candidate the opportunity to purchase

24   broadcast time described in clause (i) of subparagraph (A)

25   or (B) of this paragraph, as the case may be.

kind of legislation that, though it may be highly favored by the public, generates little intensity of concern. In a poll conducted just before the 1970 Congressional elections, Louis Harris found that 70 per cent of the sample felt there was "too much" spending by candidates for political office. He also found that 81 per cent agreed with the statement "Campaigns are so expensive these days that only a rich man can afford to run for office."[11] Withal, there was little evidence that the mass of the electorate felt intensely about reforming the system. Although significant concern was expressed by many political elites and by the media, for the average American, strong feelings on the subject were probably limited to irritation about the inundation of political commercials on television during the campaigns or the loss of a favorite program or two.

Congressmen try to ascertain how their constituents feel about issues in a variety of ways—visits back home, the mail, and, increasingly, questionnaire surveys. For example, Representative Lionel Van Deerlin, a member of the communications subcommittee that has jurisdiction over television and campaign spending, subsequently mailed a questionnaire to nearly 100,000 constituents in April, 1971. He found that the majority of his constituents who responded (over 20,000 *in total*) favored limiting over-all campaign spending [*Doc. 2-6*]

Although the American public showed considerable awareness of the problem of skyrocketing campaign costs, there was little unity of opinion as to what should be done about it. The regulation of campaign costs is a complex issue, and Congressmen were divided among themselves in determining what was the best solution.

In the House of Representatives, the Subcommittee on Communications and Power of the Interstate and Foreign Commerce Committee was given the responsibility for dealing with the legislation that was introduced in September, 1969. Its counterpart in the Senate was the Communications Subcommittee of the Commerce Committee. The two Democrats who chaired these subcommittees were Torbert Macdonald of Massachusetts in the House and John O. Pastore of Rhode Island in the Senate. Both of these veteran lawmakers had definite ideas about what was needed in the way of legislation. Both were to fight hard on behalf of their differing views. These two were instrumental in guiding the legislation out of committee and subcommittee and onto the floor of their respective chambers. They continued to play crucial roles during the debate and amending stages. Senator Pastore was to become responsible for significant changes in the original bill that was drafted by the NCEC. Representative Macdonald led his House colleagues in bringing about further reforms.

The Democratic leadership supported this legislation but clearly did not assign it a high priority. A staff member of the NCEC complained that it had to "lean on Speaker McCormack" to keep the bill moving through the House. Senate Majority Leader Mike Mansfield played only a minimal role in attempting to secure the override of President Nixon's veto.

---

[11] Louis Harris, "Too Much Campaign Spending," *New York Post*, Nov. 5, 1970.

DOCUMENT **2-6**: The Van Deerlin Poll

This is a portion of a questionnaire sent out by Congressman Lionel Van Deerlin (D., Calif.) to his constituents in the 92d Congress. Van Deerlin wanted some concrete follow-up on how the people of his district felt about this and other issues.

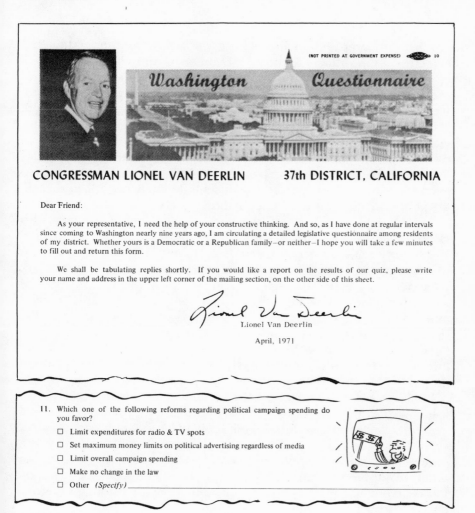

(NOT PRINTED AT GOVERNMENT EXPENSE) 10

Washington Questionnaire

CONGRESSMAN LIONEL VAN DEERLIN   37th DISTRICT, CALIFORNIA

Dear Friend:

As your representative, I need the help of your constructive thinking. And so, as I have done at regular intervals since coming to Washington nearly nine years ago, I am circulating a detailed legislative questionnaire among residents of my district. Whether yours is a Democratic or a Republican family—or neither—I hope you will take a few minutes to fill out and return this form.

We shall be tabulating replies shortly. If you would like a report on the results of our quiz, please write your name and address in the upper left corner of the mailing section, on the other side of this sheet.

Lionel Van Deerlin

April, 1971

11. Which one of the following reforms regarding political campaign spending do you favor?

☐ Limit expenditures for radio & TV spots

☐ Set maximum money limits on political advertising regardless of media

☐ Limit overall campaign spending

☐ Make no change in the law

☐ Other *(Specify)* _____

The legislation introduced in September, 1969, was initially supported by members of both parties. Although the Political Broadcast Act of 1970 was eventually passed by a bipartisan coalition, the issue had become increasingly partisan as the legislation progressed through both houses. As will be detailed in chapters 4 and 5, the bill was not passed until late fall—just before the November, 1970, Congressional elections. In those elections, more than twice as much money was to be spent on political broadcasting as in the previous midterm election, in 1966. After President Nixon's veto on October 12, the Political Broadcast Act took on increasingly partisan overtones, so that the override attempt in late November was in the main contested on party lines.

What catalyzed action on political broadcast reform in the 91st Congress? The fortunes spent by a number of candidates in the 1968 elections and the 1970 primaries certainly helped to stimulate serious consideration of campaign finance legislation. Drives toward reform were enhanced by the 1970 Senate primary campaign in New York State, where Representative Richard Ottinger spent over $700,000 for radio and television time alone. Multimillionaire Norton Simon spent well over a million dollars in an unsuccessful effort to defeat Republican incumbent George Murphy in the 1970 California Senate primary. Such excessive spending acted to concentrate attention still further on the pending campaign-reform legislation.

Partisan considerations on the part of the Democrats were also clearly a factor. In 1968, Republican Presidential candidate Richard Nixon outspent Democratic candidate Hubert Humphrey on broadcasting air time alone by a margin of more than two to one. In 1970, many Democratic Senators were facing tough re-election contests in which they knew their Republican opponent would be able to raise much more money than they could. Repeal of Section 315—and the debates that were likely to follow—might also make the incumbent President more vulnerable in 1972. Such debates could not help but give the Democratic nominee, whoever he might be, substantially greater exposure.

Although a number of external factors were important, the NCEC's leading role in galvanizing action must be acknowledged. It was instrumental in putting this broad problem into a legislative focus. Even its most lukewarm admirer would admit that "the NCEC was a catalyst in a way, a minor catalyst." Most observers would give the group major credit not only for gaining the attention of Congress on this issue but also for keeping the legislation moving through Congress once it had been introduced.

FURTHER READING

A comprehensive treatment of Congress, the Presidency, and the policy-making process is James L. Sundquist's *Politics and Policy* (Washington, D.C.: The Brookings Institution, 1968).

For an empirical study of the relationship among a Congressman's attitudes, his constituency's attitudes, and his vote on selected roll calls, see Warren E. Miller and Donald E. Stokes, "Constituency Influence in Congress," *The American Political Science Review*, vol. LVII (March, 1963).

The nature of American public opinion is analyzed thoroughly by V. O. Key, Jr., in *Public Opinion and American Democracy* (New York: Alfred A. Knopf, 1964). A useful short summary on political public opinion is Robert E. Lane and David O. Sears, *Public Opinion* (Englewood Cliffs, N.J.: Prentice-Hall, 1964).

Two very interesting articles on the seniority system in the House of Representatives are Raymond E. Wolfinger and Joan Heifetz Hollinger, "Safe Seats, Seniority and Power in Congress," *The American Political Science Review*, vol. LIX (June, 1965), and Nelson W. Polsby, Miriam Gallagher, and Barry Spencer Rundquist, "The Growth of the Seniority System in the U.S. House of Representatives," *The American Political Science Review*, vol. LXIII (September, 1969).

On the committee system, John F. Manley's *The Politics of Finance: The House Committee on Ways and Means* (Boston: Little, Brown, 1970) is an excellent case study of the House Ways and Means Committee and the leadership of its chairman, Wilbur Mills. See also Ralph K. Huitt, "The Congressional Committee: A Case Study," *The American Political Science Review*, vol. XLVIII (June, 1954), and Richard F. Fenno, Jr., "The House Appropriations Committee as a Political System: The Problem of Integration," *The American Political Science Review*, vol. LVI (June, 1962).

Interest Groups
in the
Legislative Process

INTEREST GROUPS AND THE
GOVERNMENTAL STRUCTURE

Although they are not mentioned in the Constitution, interest groups, or pressure groups as they are sometimes called, have come to play a vital role in the national policy-making process. While Congressmen ostensibly represent the manifold and often conflicting interests of their state or district, a pressure group usually represents the narrow and specific interests of its particular membership.

Interest groups develop because of a desire of a number of citizens to achieve or maintain goals. People join such groups not just because they have something in common but because they share a desire to be able to take organized action on certain interests. People with blond hair have something in common but lack any reason to take collective action on a shared purpose or goal. As David Truman, a leading authority on interest groups, defines them:

> "Interest group" refers to any group that, on the basis of one or more shared attitudes, makes certain claims upon other groups in the society for the establishment, maintenance, or enhancement of forms of behavior that are implied by the shared attitudes.[1]

Interest groups vary widely in their size, structure, and purpose. Not only do such groups as the AFL-CIO or the American Medical Association (AMA) qualify under Truman's definition but also such organizations as the National Congress of Parents and Teachers and the Council of Jewish Women. An interest group does not have to be a purely politically oriented organization. Often a group will be organized largely for philanthropic or social purposes but will occasionally take political action on a policy matter that is directly relevant to its interests.

A major function performed by interest groups in our society is public opinion linkage between the members of a group and governmental officials. They articulate and convey to government the desires and opinions of identifiable groups in the country on matters that interest them. Thus, lobbying may be conceived of as essentially a communication process. In *The Washington Lobbyists*, Lester Milbraith defines lobbying as "the stimulation and transmission of a communication by someone other than a citizen acting on his own behalf, directed to a

[1] David B. Truman, *The Governmental Process* (New York: Alfred A. Knopf, 1951), p. 33.

governmental decision-maker with the hope of influencing his decision."[2] Communication, however, is a two-way affair: These organizations also keep their members informed about those activities of government and of other groups that are pertinent to their concerns.

When a group does decide to make "certain claims upon other groups," there are a variety of means and techniques by which it may do so. As Morton Grodzins pointed out, the legislative-administrative process in our government has a "multiple-crack" nature. In other words, many different stages in the governmental process as well as the multiplicity of governmental units afford numerous points of access to an interest group seeking to influence policy. Although lobbying is an activity usually thought of as oriented toward the legislative branch of government, a great deal of interest-group work is directed toward the executive branch and administrative agencies. Commercial airlines, for example, will have less occasion to lobby in Congress because most of the policy pertinent to them will be formulated, implemented, and adjudicated by the Civil Aeronautics Board (CAB) and the Federal Aviation Agency (FAA).

The judicial branch of the government is also subject to lobbying. Because legal action demands a great deal of time and money, organizations are usually in a much better position to support litigation than are individual citizens. This is especially true when a case is appealed all the way to the Supreme Court. Pressure groups may also appear before the courts as *amicus curiae*, or "friends of the court." With the permission of the court, organizations will often be permitted to file a written brief in a case where they are not a direct party to the litigation but do have an interest in the outcome.[3]

Private interest groups not only lobby governmental institutions, they often lobby one another. Sometimes this occurs because, although two or more groups share the same general goals, they are in conflict over specific demands. At other times, one group will endeavor to enlist the aid of other groups that appear to have common interests on a specific issue in an attempt to build a coalition of support. For example, groups like the National Association for the Advancement of Colored People (NAACP), the Congress of Racial Equality (CORE), and the Southern Christian Leadership Conference (SCLC) have been able to enlist the aid of labor organizations such as the United Auto Workers (UAW) and liberal associations such as the Americans for Democratic Action (ADA) in behalf of civil rights legislation.

Lobbying is not restricted to private groups. It is common for one

---

[2] Lester Milbraith, *The Washington Lobbyists* (Chicago: Rand McNally, 1963), p. 8.

[3] A good, concise summary of the role of interest groups in the judicial process is given by Clement E. Vose, "Litigation as a Form of Pressure Group Activity," *The Annals of the American Academy of Political and Social Science* 319 (Sept., 1958), 20.

government agency to try to influence a decision that is to be made by another unit. An example of this type of institutional lobbying is when a government official appears at a Congressional committee hearing and argues for a particular policy in the hope of influencing the legislation under consideration.

There is a great variation in the size and structure of Washington lobbies. Some maintain an office in the nation's capital that is staffed by lawyers, public relations experts, and other full-time professionals. This requires substantial financial support, and only large and wealthy interest groups are able to afford a sizable, permanent staff. Most other groups are organized on a more modest scale, employing only a small cadre of professional staffers. Frequently, a Washington lobby consists of but one man and his "girl Friday."

Pressure groups that do not require the use of a full-time lobbyist may hire a "lobbyist entrepreneur" when the need arises for Washington assistance. A lobbyist entrepreneur is one who hires himself out to various interest groups to perform specific tasks for them. If a pressure group has need of a lobbyist on a periodic but steady basis, it may employ him on a fixed retainer so that the lobbyist will be available to work for the group at any time he is needed through the year. Additionally, some Washington law firms specialize in occasional lobbying for a great many of their clients.

It is all but impossible to calculate how many interest groups are active at any one time in the United States. It is difficult even to make an intelligent guess as to how many groups lobby in Washington in a given year. The Federal Regulation of Lobbying Act of 1946 requires anyone who "directly or indirectly solicits, collects or receives money or any other thing of value" for efforts to influence the defeat or passage of legislation to register with the Congress. But the Supreme Court has limited the application of that law to individuals and organizations who solicit, receive, or collect money *principally* for the purpose of influencing legislation in Congress, and then, only if their lobbying involves *direct* communications with members of Congress.[4] Consequently, many firms that actually do engage in lobbying activities from time to time do not register. During the 90th Congress, for example, the National Committee for an Effective Congress was not registered as a lobby, while the H. E. Butt Grocery Store of Corpus Christi, Texas, was.

The following table reflects the diversity of those groups that registered with the Congress between October 14, 1968, and December 23, 1969.[5]

[4] U.S. v. Harriss, 347 U.S. 612 (1954).
[5] *Congressional Quarterly Almanac, 1969* (Washington, D.C.: Congressional Quarterly Service, 1970), p. 1097.

Business	369
Citizens	83
Farm	19
Foreign	6
Foundations	35
Individuals*	51
Labor and Employee	41
Military and Vietnam Peace	4
Professional	39
	647

* "Individuals" are lobbyists who registered but did not list the concern(s) they represented.

When surveys are taken of sample populations as to how many and to which groups people belong, several significant patterns emerge. Those with low income or low education and those who are unskilled are much less likely to be members of interest groups. Conversely, the better-educated and better-off individual is much more likely to have his interests represented by private groups and, in fact, to belong to a proportionately greater number of interest groups.

An individual does not actually have to be a member of a group to be represented by it. The NAACP, for example, ostensibly represents all black Americans, but only a fraction belong to the organization. Nonetheless, as V. O. Key pointed out, "the more completely an organization encompasses its potential membership, the greater is its moral authority when it claims to speak for an interest in society."[6]

Critics of pressure groups often argue that the organizations are seldom democratic, for decision-making and policy implementation are carried out at the highest levels only; rank-and-file members may be called upon to ratify the decisions of the leaders, but they rarely take part in the actual formulation of policy. Though this may largely be true, it does not of necessity mean that leaders are always unrepresentative of the rank-and-file or that they are never guided by ideas of what the general membership desires. In fact, interest-group leaders play a role similar to Congressmen in that they are not strict delegates and must often act where they have only limited information on the views of their constituents.

Public-interest pressure groups have a special problem in communicating the interests of their constituents to Congress. Although public-interest groups like Common Cause or the League of Women Voters have a limited membership, they purport to speak for the interests of

[6] V. O. Key, Jr., *Public Opinion and American Democracy* (New York: Alfred A. Knopf, 1964), p. 503.

the public at large, or the "people." Each Congressman, however, has his own conception of what the "public interest" is and will weigh the claims of such lobbies in the light of his own perspective and experience.

Many interests in the United States remain largely unorganized. For example, Mexican-American migrant farm laborers are mobilizing in California, but their efforts to unionize in Arizona, Texas, and other states have been far less successful. Consumers, too, have long been without adequate interest-group representation although abuses by manufacturers and merchandisers have lately led to increasingly active consumer groups. Before mass unrest over the Vietnam war, it was almost unheard of for enlisted men on active duty to rally around a political cause. By and large, American students in past years were not well organized, in part because they lacked a sense of shared goals. Perhaps, as Bob Dylan suggests, "The Times They Are a Changin' "— perhaps not. With the ratification of the 26th Amendment in 1971, eighteen-year-olds gained the right to vote. Whether they will exercise that franchise, let alone organize around candidates and issues of their choice, remains to be seen.

Lobbying and Congress

Although an interest group that wants representation before Congress may hire a Washington lobbyist, a good deal of lobbying is conducted by nonprofessional members of the interest group. Groups like the Poor People's Crusade or the Vietnam Veterans Against the War would undoubtedly damage their cause if they used an intermediary between themselves and the government. Public-interest lobbyists are almost always ideologically committed to their group's cause. On the other hand, a lobbyist for a soap manufacturer or a trade association may have little personal interest in the group outside of his retainer and his reputation, which is based upon the professional services he provides.

Washington lobbyists are normally hired because they have experience and knowledge of the governmental process. A great number of lobbyists are, in fact, former White House, executive agency, or Congressional employees. Many have legal training or a public relations background, but these are not strictly necessary. A few are former Congressmen, but contrary to popular belief, most lobbyists as a rule are not people who are or have been active in campaign fund-raising and partisan politics.[7]

---

[7] For background on Washington lobbyists, see Part II, "The Lobbyist as a Political Actor," in Milbraith, *op. cit.*

A lobbyist is seldom a delegate charged merely with carrying out decisions made by the organization that hires him. Rather, he is an integral part of policy-making. A Washington-based professional staff will make the day-to-day decisions for most out-of-town pressure groups. Directly in touch with developments, the staff is more likely to know the strategies and techniques that will suit the pressure group's goals at any given time. Most lobbyists have considerable influence with the executive boards of the interest groups they represent, for group policies must be at least partially shaped by pragmatic considerations regarding what is and what is not feasible in terms of governmental reaction and response.

In theory, lobbying is an extension of the constitutional right of petition: it is a form of communication between citizens and their government. Communication is the very essence of lobbying, and it offers a convenient framework by which the process may be observed and studied. Anyone can *transmit* a message, but not everyone can *communicate* it effectively. An effective communication is one that is not merely received, but is also taken into account by the official to whom it is transmitted. It is the lobbyist's job to design such messages, but this is easier said than done. As Lewis Anthony Dexter notes, "It's partly accident if anyone's listening."[8]

Lobbyists endeavor to create and nurture the type of access to Congressmen and agency officials that will enable them to get their message across. They must pick the method and strategy that will most effectively communicate their view. Hundreds of form letters signed by individual members of an interest group have little impact because they are obviously "inspired" by the leaders of the group. On the other hand, a politically sensitive conversation between a lobbyist and a Congressman or the presentation of a concise, factual memorandum containing legislative background material to a key committee staff man may be among the most effective methods of communicating the group's position.

A fundamental problem for the lobbyist is deciding to whom he should direct his message. Time and resources are at a premium for the lobbyist: it is impossible for him to communicate with every governmental official who will have some impact on a given policy. He must know whether he is better off approaching Congress, an administrative agency, the Executive Office of the President, a court of law, or elsewhere. He must also decide which handful of individuals it would be most beneficial to approach within the one or more institutions chosen for lobbying activities. He has to know who is likely to be

---

[8] Lewis Anthony Dexter, "The Representative and His District," *New Perspectives on the House of Representatives*, 2d ed., Robert L. Peabody and Nelson W. Polsby, eds. (Chicago: Rand McNally, 1969), p. 2.

sympathetic to his cause and who is hostile or neutral. Is the committee chairman apt to be friendly? If not, who is the most sympathetic member on the subcommittee that is likely to have jurisdiction? Are there individuals or groups in the districts of neutral or hostile members who might help "educate" them? Competent assessments of such questions have a substantial bearing on whether or not the lobbyist's message will be heard or acted upon.

A lobbyist must be able to develop alternative strategies quickly if his original efforts seem headed for failure. Often a skilled lobbyist will use a sympathetic Congressman as an intermediary between himself and an administrative agency: a Congressman's office can usually obtain a far quicker response to a request or provide access for the lobbyist to key executive branch officials. Knowing *where* to lobby is much of knowing *how* to lobby. As Dexter points out, "The squeaking wheel gets the grease . . . provided that the squeaking is effectively directed and channeled, rather than at random."[9]

Part of the difficulty confronting a lobbyist is that Congressmen, like other human beings, selectively perceive the information to which they are exposed. People interpret what is presented to them in the light of their own knowledge, feelings, and past experience. The natural tendency is to ignore, downplay, or rationalize information that runs counter to one's predispositions. In communicating a message, a lobbyist must try to design and present it in a manner and form such that the Congressman perceives it in the most advantageous perspective for him. Once alerted, will he read the message and respond favorably? Probably not, unless he sees the benefits for himself or his district.

An awareness of the importance of communication between lobbyist and Congressman must not lead us to a wholesale acceptance of the standard American stereotype: the pressuring of Congressmen by lobbyists who, by one means or another, convert a Representative or Senator to the desired point of view. In the cartoon stereotype, the fat, sinister, cigar-smoking lobbyist seems all too ready to buy as many votes as are needed from all-too-willing legislators. In fact, instances of outright bribery of Congressmen are very rare. The same may be said for cases of "conversion." Research has shown that the vast majority of lobbying activities are aimed at Congressmen who are already favorably disposed toward the lobby's point of view. In other words, lobbyists concentrate on seeing their "friends" and tend to leave their "enemies" alone. Because resources are often scarce and never unlimited, it does little good to expend them in attempts to convert those who are already on record against the group's position. Effort is much

[9] Lewis Anthony Dexter, *How Organizations Are Represented in Washington* (Indianapolis: Bobbs-Merrill, 1969), p. 19.

better expended on trying to convince the undecided and to keep supporters concerned and active in the group's interest.

The Strength of Congressional Lobbying

Congressmen and interest groups attempt to pass a bill
by building winning coalitions at each stage of the legislative process.
"Logrolling" is one method of building such coalitions. Basically, logrolling is a form of bargaining that occurs when one Congressman
promises to vote for a bill favored by a second if the second Congressman will, in return, vote for legislation supported by the first.

Logrolling in legislatures is cushioned by a broad and pervasive
climate of exchange, trust, and accommodation. It is much more
difficult for lobbies to logroll or trade off support. Unlike a Congressman on the floor of the House or Senate, one lobby does not have a
co-equal vote to offer another lobby. And, whereas a Congressman
may gain the support of other Congressmen who have little or no
interest in a particular bill but whose votes may nonetheless be quite
valuable, for a lobby, the support of another group that has little
self-interest in the outcome of a particular bill may be of negligible
use. This stems from the very nature of lobbying. Lobbyists gain much
of their access and influence because they are able to transmit valuable information to Congressmen, but a pressure group is unlikely to
commit the time, money, and staff necessary to research, prepare,
and circulate information unless it has a *direct* interest in a certain
policy. Still, without expending much in the way of resources, a
lobby that is not directly interested in a piece of legislation may be of
some help to other groups that are vitally concerned. For example,
lobbies may exchange information about certain Congressmen and
how best to approach them or who to see on their staff.

When lobbies do coalesce it is usually on a highly informal and
often uncoordinated basis among groups that are directly interested
in specific legislation. In light of their restricted resources, organizations seldom lobby on everything their group has an interest in. Most
lobbies concentrate their efforts on a small number of issues on
which they have placed a high priority. In one important study of
foreign trade legislation, *American Business and Public Policy*, the
authors found that many groups they thought would be highly active
were doing little if any lobbying, despite an apparent interest in the
legislation. Finding few lobbies to be well-oiled machines capable of
acting with effectiveness on a wide variety of issues, the authors
concluded:

> The failure to recognize the multiplicity and diversity of spending bodies,
> each with its individual goals, leads to a false image of pressure group proc-

esses. . . . Wherever one looked at the persons actually spending their money, one saw only harassed men with tight budgets and limited campaign funds, once their essential organizational overheads had been met.[10]

Are Congressmen overly pressured by special interest groups? The purpose of a lobbyist is to gain effective access for information transmitted from an interest group. But, is it "pressure" for a Congressman to accept proffered information and be influenced by it? What may appear to an outsider as pressure is likely to be perceived in an entirely different light by a Congressman; for him, it is merely part of his day-to-day interaction. Most Congressmen take the activities of interest groups in stride, and the most competent legislators often turn the relationship around, using lobbyists for their own legislative ends.

It is often assumed that interest groups can exert pressure on a Congressman because they can help to vote him out of office at the next election. As V. O. Key has argued, however, this is rarely the case.[11] It may be possible in a district or state where one well-organized interest is clearly dominant—for example, the Boeing Aircraft Company in Seattle—but the fact is that few interest groups by themselves are strong enough to defeat a Representative, let alone a Senator, at the polls. Most districts and states have numerous interest groups, many of which have conflicting goals. Boeing workers, for example, are likely to vote differently than the company's middle or top management. A skilled Congressman can sometimes play one group off against another.

In responding to a group's interest, a Congressman may consciously feel he is representing his constituents whether he considers them to be part of his district, state, or national constituency. Most Representatives and Senators are relatively free agents; within limits they have some choice as to which interests they will represent. Of course, over time a Congressman usually develops a fairly stable set of interests he feels comfortable with.

Campaign contributions are, however, a major form of securing access to a Congressman's office for an interest group. A Representative or Senator is careful not to alienate those groups that have in the past given him $100, $1,000, or $5,000 for campaign expenses. Critics of pressure groups often question the ethics of direct campaign contributions. For example, is it proper for a chairman whose committee determines how many miles of interstate highway are to be built each year to accept money for campaign expenses from large highway con-

[10] Raymond A. Bauer, Ithiel de Sola Pool, and Lewis Anthony Dexter, *American Business and Public Policy* (New York: Atherton Press, 1968), p. 345.

[11] V. O. Key, Jr., *op. cit.*, pp. 518–19.

tractors? The question of from whom a Congressman may ethically accept campaign contributions is one Congress has never resolved: Instead, each House and Senate member makes his own determination.

INTEREST GROUPS AND THE
POLITICAL BROADCAST ACT

The activities of interest groups during attempts to pass the Political Broadcast Act mainly support the conclusions reached by recent studies of American pressure groups. Probably the most striking aspect of pressure-group activity in this case was the *lack* of it. Considering the importance of the measure and the potential impact of the various versions of the bill upon the broadcasting industry, it is somewhat surprising that more intense lobbying did not occur.

Before the President's veto, few Congressmen were visited by representatives of any interest groups other than the National Committee for an Effective Congress. Except for what they heard at the House or Senate hearings, Senators and Representatives received little information from lobbies until the attempt to override the veto was underway. Prior to October–November, 1970, few Congressmen were contacted either by the National Association of Broadcasters or by local television and radio stations. Contrary to the popular stereotype of lobbyists freely spending money to influence votes, there is little evidence that significant amounts were spent on lobbying directly related to the Political Broadcast Act of 1970. Of course, NCEC had supported a number of Congressmen in past elections and would contribute more than $800,000 to campaigns in the 1970 elections. But such support could and did cut both ways: Incumbents who were denied contributions in previous elections, and especially those who had withstood the challenge of NCEC-supported candidates, would not easily forget or forgive this affront. Moreover, because most of NCEC's direct contributions were being channeled to friends or early supporters of campaign reform, their political impact vis-à-vis the act was further diminished.

Aside from its campaign contributions, the NCEC spent little more than its normal operating overhead during its intensive effort to pass the Political Broadcast Act. Susan King, the Washington director, gave this project top priority throughout most of the 91st Congress. Russell Hemenway, the national executive director, commuted to Washington from New York during peak periods of lobbying activity in the spring, summer, and fall of 1970. Although only modest amounts of money were spent, major efforts were made to cultivate reporters and editorial writers in order to generate the broadest possible base of public opinion support. The NCEC staff also took advantage of the FCC "fairness doctrine," thereby gaining editorial time on television, and continued its efforts to hold or convert Congressmen through personal contacts or letters. [*Doc. 3-1 and Doc. 3-2*]

DOCUMENT **3-1**: NCEC Rebuts a WTOP Editorial

NCEC Director Russell Hemenway replies to a TV editorial that had recommended a veto of the Political Broadcast Act.

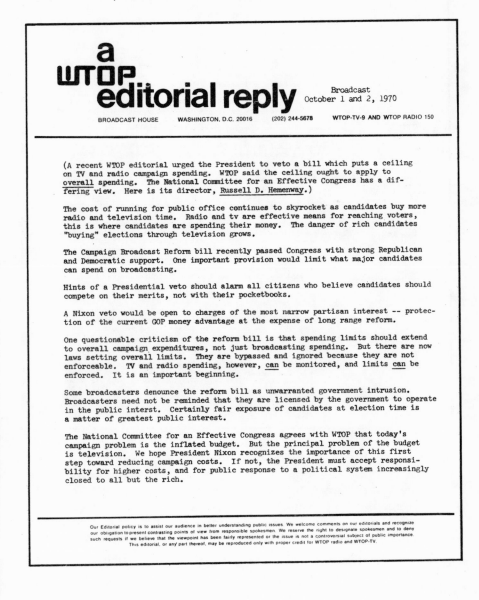

a
WTOP
editorial reply   Broadcast
October 1 and 2, 1970

BROADCAST HOUSE   WASHINGTON, D.C. 20016   (202) 244-5678   WTOP-TV-9 AND WTOP RADIO 150

(A recent WTOP editorial urged the President to veto a bill which puts a ceiling on TV and radio campaign spending. WTOP said the ceiling ought to apply to <u>overall</u> spending. The National Committee for an Effective Congress has a differing view. Here is its director, <u>Russell D. Hemenway</u>.)

The cost of running for public office continues to skyrocket as candidates buy more radio and television time. Radio and tv are effective means for reaching voters, this is where candidates are spending their money. The danger of rich candidates "buying" elections through television grows.

The Campaign Broadcast Reform bill recently passed Congress with strong Republican and Democratic support. One important provision would limit what major candidates can spend on broadcasting.

Hints of a Presidential veto should alarm all citizens who believe candidates should compete on their merits, not with their pocketbooks.

A Nixon veto would be open to charges of the most narrow partisan interest -- protection of the current GOP money advantage at the expense of long range reform.

One questionable criticism of the reform bill is that spending limits should extend to overall campaign expenditures, not just broadcasting spending. But there are now laws setting overall limits. They are bypassed and ignored because they are not enforceable. TV and radio spending, however, <u>can</u> be monitored, and limits <u>can</u> be enforced. It is an important beginning.

Some broadcasters denounce the reform bill as unwarranted government intrusion. Broadcasters need not be reminded that they are licensed by the government to operate in the public interst. Certainly fair exposure of candidates at election time is a matter of greatest public interest.

The National Committee for an Effective Congress agrees with WTOP that today's campaign problem is the inflated budget. But the principal problem of the budget is television. We hope President Nixon recognizes the importance of this first step toward reducing campaign costs. If not, the President must accept responsibility for higher costs, and for public response to a political system increasingly closed to all but the rich.

DOCUMENT 3-2: The NCEC Acts in Support of the Override

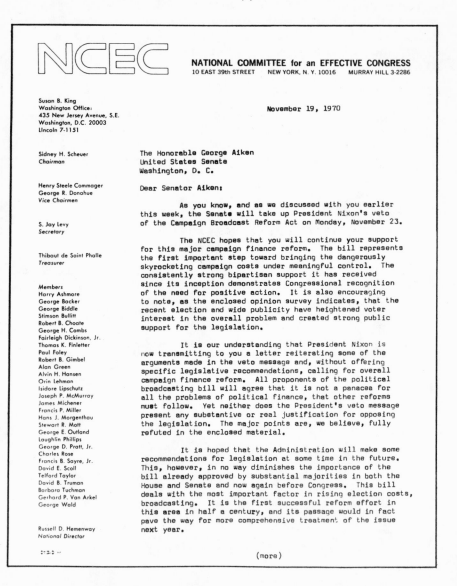

NCEC

NATIONAL COMMITTEE for an **EFFECTIVE CONGRESS**
10 EAST 39th STREET   NEW YORK, N. Y. 10016   MURRAY HILL 3-2286

Susan B. King
Washington Office:
435 New Jersey Avenue, S.E.
Washington, D.C. 20003
Llncoln 7-1151

November 19, 1970

Sidney H. Scheuer
Chairman

The Honorable George Aiken
United States Senate
Washington, D. C.

Henry Steele Commager
George R. Donahue
Vice Chairmen

Dear Senator Aiken:

S. Jay Levy
Secretary

As you know, and as we discussed with you earlier
this week, the Senate will take up President Nixon's veto
of the Campaign Broadcast Reform Act on Monday, November 23.

Thibaut de Saint Phalle
Treasurer

The NCEC hopes that you will continue your support
for this major campaign finance reform. The bill represents
the first important step toward bringing the dangerously
skyrocketing campaign costs under meaningful control. The
consistently strong bipartisan support it has received
since its inception demonstrates Congressional recognition
of the need for positive action. It is also encouraging
to note, as the enclosed opinion survey indicates, that the
recent election and wide publicity have heightened voter
interest in the overall problem and created strong public
support for the legislation.

Members
Harry Ashmore
George Backer
George Biddle
Stimson Bullitt
Robert B. Choate
George H. Combs
Fairleigh Dickinson, Jr.
Thomas K. Finletter
Paul Foley
Robert B. Gimbel
Alan Green
Alvin H. Hansen
Orin Lehman
Isidore Lipschutz
Joseph P. McMurray
James Michener
Francis P. Miller
Hans J. Morgenthau
Stewart R. Mott
George E. Outland
Laughlin Phillips
George D. Pratt, Jr.
Charles Rose
Francis B. Sayre, Jr.
David E. Scoll
Telford Taylor
David B. Truman
Barbara Tuchman
Gerhard P. Van Arkel
George Wald

It is our understanding that President Nixon is
now transmitting to you a letter reiterating some of the
arguments made in the veto message and, without offering
specific legislative recommendations, calling for overall
campaign finance reform. All proponents of the political
broadcasting bill will agree that it is not a panacea for
all the problems of political finance, that other reforms
must follow. Yet neither does the President's veto message
present any substantive or real justification for opposing
the legislation. The major points are, we believe, fully
refuted in the enclosed material.

It is hoped that the Administration will make some
recommendations for legislation at some time in the future.
This, however, in no way diminishes the importance of the
bill already approved by substantial majorities in both the
House and Senate and now again before Congress. This bill
deals with the most important factor in rising election costs,
broadcasting. It is the first successful reform effort in
this area in half a century, and its passage would in fact
pave the way for more comprehensive treatment of the issue
next year.

Russell D. Hemenway
National Director

(more)

It is ironic that on this vital issue the NCEC, not normally involved in legislation, was the most active interest group. Its primary function has been and continues to be raising money and helping to elect the Congressmen it feels will best serve the needs of the nation. As already noted, its criteria for evaluating candidates for endorsement center mainly on their moderate-to-liberal political ideology, their chances for winning the election, and whether or not they are clearly

Doc. 3-2 *(cont.)*

Unfortunately, through an erroneous newspaper story, the vote on Monday has been described as a test of wills between President Nixon and Democratic leaders. This is simply not true. The original bipartisan sponsors of the legislation, Senators Pearson, Hart, Pastore and Goodell, continue to lead this fight for reform for the same reason they did 18 months ago -- it is desperately needed. They and other sponsors will undoubtedly be in the forefront of the continuing effort for other badly needed reform.

The NCEC appreciates and understands the immense pressures to which members of the President's party are subject at such a time. We can only ask that you not allow extraneous arguments to distort the issue, and that you accord it the consideration which a measure of this importance deserves, determination on the merits.

We urge you to support the legislation on Monday, as you have done earlier.

With all best regards.

Sincerely,

Russell D. Hemenway
NCEC National Director

Enclosures (2)

preferable to their opponents. Still, the NCEC's effectiveness in campaign support was obviously being endangered by the sharply increasing costs of political campaigning, in turn due mainly to the greater use of television. As Susan King explained the NCEC's legislative sponsorship, "We sort of backed into this one by default. No one else would take the issue."

The NCEC decision to become active in trying to stimulate Congressional action on campaign finance was not the product of a grass-roots movement on the part of the NCEC membership. Rather, the decision was made primarily by Russell Hemenway and Susan King, both of whom felt keenly the severity of the problem. Their plan to sponsor legislation was readily endorsed by a sympathetic NCEC executive board. Hemenway summed up his feelings when he told the Senate Communications Subcommittee, "At any given time when a society finds a large percentage of its members are frozen out of public service because they can't afford to run, obviously we have a serious crisis." For Mrs. King, "The bill would help to keep politics and elective office open to the little guy, the qualified, capable but unknown and unrich candidate."

The primary thrust of opposition to the bill was led by the National Association of Broadcasters (NAB), the major trade association and spokesman for the majority of individual radio and television stations throughout the country. Many people mistakenly assume that the three large national television networks—CBS, NBC, and ABC—own the stations that carry their programs. By law, however, the networks are limited to ownership of five individual stations. In May, 1971, the NAB listed its membership as 2,124 AM radio stations, 1,250 FM stations, 538 TV stations, all four radio networks, the three major television networks, and 278 associative members (producers of television equipment, for example, and others who have an interest in broadcasting). Somewhere between 50 and 60 per cent of the nation's radio stations and over 60 per cent of the television stations are members of the NAB.

The NAB is governed by a forty-four-man board of directors—twenty-nine from radio and fifteen from television. The directors are a representative cross-section of the country's television and radio stations in terms of size and market area. The board of directors, like the entire membership, represents a broad spectrum of beliefs about politics and about the broadcasting industry.

Given the size of the board and the wide range of opinions held by it and the total membership, one could expect a rather ponderous and slow-to-react interest group. Indeed, on most legislative matters, save those absolutely vital to broadcaster survival, the NAB is not quick to enter the fray. Renewal of owner selection and licensing regulations would receive top priority; campaign finance reform, even with restrictive television broadcast provisions, would probably be seen as less central to many broadcasters.

Save for the testimony before the House hearings, the NAB appeared to be doing little as the Political Broadcast Act evolved through the Congress. Since they vigorously opposed the original NCEC bill introduced by Representative Macdonald and Senators Hart and Pearson, their lack of public lobbying is rather surprising. In the main, what they objected to was the provision that required television stations to charge only 30 per cent of the normal commercial rate for spot advertisements and 20 per cent of the normal rate for a full half-hour show. The NAB may well have been more effective working behind the scenes, for the Pastore subcommittee later deleted these provisions. On the other hand, the NAB's apparent inactivity may have been a consequence of its attitude, shared by others in and out of Congress, that there was no real chance of the bill's passage despite numerous cosponsors and public declarations to the contrary.

The NAB was also opposed to the section of the Political Broadcast Act, which passed both the House and the Senate, that required stations to charge the "lowest unit rate"—that is, the price for a specific time spot that was accorded the station's best customers. Thus, for the brief period of the campaign a political candidate could obtain the same price as a business that bought over 1,000 spots during the full course of a year. The NAB argued that this provision was discriminatory against the broadcasting industry because it did not apply to other media. Jon Bednerik, a governmental relations staff member at the NAB, characterized the lowest unit rate as a "bad bullet to bite." Since individual stations would no longer be able to charge medium or even top rates for political advertisements, it is easy to understand why the NAB would be so firmly opposed to the lowest-unit-rate clause.

After offering critical testimony at the House hearings, the NAB did not again indulge in much open lobbying activity until, late in the fall, following passage of the bill by both houses, it resurfaced. Willard E. Walbridge, the chairman of the NAB board, wrote to President Nixon calling for a veto. "This bill," said Walbridge, "is very unfair to the nearly 700 television stations and more than 6,000 radio stations throughout the nation." [*Doc. 3-3*]

Did his letter carry great weight with President Nixon? The opposition of the major industry voice certainly made it easier for the President to justify his veto.

Once President Nixon vetoed the Political Broadcast Act, the NAB went into high gear. Through its regional representatives, it asked local stations to contact their Congressmen and express the industry's opposition to the bill. Just how many individual stations followed through and approached their Representatives or Senators is impossible to estimate. Lobbyists from the NAB, led by their vice-president in charge of governmental relations, Paul Comstock, intensified their direct efforts to convert Senators. Even greater impact was obtained by local broadcast owners, especially those from southern and border states. Given the increasingly partisan nature of the bill by this stage—a majority of Democratic Senators trying to override a Republican President's veto—the NAB lobbyists had to tread most delicately. As Bednerik noted at the time, "We have to be very careful not to get identified with one party or the other."

Throughout the legislative stages, the three major national broad-

DOCUMENT **3-3**: The NAB Urges President Nixon to Veto

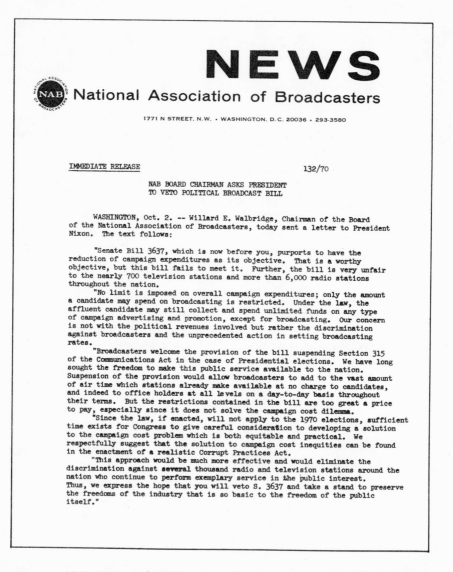

NEWS

National Association of Broadcasters

1771 N STREET. N.W. · WASHINGTON. D.C. 20036 · 293-3580

IMMEDIATE RELEASE   132/70

NAB BOARD CHAIRMAN ASKS PRESIDENT
TO VETO POLITICAL BROADCAST BILL

WASHINGTON, Oct. 2. -- Willard E. Walbridge, Chairman of the Board
of the National Association of Broadcasters, today sent a letter to President
Nixon. The text follows:

"Senate Bill 3637, which is now before you, purports to have the
reduction of campaign expenditures as its objective. That is a worthy
objective, but this bill fails to meet it. Further, the bill is very unfair
to the nearly 700 television stations and more than 6,000 radio stations
throughout the nation.

"No limit is imposed on overall campaign expenditures; only the amount
a candidate may spend on broadcasting is restricted. Under the law, the
affluent candidate may still collect and spend unlimited funds on any type
of campaign advertising and promotion, except for broadcasting. Our concern
is not with the political revenues involved but rather the discrimination
against broadcasters and the unprecedented action in setting broadcasting
rates.

"Broadcasters welcome the provision of the bill suspending Section 315
of the Communications Act in the case of Presidential elections. We have long
sought the freedom to make this public service available to the nation.
Suspension of the provision would allow broadcasters to add to the vast amount
of air time which stations already make available at no charge to candidates,
and indeed to office holders at all levels on a day-to-day basis throughout
their terms. But the restrictions contained in the bill are too great a price
to pay, especially since it does not solve the campaign cost dilemma.

"Since the law, if enacted, will not apply to the 1970 elections, sufficient
time exists for Congress to give careful consideration to developing a solution
to the campaign cost problem which is both equitable and practical. We
respectfully suggest that the solution to campaign cost inequities can be found
in the enactment of a realistic Corrupt Practices Act.

"This approach would be much more effective and would eliminate the
discrimination against several thousand radio and television stations around the
nation who continue to perform exemplary service in the public interest.
Thus, we express the hope that you will veto S. 3637 and take a stand to preserve
the freedoms of the industry that is so basic to the freedom of the public
itself."

casters—ABC, CBS, and NBC—were also largely inactive. Their spokesmen testified at both Senate and House hearings, strongly objecting to
the NCEC bill because of the percentage-rate charges it would have
imposed. But they did little lobbying after the Senate hearings. Once
the objectionable provision was removed by the Pastore subcommittee,
the networks maintained the appearance of neutrality toward the
passage of the bill. While not enthusiastic about the version of the bill
that passed, they did not campaign against it. Passive acceptance of the

limited bill seemed better than the dangers of opening up the entire range of problems inherent in television involvement in elections.

The FCC, as the federal agency that regulates the broadcasting industry and licenses individual stations, also remained neutral during most of the bill's passage through Congress, despite the fact that its initial responsibility would be to enforce any campaign broadcast legislation that was enacted. Early in his tenure, President Nixon had appointed former Republican National Chairman and Goldwater aide Dean Burch as FCC chairman. Thus, the FCC was a medium by which the Administration could have presented its views. However, Burch and his FCC colleagues largely remained aloof from the conflict.

Most interest groups got involved only *after* President Nixon's decision to veto the Political Broadcast Act. [*Doc. 3-4*] United Auto Workers President Leonard Woodcock had sent a telegram to President Nixon urging him to sign the bill after it was sent to him.

DOCUMENT **3-4**: The UAW Telegram

This is the original draft of the telegram sent by UAW President Leonard Woodcock to President Nixon, urging him to sign the Political Broadcast Act.

UAW WSH
TELEX PD 10/5/70 WASH DC
RICHARD M. NIXON
THE WHITE HOUSE
WASHINGTON, D.C.

ON BEHALF OF THE UNITED AUTO WORKERS, I EARNESTLY REQUEST THAT YOU SIGN THE POLITICAL SPENDING BILL, HR-18434, WHICH IS NOW ON YOUR DESK.

THE EVER ESCALATING COSTS OF POLITICAL CAMPAIGNS ARE OF SPECIAL CONCERN TO WORKING PEOPLE IN OUR COUNTRY. UNLESS CAMPAIGN EXPENSES CAN BE REALISTICALLY REDUCED, THE CONTESTS FOR MAJOR POLITICAL OFFICE WILL BE EXCLUSIVELY OPEN ONLY TO THE VERY RICH OR TO THOSE INDEBTED TO SPECIAL INTERESTS.

WE IN THE UAW BELIEVE, AS DOES A BIPARTISAN MAJORITY IN CONGRESS, THAT THE CAMPAIGN SPENDING BILL AWAITING YOUR SIGNATURE, WILL BROADEN POLITICAL OPPORTUNITY FOR MEN AND WOMEN IN BOTH PARTIES AND WILL, IN ADDITION, PLACE HEALTHY RESTRAINTS TO THE MOUNTING CAMPAIGN COSTS WHICH FACE ALL FEDERAL CANDIDATES TODAY.

FOR MANY YEARS THE UAW HAS FOUGHT IN THE STRUGGLE FOR EQUITY IN THE POLITICAL ARENA, AND THIS CAMPAIGN SPENDING BILL CAN BECOME THE LAW OF THE LAND, WITH YOUR SIGNATURE.
LEONARD WOODCOCK
PRESIDENT
UNITED AUTO WORKERS

The Autoworkers' newsletter also suggested to their rank-and-file that they write their Congressmen in behalf of the legislation. In the main, however, interest-group activities in regard to the legislation fit the proverbial case of "too little and too late."

Once the President acted, labor unions were quick to proclaim support for the Political Broadcast Act, but their efforts on its behalf were spasmodic and far from effective. The AFL-CIO did contact a few Senators, but other lobbying projects received higher priority. The Communications Workers of America, a labor union composed of 450,000 employees in the communications field, sent a lengthy letter to Congressmen calling on them to override the President's veto. Overall, however, labor's lobbying seemed more symbolic than substantive.

The American Association of Political Consultants, which is made up of campaign managers and political and media consultants, passed a resolution in support of the Political Broadcast Act. Two early drafters of the bill, Russell Hemenway and Robert Squier, were the chief instigators of the resolution. Since the resolution did not represent a united position, its impact was at best marginal.

Common Cause claimed this issue as one of its top priorities, but John Gardner, the chairman of the organization, was able to reach only a handful of Senators during the override effort. The headquarters staff in Washington contacted a number of their citizen members and asked them, in turn, to contact their Congressmen. This exercise appeared to have little direct pay-off. Few Senators were to be swayed by isolated telephone calls or letters.

Congressmen were not, in short, besieged by lobbyists or constituents vigorously trying to persuade them how to vote on the Political Broadcast Act, although more interest-group activity did occur during the attempt to override the President's veto. Some local broadcasters were apparently able to get the ears of a few Senators, particularly those from southern and border states, but most of the lobbying that went on was of questionable effectiveness. Only the NCEC put on a sustained and reasonably effective effort. In terms of the intensity and range of pressure-group activity, the Political Broadcast Act seemed typical of most issues before Congress—relatively limited and rather late in developing. Only the rare major confrontations—a Landrum-Griffin Act, the fight over the supersonic transport, or the 1964 Civil Rights Act—generate sustained activity. It is the unusual issues, seldom more than four or five per session, that intensely involve many different groups over a prolonged period of time. Clearly, only a few groups can commit major resources—staff, time, and money—to more than a handful of issues. Instead, most bide their time, monitoring specialized legislation, waiting for those one or two issues that may never surface in newspapers but that are vital for their group or client's interests. If the group is effective, it will make its weight felt early in the committee stage. And, of course, it is far easier to defeat or seriously weaken unfavorable legislation than to maintain working majorities throughout Senate and House consideration of strong, favorable legislation.

FURTHER READING

Two excellent case studies of the legislative process that bring out the diverse roles of pressure groups are Stephen K. Bailey, *Congress Makes a Law* (New York: Columbia University Press, 1950) and Eugene Eidenburg and Roy D. Morey, *An Act of Congress* (New York: W. W. Norton, 1969). The first study traces the passage of the Employment Act of 1946; the second deals with the enactment of the Elementary and Secondary Education Act of 1965.

Much of what we know about contemporary interest groups and Congress comes from Raymond A. Bauer, Ithiel de Sola Pool, and Lewis Anthony Dexter, *American Business and Public Policy* (New York: Atherton Press, 1968).

A general introductory work on interest groups is Graham Wooton, *Interest Groups* (Englewood Cliffs, N.J.: Prentice-Hall, 1969). Another useful general treatment of interest groups is V. O. Key, Jr., *Politics, Parties and Pressure Groups*, 5th ed. (New York: Thomas Y. Crowell, 1964). For a comprehensive analysis of the role of interest groups in American society see David B. Truman, *The Governmental Process* (New York: Alfred A. Knopf, 1951).

On the subject of lobbyists, who they are and what they do, see Lester W. Milbraith, *The Washington Lobbyists* (Chicago: Rand McNally, 1963) and Lewis Anthony Dexter, *How Organizations Are Represented in Washington* (Indianapolis: Bobbs-Merrill, 1969).

A provocative theory of "interest-group liberalism" is developed by Theodore J. Lowi, *The End of Liberalism* (New York: W. W. Norton, 1969). Lowi describes how private power becomes public power through the delegation of authority by the federal government.

The Senate Acts

THE LEGISLATIVE PROCESS IN THE SENATE

The Structure of the Senate

How best to characterize the United States Senate? For some it is "the greatest deliberative body in the world." For others it is an "ego jungle." Still others would describe it as an assembly of a hundred ambassadors representing the fifty sovereign states. It is a "body of equals" where a few, the more senior members, are more equal than others. The Senate is all of these things and more.

An understanding of how the Senate operates must begin with the recognition that this august assembly is a continuing legislative body. The Constitution provides that one-third of the Senate's members are to be chosen every two years, with the term of office being six years. Unlike the House, there is never a time when the entire Senate stands for re-election.

The Senate's seating arrangement delineates the partisan character of the institution. Facing the rostrum, the Republicans occupy the right side of the chamber and the Democrats the left side. The center aisle separates the two groups, but the division by no means unifies each side. East Coast liberal Republicans may frequently vote with mainstream Democrats; southern Democrats often find compatibility with a majority of GOP party stalwarts.

Leadership in the Senate. The Vice-President, according to the Constitution, is also the President of the Senate—its presiding officer—but this aspect of his duties is accompanied by little influence or power, except for the casting of a deciding vote in the rare event of a tie. Since the Vice-President rarely attends Senate sessions, the job of presiding rests on the President Pro Tempore, which is also a constitutionally mandated position. In recent years, this position has been filled by the member of the majority party with the longest continuous service in the Senate.[1] In the absence of the President Pro Tempore, the job of presiding over the Senate sessions usually falls upon the freshman members of both parties. The job is looked upon as a burden because of the many hours expended with little pay-off in power or influence. Senior Senators consider this task a necessary apprenticeship, however, since presiding over the Senate enables new members to become acclimated to the formal and informal procedures of the institution. The presiding officer is assisted by a professional employee

[1] Senator Allen J. Ellender of Louisiana, a member of the Senate since Jan. 3, 1937, serves as President Pro Tempore in the 92d Congress.

of the Senate called the Parliamentarian who is the main authority on the Senate's rules and procedures.

The principal leaders of the Senate are called floor leaders, one for each party, majority and minority. At the beginning of each new Congress, the two parties meet in caucuses (Democrats) or conferences (Republicans) to elect their principal officers. Effective leaders such as Majority Leader Lyndon B. Johnson of Texas (1955–60) or the late Minority Leader Everett McKinley Dirksen of Illinois (1959–69) exercise more influence in the Senate than even the strongest of committee chairmen. But the Senate is inherently "a body of equals," so all leaders end up depending a great deal on personal persuasion rather than formal powers.

The current Majority Leader, Mike Mansfield of Montana, and his Republican counterpart, Hugh Scott of Pennsylvania, have purposely chosen to play a more "low profile" leadership role than their immediate predecessors. The soft-spoken Mansfield took over in January, 1961, when Johnson advanced to the Vice-Presidency. Scott replaced Dirksen in September, 1969, following the latter's death.

Assistant floor leaders, known as Whips, aid the top leaders in scheduling legislation, arranging for unanimous-consent agreements,[2] seeing that members are present for key votes, and, generally, expediting the work of the Senate. In recent years, the Whip's position has frequently served as a stepping stone to the floor leadership. Johnson and Mansfield, Dirksen and Scott—all four served prior apprenticeships as Whips before becoming floor leaders.

The Committee System. The table that follows indicates the number and kinds of measures introduced and passed in the Senate during the 91st Congress. [Doc. 4-1] One reason the Senate operates under a decentralized committee system is because of this sizable workload. Organized by subject matter and roughly paralleling executive branch departments, the various committees allow an expertise to develop among both members and staff. Informed judgments can be made in committee before complex issues are brought to the floor for final disposition by the 100-member Senate. The history of Senate committees indicates that most often they are created on the heels of the recognition of important problems. Consider the Aeronautical and Space Sciences Committee. It did not come into existence until 1959, following the post-Sputnik crisis. Committees have had a tendency to proliferate since the adoption of standing committees in 1816. In 1945, standing committees in the Senate numbered thirty-

---

[2] A *unanimous-consent agreement* is the standard device by which the Senate programs itself to consider legislation and amendments. If one Senator objects, then the Majority Leader must *move*, and obtain, majority support for his proposals; that is, he must get 50 per cent plus one of those Senators present and voting.

DOCUMENT **4-1**: Workload of the Senate

Workload of the United States Senate, 91st Congress
(1st and 2d sessions, 1969–70).

Measure	Designation When Introduced	Total Number Introduced	Number Passed
Bill[a]	S. + number	4,616	464
Joint resolution[b]	S. J. Res. + number	251	60
Concurrent resolution[c]	S. Con. Res. + number	89	30
Resolution[d]	S. Res. + number	509	22

[a] A *bill* is a legislative proposal of a public or private character. When a bill is passed by both the House and the Senate in identical form and signed by the President, it becomes a public or private law.

[b] A *joint resolution* most often embodies a single matter of a public or private character, such as the extension of a legal agreement. When it is passed by the House and the Senate in identical form and signed by the President, a joint resolution becomes a law. Amendments to the Constitution are submitted as joint resolutions and do not require the President's signature.

[c] A *concurrent resolution* deals with matters strictly within the limits of Congress, as in the expression of Congressional intent or purpose. Its authority is limited to Congress, and it does not have the force of law. A concurrent resolution must be passed by both the House and the Senate, but it does not require the President's signature.

[d] A *resolution* is strictly within the authority of the body in which it is introduced. It does not require passage in the other body nor does it require the President's signature. Such resolutions are used to create special committees or to express the will of the body originating it on some matters. Often, resolutions deal with the rules of the body in which it is introduced.

---

three. Under the Legislative Reorganization Act of 1946, these were consolidated and reduced to fifteen. Since that time, two additional committees have been created: Space, in 1959, and Veterans' Affairs, in 1971. [*Doc. 4-2*] Rule XXV of the Senate lists the standing committees and carefully sets forth their respective jurisdictions.

The size of each committee, ranging from a high of twenty-seven members on Appropriations to a low of seven members on the District of Columbia Committee, is also set forth in the Senate rules. The party ratio on each committee, closely approximating the over-all ratio of Democrats to Republicans in the Senate, is determined by the majority-

DOCUMENT **4-2**: Standing Committees of the Senate (91st Congress)*

Aeronautical and Space Sciences	Government Relations
Agriculture and Forestry	Interior and Insular Affairs
Appropriations	Judiciary
Armed Services	Labor and Public Welfare
Banking and Currency	Post Office and Civil Service
Commerce	
District of Columbia	Public Works
Finance	Rules and
Foreign Relations	Administration

* In the 92d Congress, the Senate added a seventeenth standing committee, Veterans' Affairs.

party leadership in consultation with the minority. The selection of committee assignments is made by the Democratic Steering Committee and the Republican Committee on Committees. There is a "pecking order" of assignments for which Senators compete. Appropriations, Finance, and Foreign Relations are generally considered the most prestigious assignments. Most Senators serve on three committees, one of which will usually be high ranking.

The Committee Chairman. The chairmanship of a committee is determined by the seniority system. Although this is not a formal requirement embodied in the Senate's rules, it is an accepted feature (and some argue, a necessary condition) of the Senate's life. A Senator's seniority is determined by his length of continuous service as a Senator in the same political party. A committee member of the majority party with the longest service on that committee becomes its chairman. Should his party lose its majority status, the chairman then becomes the ranking minority member. Assignments to committees as vacancies occur are generally based on Senate seniority. A Senator who changes his committee becomes last in seniority on the new committee, whatever his over-all seniority in the Senate.

Ralph K. Huitt, a perceptive observer of the Senate, has characterized the chairman's influence in the following way:

The chairman of a major standing committee in the Senate is an influential and important man indeed. He usually is in virtual control of his committee. He calls committee meetings, decides what bills will be considered, appoints subcommittee chairmen, controls the selection of witnesses and, excepting bills of overriding importance, determines which bills favorably reported by his committee really will be pressed for floor consideration. He probably will lead the floor fight for it or designate the man who will. In practice, he chooses committee members who will go to conference with the House on committee bills and may choose to lead the group himself. The chairman decides whether the staff will be as large and expert as money will buy or funds will be returned to the Treasury; whether the staff will be encouraged to be aggressive or passive; and whether a real fight will be made to carry the bill through floor and conference as the committee wrote it or the effort will be half-hearted.[3]

Although the Legislative Reorganization Act of 1946 reduced the number of Senate standing committees, it in no way reduced the volume of legislative business. One way in which Senators compensated was to increase the number of subcommittees. In 1950, some four years after consolidation, there were sixty-six. At the beginning of the 91st Congress (1969–70) there were an even hundred Senate subcommittees. It is in these "miniature legislatures"—sometimes consisting of as few as three Senators, seldom more than a dozen— that the fate of most bills is decided.

The Stages of Legislation

The origins of legislation—usually amorphous, seldom traceable to a single source, almost always with some grounding in legislation developed in previous Congresses—become a little clearer once a bill is drafted and introduced. In contrast to the House, where bills are merely dropped into a hopper at the Speaker's rostrum, a Senator usually seeks floor recognition in order to introduce his proposed legislation. Introduction takes place during the "morning hour" of the Senate, a period of time that may run for an hour or more and that is generally characterized by solitary Senators gaining recognition, often speaking for home-state consumption or striving for national headlines, and then yielding the floor to still another colleague. The galleries may be full of mystified tourists, but the balance of the audience is seldom more than one or two Senators patiently waiting their turns, a few staffers, a bored newspaperman or two, and several Senate officials awaiting the calling of the day's legislative calendar early in the afternoon.

Once a bill is introduced, the presiding officer routinely approves the referral of the bill to a committee under fixed jurisdictions prescribed by the Senate's Rule XXV. On rare occasions when bills

---

[3] Ralph K. Huitt, "The Internal Distribution of Influence: The Senate," in David B. Truman, ed., *The Congress and America's Future* (Englewood Cliffs, N.J.: Prentice-Hall, 1965), p. 89.

overlap jurisdictions, the Parliamentarian may decide or a floor fight may even occur. Another way out of the dilemma is to refer the bill to two or more committees. In this way, a particularly insistent chairman can see to it that his committee will deal with the legislation, if not in whole, then in part. Sometimes a bill may be drafted in such a way as to avoid a hostile committee and insure that legislation initially lands within a friendly committee's jurisdiction. The 1964 Civil Rights Act was designed so that its constitutionality hinged on the commerce clause of the Constitution. This was done to assure that the bill would be sent first to the Committee on Commerce, where Chairman Warren Magnuson of Washington was favorably disposed to the legislation, and only later to the Committee on the Judiciary, whose chairman, James Eastland of Mississippi, was strongly opposed.

The Hearing. The decision to hold a hearing on a measure before a committee or subcommittee is usually made by the chairman. Most bills with a modicum of public support are eventually given a hearing. If there is no hearing—a prerogative of the chairman—there is a strong possibility that no further action will be taken on the measure. Occasionally, a strong campaign will be waged to change the chairman's mind in order to get a hearing scheduled and give the bill a chance to reach the floor.

Congressional committees hold hearings for a variety of reasons. First, a chairman may utilize a hearing to bolster his own initial position on legislation, chiefly through the device of calling favorable witnesses. Second, a hearing provides a vehicle for reaching a broader audience, initially the chairman's own committee associates; later, through printed committee hearings, other Senators; and finally, through the mass media, a broader base of public support. Any experienced staff director knows how to schedule witnesses so they will derive maximum (or minimum) exposure and, thus, facilitate his chairman's ends. Hearings also play an important informational role: Expert witnesses can help the committee arrive at a more rational judgment about the complex legislative issues to be decided. Furthermore, testimony for or against the legislation allows a chairman to discover or affirm which individuals or groups are likely to support or oppose the legislation. Finally, each participating Senator is better able to assess the political advantages and disadvantages of voting for or against the legislation, both within the committee and later when the legislation is scheduled for floor debate.[4]

Since the chairman controls the professional staff of the committee, he has considerable discretion in developing hearings to his liking.

[4] Julius Cohen, "Toward Realism in Legisprudence," *Yale Law Journal* LIX (Apr., 1950), 892; and George B. Galloway, *The Legislative Process in Congress* (New York: Thomas Y. Crowell, 1953), p. 301.

The chairman may leave matters in the hands of his staff, or he may give them specific directions as to the witnesses to be called and the questions to which the witnesses are to address themselves. A chairman who has been forced to call a hearing on an issue to which he is opposed can subvert the hearing by delaying it, by canceling it at the last moment, or simply by changing the room around without prior notice as a means of preventing the press or interested parties from reporting or attending.

The staff takes care of the committee's housekeeping function— seeing to it that prepared statements of witnesses are available at or before the testimony; that the witnesses are present; and that the hearings run smoothly and efficiently. The legal counsel on the sub-committee staff may prepare memoranda at the direction of the chairman to brief committee members before or after a hearing. It is a general maxim that "a good staff man knows the answer to the boss's question before the boss has asked it."

Executive Sessions. After hearings have been concluded, the most important part of the subcommittee's work begins. At the discretion of the chairman, the subcommittee may meet in executive session (closed to all but members), to consider the legislation before it as well as the suggestions culled from the hearing and other sources prepared by the subcommittee members or the staff. Often, the secrecy of the meetings is broken by a "leak" to a sympathetic reporter or a phone call to an interested group so that pressure can be placed on neutral or opposing members. Of course, discussion of legislation need not be confined to the subcommittee sessions; frequently, several Senators will meet in advance of an executive session to plot their strategy on amendments. The stereotype conception of a subcommittee session—a group of reasonable men arranged on two sides of a table deliberating a bill on its substantive merits—is all too seldom met. A Senate staff member provides an opposite, more irreverent caricature:

> Seven men sitting around a table, most of them over seventy years old. Only one or two know what's in the bill. One will ask the chairman, "You for it, Bill?" He'll reply laconically, "Yeah, it's a good bill." And the others will just fall in line.

Most subcommittee executive sessions probably fall somewhere between these two extremes. The chairman will preside; sitting on his left will be the ranking minority member. Those subcommittee members who cannot attend will usually give their proxy, the right to cast their vote, to their ranking party leader; however, with the passage of the Legislative Reorganization Act of 1970, *general* proxies are prohibited, and proxy votes must now be keyed to specific amendments or issues. Members may be absent for a variety of reasons. Perhaps they are out of town; more likely they got caught in a cross-pressure of two or more subcommittees meeting at the same time. If they cannot attend, they may be represented by staff. The chairman can, of course, call meetings when opposing members must necessarily be absent, or delay meetings to allow "the heat" to be turned on by external forces. Occasionally, the chairman may even invite "interested parties"—executive branch officials, a lobbyist or two—to sit in on these early discussion sessions.

After considering one or more working drafts of a bill, the subcommittee may decide to take no action. This invariably means the death of the proposal, unless the other House passes a similar measure— in which case the "dead" bill may be reviewed.

If the subcommittee finds itself favorably disposed to the issue before it, it proceeds to the "mark-up" stage. Here, the legislation that was the subject of the hearings is changed as the chairman and the committee deem necessary. Language in the bill is crossed out, new phrasing is substituted, whole new sections may be added. "Reading the bill" is the usual procedure by which the mark-up proceeds. Usually, a staff member will read the measure line by line to the subcommittee. The chairman's hope is to eliminate ambiguities and strengthen, or perhaps weaken, the measure as a majority of the members decide.

Once this task is completed, the subcommittee will usually report the original legislation back to the full committee with the amendments the subcommittee has made. The full committee, meeting in executive session, can then act on the subcommittee recommendations, which will often be approved without much further consideration. Still, if the subcommittee is sharply divided or quite unrepresentative of the full committee (mostly northerners on a committee dominated by southerners, for example), then a new round of hearings or a full committee mark-up session may be in order. Again, without a majority of committee members behind it, the measure has only a remote chance of being scheduled for floor action.

Reporting a Bill. If the committee acts favorably on the measure before it, it discharges the bill by filing a report with the presiding officer of the Senate in which the committee's recommendations and reasons are indicated. The report is usually submitted by the chairman of the committee or by the chairman of the subcommittee who dealt with the legislation.

If there are many changes in the legislation during the mark-up, an entirely new bill (called a "clean" bill) may be introduced in the Senate. The clean bill, with its new "S" number, can be referred to the committee, but this is merely a formal requirement of the Senate rules. This clean bill procedure is a time-saver because it enables the Senate to avoid floor consideration of each of the changes made in the original bill. At the same time, a committee report will be issued outlining the major provisions of the new bill. Should there be a strong dissent in committee, minority views can be included, or a minority report may even be filed as well. These reports and the clean bill are then printed and distributed to all the members of the Senate.

When the bill is reported out of committee and filed in the Senate, it is placed on the Calendar of General Orders.[5] The calendar is an agenda of the legislative business pending before the Senate. All measures on the calendar are listed in the order in which they are filed, but they may be called up for consideration out of this time sequence either by a unanimous-consent agreement or by a formal motion, usually offered by the Majority Leader. Much more so than in the House of Representatives, scheduling of legislation is a matter of continuous negotiation and compromise between the Democratic and Republican floor leaders. Most of the time, all that is needed is the concurrence of the chairman and ranking minority member—and perhaps one or two other deeply interested Senators. However, the threat of a filibuster—one or more Senators threatening to "talk" a bill to death—lurks forever in the background.

Once the time to debate a bill arrives, either through a unanimous-consent agreement or a formal motion to consider, attendance on the floor usually picks up. At a minimum, most of the members of the committee that held hearings on the legislation will be there to participate in the debate. By the time a bill is considered on the floor, the sides are usually well drawn. A floor manager, generally the chairman of the subcommittee, will lead the fight. The opposition will typically be led by the ranking minority member from the same subcommittee. If the legislation is major in consequence, the chairman of the full committee may assume management. Meanwhile, the respective party floor leaders stand by to aid in parliamentary maneuvering.

Opponents may try to kill the measure by adding a crippling amendment. For example, on campaign finance legislation, they may try to add a full-disclosure provision that would make the legislation unpalatable to the House. Or they may consider raising the cost-per-vote television expenditure to such a level as to force a Presidential veto. Perhaps they make the bill so "comprehensive" that the accretion of opposition, part to one section, part to another, will sink the bill under its combined weight. The proponents of a bill may soon find themselves on the defensive, attempting to fight off amendments, trying to salvage what they can.

[5] There is a second calendar in the Senate called the Executive Calendar. It is used for executive branch nominations and treaties, not legislation.

One of the most well-known methods for killing a bill on the Senate floor is the filibuster. It is not used frequently, but it has been a powerful weapon in the hands of anti–civil rights forces. Increasingly, Senate liberals have used the threat of a filibuster to force vital concessions on such legislation as draft extension and the SST. According to the Rules, debate in the Senate can be limited only by agreement of two-thirds of the members present and voting. This is known as a vote of cloture. If this extraordinary majority cannot be obtained, a bill can be killed by continuous extended debate that prevents the Senate from proceeding with its pending business. Especially toward the end of a session, a small band of determined Senators can bring legislation to a halt. Thus, a minority that means business can succeed in defeating legislation when all other methods of gathering a majority to its cause have failed.

Voting in the Senate. Most votes in the Senate are by voice, with the presiding officer the judge of whether the "yeas" or "nays" have it. Any member can request a roll-call vote in which each Senator's vote is made part of the official record, but the motion must have the support of at least one-fifth of the members present. Whenever a roll-call vote is ordered in the Senate, bells will sound throughout the Senate wing of the Capitol and in the Senate Office Building as well, alerting members to the impending vote. [*Doc. 4-3*]

The process of legislating does not come to an end with the act of voting on the Senate floor. There are still many challenges to be faced—the House, the conference committee, the threat of a Presidential veto—in the process of enacting legislation. The stages of enacting a bill into law will become more understandable by examining the particular fate of a major piece of legislation, the Political Broadcast Act of 1970.

THE BEGINNINGS OF CAMPAIGN-REFORM LEGISLATION

On September 10, 1969, Senators Philip A. Hart (D., Mich.) and James B. Pearson (R., Kans.) introduced the campaign broadcast reform bill drafted by the National Committee for an Effective Congress. As initially presented, the bill was cosponsored by a total of thirty-six Senators—twenty-five Democrats and eleven Republicans.[6] It is generally believed that cosponsoring can aid in the passing

[6] On October 20, 1969, two other Senators added their names to the list of cosponsors, increasing the total party support to twenty-seven Democrats and eleven Republicans.

DOCUMENT **4-3**: For Whom the Bells (and Buzzers) Toll

When you visit Capitol Hill, and no student of the legislative process can hope to comprehend all of its complexities and fascinations without first-hand expo- sure, you will find numerous systems of bells, buzzers, and electric lights located throughout the Capitol, the two Senate and the three House office buildings. Indeed, most of the adjacent restaurants are also equipped with devices to alert lawmakers to quorum calls or votes on the floor. Floor debate seldom preoccupies more than a small number of Representatives or Senators at any one time. The others are generally concerned with committee work, meeting with constituents, answering mail, or the other wide-ranging tasks that keep members of Congress busy. But when the bells ring or the buzzer sounds, the Congressmen will abandon their current activity and either walk across, ride the "Toonerville Trolley" (the local railway transport), or scurry along through the tunnels that connect the office buildings with the legislative cham- bers. No one wants to miss a quorum call or a vote if he can possibly help it. The communication systems are somewhat different for the two bodies:

No. of Bells	House	Senate
1	Teller vote	Record vote
2	Record vote ("Yeas" and "Nays")	Roll call (for quorum)
3	Quorum call	Opening of executive session*
4	Adjournment	Adjournment
5	Recess	Five minutes remaining on a roll call vote
6	——	Recess
7	——	Doors closed (secret proceedings)

* Executive sessions are used to consider treaties and executive nominations.

of a bill, but in the opinion of Susan King, "Probably one reason we were able to secure thirty-eight sponsors was because few thought it would pass." Here, the effect and ultimate purpose of cosponsorship was "to build a record so that reticent legislators could not back out of it."

The introduction of legislation takes place during the "morning hour" that follows the perfunctory ceremonies upon the convening of the Senate. It is the practice of the Senate that a member be on the floor, gain recognition from the presiding officer, and then formally introduce his measure. Statements made by sponsors of legislation on introduction are invariably limited—by unanimous consent—to three minutes, but this rule (like so many others in the Senate) is observed more in the breach than in the practice.

Senator Pearson's remarks were no exception. A selection from his remarks as they were printed in the *Congressional Record* follows. [*Doc. 4-4*]

DOCUMENT **4-4**: Introduction of S.2876—The NCEC Bill

S.2876—INTRODUCTION OF THE CAMPAIGN BROADCAST RE-FORM ACT

Mr. PEARSON. Mr. President, today it is my privilege to introduce the Campaign Broadcast Reform Act of 1969, together with the distinguished senior Senator from Michigan (Mr. HART) and Senators ANDERSON, BROOKE, BURDICK, CASE, CRANSTON, DODD, EAGLETON, FULBRIGHT, GOOD-ELL, GRAVEL, HARRIS, HARTKE, HAT-FIELD, HOLLINGS, HUGHES, INOUYE, KENNEDY, McGOVERN, MATHIAS, MET-CALF, MUSKIE, MONTOYA, NELSON, PELL, PERCY, RANDOLPH, SAXBE, SCOTT, SCHWEIKER, SMITH, SPONG, TYDINGS, YARBOROUGH, and YOUNG of Ohio.

Earlier this year I resubmitted the Campaign Finance Act (S.1692) which was originally introduced several years ago. That bill is designed to broaden the contributions base in

public affairs by offering tax incentives to small- and medium-sized donors to political campaigns. The bill would also require much more stringent reporting of all campaign spending. At that time I noted that the rising costs of political campaigns was rapidly pricing many qualified men of modest means out of the public arena. A better system of reporting and a broadened contributions base would help alleviate the problem, of course, but they could not alone halt the costly trend that is rapidly making a mockery of our democratic election philosophy. Thus, something must also be done to directly reduce the major costs of seeking public office. That is the purpose of the legislation we introduce today, for it is obvious that the greatest expense faced by serious candidates for Federal office is incurred in the purchase of television time.

Once received by the presiding officer, the bill was numbered and designated by the letter "S"—for the chamber in which it was introduced. As with all bills, S.2876 was then ordered to be printed so that copies might be obtained by any interested party. Of all the formal procedures immediately following a bill's introduction, the most important is the referral to committee; there, the fate of legislation is initially determined. [*Doc. 4-5*] Sometimes there is latitude in the assignment of a bill, but in the case of the Political Broadcast Reform Bill it was a simple task to refer it to the Committee on Commerce. Thus, on September 10, 1969, the bill went to committee.

Senator Warren G. Magnuson (D., Wash.), in his capacity as chairman of the Committee on Commerce, referred S.2876 to the Com-

DOCUMENT **4-5**: Rule XXV on the Jurisdiction of the Committee on Commerce, Standing Rules of the Senate

(f) *Committee on Commerce,*[1] to consist of seventeen[2] Senators, to which committee shall be referred all proposed legislation, messages, petitions, memorials, and other matters relating to the following subjects:

1. Interstate and foreign commerce generally.

2. Regulations of interstate railroads, busses, trucks, and pipe lines.

3. Communication by telephone, telegraph, radio, and television.

4. Civil aeronautics,[3] except aeronautical and space activities of the National Aeronautics and Space Administration.

5. Merchant marine generally.

6. Registering and licensing of vessels and small boats.

7. Navigation and the laws relating thereto, including pilotage.

8. Rules and international arrangements to prevent collisions at sea.

9. Merchant marine officers and seamen.

10. Measures relating to the regulation of common carriers by water and to the inspection of merchant marine vessels, lights and signals, life-saving equipment, and fire protection on such vessels.

11. Coast and Geodetic Survey.

12. The Coast Guard, including life-saving service, lighthouses, lightships, and ocean derelicts.

13. The United States Coast Guard and Merchant Marine Academies.

14. Weather Bureau.

15. Except as provided in paragraph (d), the Panama Canal and interoceanic canals generally.

16. Inland waterways.

17. Fisheries and wildlife, including research, restoration, refuges, and conservation.

18. Bureau of Standards, including standardization of weights and measures and the metric system.

[1] Name changed from Committee on Interstate and Foreign Commerce, S. Jour. 27, 87–1, Apr. 13, 1961.

[2] Number changed from thirteen to fifteen, S. Jour. 56–57, 83–1, Jan. 9, 1953; number changed from fifteen to seventeen, S. Jour. 42, 86–1, Jan. 14, 1959.

[3] As amended, S. Jour. 508, 85–2, July 24, 1958.

munications Subcommittee, one of the six Commerce subcommittees in the 91st Congress. [*Doc. 4-6*] Of course, Magnuson could have done any number of things with the bill—for example, refuse to refer it to a subcommittee; refer it to a subcommittee chaired by himself; have the full committee deal with the legislation—but S.2876 was given no special treatment.

DOCUMENT **4-6**: Membership of the Communications Subcommittee

Democrats	*Republicans*
John O. Pastore, R.I., Chairman†	Hugh Scott, Pa.*†
Vance Hartke, Ind.*†	Robert P. Griffin, Mich.
Philip A. Hart, Mich.*†	Howard H. Baker, Jr., Tenn.
Russell B. Long, La.	Charles E. Goodell, N.Y.*†
Frank E. Moss, Utah†	
Howard W. Cannon, Nev.†	

* Cosponsor of S.2876.
† Up for re-election in 1970.

The Communications Subcommittee of the Senate Commerce Committee was chaired by John O. Pastore, a Democrat from Rhode Island with almost twenty years of service in the United States Senate. Born in 1907, Pastore had served as Governor of his home state for two terms prior to winning a special election for a vacated seat in 1950. Regarded as one of the foremost orators in the Senate, the fiery Italian–American delivered a memorable lashing keynote address at the Democratic Convention in 1964. In 1965, he lost out to Senator Russell B. Long of Louisiana in a three-way battle for the number-two position in the Senate Democratic hierarchy, the party Whip. His 1969 committee positions—top-ranking (just below Chairman Magnuson) on Commerce, vice-chairman of the Joint Atomic Energy Committee (alternating as chairman every two years with a House counterpart), and middle-ranking on Appropriations—illustrate the kind of overlapping power bases that most Senators gradually acquire with tenure.

If his critics considered him a "broadcasters' man," that is, one familiar with and friendly to their interests after years of contact with the National Association of Broadcasters and individual station owners, his leadership on the Political Broadcast Act of 1970 was to challenge that presumption. No one could accuse him of lack of interest or of not doing his legislative homework. But others did accuse him of "operating with a short fuse" or sometimes tending to be "dogmatic, if not inflexible." In the months ahead, Pastore would display considerable legislative acumen and a tendency toward stubbornness.

Hugh Scott, the ranking Republican on the Communications Subcommittee, was to play a less central role in the shaping of this legislation, but the wily veteran Senator from Pennsylvania was in the end to see his view prevail. Scott had less to say about the provisions of S.2876, in part because he was a member of the minority. But more critically, he was to find himself spread rather thin because of his newly acquired duties as Minority Leader. On September 24, 1969, Scott succeeded the late Everett McKinley Dirksen as leader of the Republican Party in the Senate, defeating Howard Baker of Tennessee, Dirksen's son-in-law, by a vote of 24 to 19.

A number of weeks passed with no indication that the Communications Subcommittee would take action on S.2876. Senator Pastore could determine, at his own discretion, if hearings were to be held, and it was possible that he might just "sit on the bill," thereby increasing the chance of its demise. In mid-October, however, the Digest section of the Congressional Record indicated that public hearings on political broadcasting were scheduled for October 21–23, 1969. What prompted Pastore to act? The list of cosponsors, at this point numbering thirty-eight, probably served as a general stimulus, but of greater importance was the presence of four cosponsors on Pastore's subcommittee. And not to be discounted were the continued promotional efforts of the NCEC. "We were papering the Senators to death urging action on the bill," Russell Hemenway later recalled. [Doc. 4-7]

Over a period of three days, eighteen witnesses testified at the subcommittee hearings. The first witness to be called to testify, as a matter of courtesy and relative importance, was Senator James B. Pearson, the chief Republican sponsor of the NCEC bill. Among the other witnesses called were Russell Hemenway, NCEC's national director, the presidents of the major television networks, various representatives from communications-related industries, and the cosponsors of S.2876 in the Senate as well as those cosponsoring the identical measure in the House of Representatives. Throughout the hearings, witnesses were heard in a spirit of cordiality and cooperation; acrimony or heated exchange was almost nonexistent.

The following dialogue, which took place between Senator Pastore and Hemenway, is illustrative of much of the give-and-take of a friendly Senate subcommittee hearing. [Doc. 4-8] (The examination of hostile witnesses would present quite a different atmosphere and tone. Though the public is, for obvious reasons, more aware of acrimonious legislative hearings, these are in fact far less frequent.) In the exchange quoted, both men are exploring the usefulness of the typical campaign spot commercial. The original NCEC bill would have made available for purchase at reduced rates up to 60 one-minute announcements for House candidates and up to 120 one-minute spots for legally qualified Senate candidates.

Hemenway finished his testimony with a candid explanation of the need for legislation. Note how he plays to Pastore in the process. [Doc. 4-9]

DOCUMENT **4-7**: Title Page of the Senate Subcommittee Hearings

THE CAMPAIGN BROADCAST REFORM ACT OF 1969

HEARINGS

BEFORE THE

COMMUNICATIONS SUBCOMMITTEE

OF THE

COMMITTEE ON COMMERCE

UNITED STATES SENATE

NINETY-FIRST CONGRESS

FIRST SESSION

S. 2876

TO AMEND THE COMMUNICATIONS ACT OF 1934 TO PROVIDE
CANDIDATES FOR CONGRESSIONAL OFFICES CERTAIN
OPPORTUNITIES TO PURCHASE BROADCAST TIME FROM
TELEVISION BROADCAST STATIONS AT REDUCED RATES

OCTOBER 21, 22, AND 23, 1969

Serial No. 91–29

Printed for the use of the Committee on Commerce

U.S. GOVERNMENT PRINTING OFFICE

36–512   WASHINGTON : 1969

For sale by the Superintendent of Documents, U.S. Government Printing Office
Washington, D.C. 20402 - Price 70 cents

DOCUMENT **4-8**: Exchange Between Pastore and Hemenway*

Senator PASTORE. Do you have a strong feeling on these sixty 1-minute or 120 1-minute spot announcements? Do you think they will play a part in educating the electorate?

Fundamentally, I think the whole process here is not so much the idea that you want to be helpful to the candidate as much as it is an idea that if you do help the candidate you do promote the public interest. You give him a proper exposure that the people are entitled to.

Of course, the legislation would never pass the Congress unless it did affect the public interest.

The thing that came up yesterday was this matter of spot announcements. You said you backed off on that a little bit. Do you have a strong feeling with reference to that, or do you have a strong argument or rationale that would sustain that being left in the bill if the bill were to be reported?

Mr. HEMENWAY. The only argument I have, Senator, are the facts. Seventy-five cents of every dollar spent on television by political candidates is spent on political spots. This is what the candidate wants. And when the candidate goes to a broadcaster, this is the kind of time he finds most readily available. The broadcaster prefers to sell spots.

Senator PASTORE. I realize that is what the candidate likes. That is what I like truly, but the question is should I receive a discount just because I like it. Does it serve the public interest. That is the question. Do you feel a spot announcement of 1 minute does serve the public interest? Maybe it does or maybe it does not, but I would like to hear you on it.

Mr. HEMENWAY. I have been involved in a great many campaigns, Senators. I have been involved in buying and selling television time. I have been involved with both incumbent and challenger. I can tell you that as a challenger, there is almost no other way today to get voter identification except with the use of spots.

You identify yourself to the public as a candidate and you can identify yourself with issues. Intelligent use of spots would negate this argument that some people have made that they are not in the public interest.

There have been some very excellent television spots produced and used by candidates. I agree that in some instances there are spots that are oversimplifications, some that may be in fact demagogic.

How we protect ourselves as a people from this I just do not know, but the fact is the money that is spent on television, to win a campaign, is spent on spots, and we have not tried to change this balance any more than we have tried to change the balance of how television is used in this country.

We contend, and let me reiterate this, very few of those people who do not now use television will use it under this bill. It is just too inefficient a use of campaign resources and campaign funds. This is not the way a candidate will decide to use his money.

* *Senate Hearings,* p. 87.

DOCUMENT **4-9**: Hemenway Summary*

Mr. HEMENWAY. This bill has been pretty carefully thought through in terms of the dynamics of present day American politics. It does not accomplish all the things that we would like to, many of the things that we would like to, but it does, we think, meet with the immediate problem. It is, we think, a very intelligent first step. It limits itself to the House and Senate races because we know we have to begin somewhere, Senator.

If we begin to think about expand-ing this to all statewide races, to all the political races in this country, I do not think we are going to do anything. You said yourself, Mr. Chairman, some time ago that television is an indispensable means of political cam-paigning but its costs are appalling. I cannot add anything to that sentence.

You went on to say that a candi-date may have to spend $2 million on television to win a Senate seat paying $42,500 a year. That sums it up about as well as anyone I have heard.

* *Senate Hearings*, p. 90.

But, if the hearings were free of hostility, they were not lacking in disagreements. Much of the conflict in opinion that did occur centered around Section 315. Although the NCEC bill did not recommend repeal of Section 315(a), Senator Pastore made his position clear early in his opening statement.

> The suspension of the equal-time requirement for the 1960 Presidential campaign permitted the "Great Debates," and I think everyone would agree the voting public was better informed as a result.
>
> I have frequently advocated that a similar suspension be extended to candidates for other public office.[7]

Later in the hearings, the Rhode Island Senator voiced his opinion in stronger terms:

> We have many Members of Congress who for one reason or another have considered themselves burned at times. It may be that a politician is a pretty sensitive fellow at campaign time, and that he exaggerates. Never-theless, there have been some occasions. It came up on the floor the last time we amended 315, and there were certain strong statements made by certain Senators who had had sorrowful experiences. . . .
>
> I'm afraid that the Congress at this time is not ready to repeal 315, and I know how you gentlemen [the broadcasting networks] feel about it. But

[7] Senate Committee on Commerce, *Hearings on the Campaign Broadcast Reform Act of 1969*, 91st Congress, 1st Session (Washington, D.C.: Government Printing Office, 1969), p. 3. [Hereinafter cited as *Senate Hearings*.]

somewhere along the line if this isn't the proper legislation, there has to be some other.[8]

While generally sympathetic to the proposed modification of Section 315(a), the major broadcast networks were strongly opposed to the discount provision of the NCEC bill. From their point of view, such a provision discriminated against the television industry since none of the other media would be covered. In addition, they feared that TV stations serving large metropolitan areas would be inundated by Congressional candidates whose districts were within their broadcasting reach. New York City stations, for example, broadcast in all or parts of thirty-eight House districts. In short, the discount formula would make television advertising even more attractive because of its low cost. Hence, it was feared that large-city TV stations would have to make available unreasonable amounts of prime commercial time. Dr. Frank Stanton, President of CBS, summed up many of these feelings in his testimony.

> Notwithstanding the inefficiency of this use of television, the 70- and 80-per cent discount rates contemplated by this legislation, by making it much more attractive for congressional candidates to purchase time, will force a competition in the use of television by congressional candidates who have not previously found it practical or feasible. Since there is no reason to expect that candidates will turn away from such traditionally effective campaign methods such as direct mail, hand bills, and newspaper advertising, the net result may well be a substantial increase in campaign costs. . . .
> The cure as proposed by S.2876, I submit, is far worse than the ailment it purports to remedy.[9]

Nor were the broadcasters alone in their general distrust of a discount approach. For Senator Pastore all it could do "would be to allow the rich guy to buy more TV time, the poor guy to buy some." Quite clearly, Pastore had plans to move beyond the NCEC bill and include language treating Section 315. After the hearings had ended and the transcript of the testimony was prepared, the chairman met with his chief counsel, Nicholas Zapple,[10] to plan almost entirely new legislation. Now, repeal of Section 315 was to receive equal billing with reduced rates on television costs. The discount formula in the NCEC bill, which would have allowed candidates to purchase time at 20 to 30 per cent of normal commercial rates was scrapped in favor of a proposal whereby

---

[8] *Ibid.,* p. 126.

[9] *Ibid.,* p. 107.

[10] A veteran of more than twenty years of Congressional experience, Zapple has earned a reputation as a resourceful and innovative staff assistant. His knowledge of federal communications law is probably unsurpassed on Capitol Hill.

candidates could buy time at the "lowest-unit-charge" rate.[11] The NCEC discount rates would have produced cheaper broadcast costs for candidates than the lowest-unit-charge provision. When, in the early spring of 1970, Pastore began reconvening his subcommittee in executive session, it was his bill, not the NCEC proposal, that was to receive the bulk of the subcommittee's attention.

In an effort to rally support for a compromise version that would include an NCEC discount formula as well as the lowest unit charge provision of the Pastore proposal, NCEC distributed a fact sheet showing the effect such an amended bill would have on each of the subcommittee members. [Doc. 4-10] The revised discount formulas and the amount of permissible spot and program time were spelled out for each of the subcommittee members. The effect of the bill on each broadcasting station was noted; and the maximum amount of broadcasting time used by each candidate in the thirty-five days preceding the election was also indicated.

In the end, the subcommittee chairman for the most part had his way. It was Pastore who had the subject–matter experience; it was Pastore who controlled the staff. If his conduct of the executive ses-

DOCUMENT **4-10**: NCEC Fact Sheet for Rhode Island

The fact sheet for Rhode Island spells out the amount of television time permissible under the bill for House, senatorial, and gubernatorial candidates in that state. It shows that a Rhode Island candidate for a U.S. Senate seat, for instance, would be entitled to purchase at a 50 per cent discount a total of 120 one-minute spots, divided equally among the state's three television stations. Thus, he would be allowed to purchase forty one-minute spots on each station at a 50 per cent discount. With an additionally permitted twenty minutes per station purchased at the lowest unit rate, the candidate would be allowed a total of one hour of spot time per station, which amounts to three hours statewide. In addition to spot time, the senatorial candidate could purchase a half hour of program time on each station. The fact sheet provides similar information for gubernatorial and House candidates. Finally, the fact sheet translates these limits into individual station requirements, showing that over the thirty-five days preceding the election each station would have to provide an average of less than seven minutes per day of both spot time and program time.

---

[11] In the past, candidates for public office were typically saddled with the highest rates for television time, as much as $3,000–$4,000 for a twenty-second prime-time announcement in New York City. Although the concept of "lowest unit charge" was to prove difficult to define in the months ahead, proponents of the language had in mind charges equal to those paid by heavy users of television time, such as major food and cosmetics companies.

Doc. 4-10 *(cont.)*

STATE: *RHODE ISLAND*

Commercial Stations ___**3**___ (___**3**___ VHF; ___**0**___ UHF)

Other Markets:
Boston - but candidates not eligible for discounts on Boston stations -

SENATE AND GUBERNATORIAL CANDIDATES ENTITLED TO:

Spots: 120 one-minute spots per candidate, equally divided among stations, at 50% discount.

___*40*___ minutes per station (at 50% discount).

___*20*___ minutes additional per station at the lowest actual commercial charge (bringing candidate to full one hour spot limit per station).

___*3*___ hours total spot time statewide.

Program: ½ hour per station per candidate at 50% discount.

___*1½*___ hour(s) total program time (statewide) per candidate at 50% discount.

HOUSE CANDIDATES ENTITLED TO:

Spots: 60 one-minute spots per candidate, equally divided among stations, at 50% discount.

Program: ½ hour per station per candidate at 50% discount.

Example: District ___*1 & 2*___ Market ___*Providence*___ Stations ___*3*___

Spots: ___*20*___ minutes per station (at 50% discount).

___*40*___ minutes additional per station at lowest actual commercial charge (bringing candidate to full one hour spot limit per station).

___*3*___ hours total spot time districtwide.

Program: ___*1½*___ hour(s) total program time (districtwide) per candidate at 50%.

MAXIMUM INDIVIDUAL STATION REQUIREMENTS:

Spots: ___*4*___ Senate and Gubernatorial, ___*40*___ minutes each * = ___*160 min.*___

___*4*___ House candidates, ___*20*___ minutes each * = ___*80 min.*___
___*240 min. total (4 hr.)*___

___*6 6/7*___ minutes per day if evenly distributed throughout 35 day period.

Program: ___*4*___ Senate and Gubernatorial, ___*30*___ minutes each = ___*2 hrs.*___

___*4*___ House candidates, ___*30*___ minutes each = ___*2 hrs*___
___*4 hr. total*___

___*6 6/7*___ minutes per day if evenly distributed throughout 35 day period.

* Stations not <u>required</u> to sell additional time above 50% discount time; <u>may</u> *discount* to one hour limit.

sions was not a textbook process, it nevertheless got results. Sometimes he could be testy or unyielding, but the end product would be a bill that the broadcasting industry and most of his colleagues could live with.

Some four months after the hearings had been concluded, the subcommittee reported its findings, recommendations, and suggested new language of the bill to the full committee meeting in executive session. After further consideration of the various proposals, the full committee quietly went along with the subcommittee's unanimous recommenda-

tions: to support permanent repeal of the equal-opportunities requirement of 315(a) insofar as it applied to legally qualified candidates for
President and Vice President, and to urge adoption of the lowest-unit
rate proposals. Democrats and Republicans were in wide disagreement,
however, as what to do about limits on broadcast spending. Finally,
Pastore and Senator Cotton, the ranking Republican on the full committee, agreed to hold off on any recommendation until the measure
reached the floor. An excerpt from the Committee on Commerce's
Report 91-751, released on March 25, 1970, summed up the accord:

> The committee was impressed by the spiraling costs of campaigning via
> the electronic media and the various proposals that would bring relief to
> the candidates for congressional and gubernatorial offices. However, it
> decided to withhold any specific recommendation in this area so that the
> entire Senate may have the benefit of considering all the various proposals
> on the subject when the bill is before it on the floor.[12]

That same day, during the course of routine morning business, Senator
Pastore filed the Commerce Committee's report on political broadcasting with the Senate. [*Doc. 4-11*] The report was accompanied by
a clean bill—which meant giving it a new "S" number (S.3637)—
introduced on March 25, 1970 by Pastore and placed that day on the
Senate calendar. [*Doc. 4-12*]

The Pastore Bill

What was S.3637 designed to accomplish? First, it
would repeal the equal-time provision of Section 315(a) of the Communications Act for Presidential and Vice-Presidential campaigns.
This action would remove a major obstacle to debates between the
major-party candidates who, in the past, had had to share the public
spotlight with candidates from such organizations as the Vegetarian
Party and the Prohibitionists.

Second, S.3637 would require radio and television broadcasters to
charge candidates for public office no more than the lowest price
charged commercial buyers of the same time period. In the past, the
charges for television and radio time for political candidates had been
fixed at a rate no higher than that charged to any other advertiser, but
the over-all effect had been that candidates ended up paying the high-

---

[12] Senate Committee on Commerce, *Repeal of Section 315 of the Communications
Act of 1934 for Presidential and Vice Presidential Candidates, and Amendment of the
Provision with Respect to Charges*, 91st Congress, 1st Session, Report 91-751 (Washing-
ton, D.C.: Government Printing Office, 1970), p. 4.

Document **4-11**: Report of the Committee on Commerce, Excerpt

Calendar No. 747

91ST CONGRESS	SENATE	REPORT
2d Session		No. 91-751

REPEAL OF SECTION 315 OF THE COMMUNICATIONS ACT OF 1934 FOR PRESIDENTIAL AND VICE PRESIDENTIAL CANDIDATES, AND AMENDMENT OF THE PROVISION WITH RESPECT TO CHARGES

MARCH 25, 1970.—Ordered to be printed

Mr. PASTORE, from the Committee on Commerce,
submitted the following

REPORT

[To accompany S. 3637]

The Committee on Commerce report favorably an original Senate bill to repeal the equal opportunities requirements of section 315 of the Communications Act of 1934 for legally qualified candidates for the office of President and Vice President, and to amend the provision of that section regarding the charges made for the use of broadcasting facilities, and recommend the bill do pass.

Resolved by the Senate and House of Representatives of the United States of America in Congress assembled, That (a) the first sentence of section 315(a) of the Communications Act of 1934, as amended (47 U.S.C. 315(a)), is amended by striking out the colon and inserting in lieu thereof a comma and the following: "except that the foregoing requirement shall not apply to the use of a broadcasting station by legally qualified candidates for the office of President and Vice President of the United States:".

(b) Section 315(b) of that act is amended to read as follows:

"(b) The charges made for the use of any broadcasting station by any person who is a legally qualified candidate for any public office shall not exceed the lowest unit charge of the station for any time period."

37-010

DOCUMENT **4-12**: S.3637

Calendar No. 747

91st CONGRESS
2d Session

S. 3637

[Report No. 91–751]

IN THE SENATE OF THE UNITED STATES

MARCH 25, 1970

Mr. PASTORE, from the Committee on Commerce, reported the following bill;
which was read twice and ordered to be placed on the calendar

---

A BILL

To amend section 315 of the Communications Act of 1934 with
respect to equal-time requirements for candidates for public
office, and for other purposes.

1   *Be it enacted by the Senate and House of Representa-*

2 *tives of the United States of America in Congress assembled,*

3 That (a) the first sentence of section 315(a) of the Com-

4 munications Act of 1934, as amended (47 U.S.C. 315(a)),

5 is amended by striking out the colon and inserting in lieu

6 thereof a comma and the following: "except that the fore-

7 going requirement shall not apply to the use of a broadcast-

8 ing station by legally qualified candidates for the office of

9 President and Vice President of the United States:".

   II

Doc. 4-12 (*cont.*)

2

1   (b) Section 315 (b) of that Act is amended to read as

2 follows:

3   " (b) The charges made for the use of any broadcasting

4 station by any person who is a legally qualified candidate

5 for any public office shall not exceed the lowest unit charge

6 of the station for any time period."

Calendar No. 747

91st CONGRESS
2d Session

S. 3637

[Report No. 91–751]

A BILL

To amend section 315 of the Communications Act of 1934 with respect to equal-time requirements for candidates for public office, and for other purposes.

By Mr. PASTORE

MARCH 25, 1970

Read twice and ordered to be placed on the calendar

est rate possible. Few could command the discounted saturation rates available to year-round heavy users.

Why should Pastore have moved so far from the original legislation?[13] Certainly, a part of the reason was that Pastore was motivated by a desire to produce legislation that would pass. Free from the NCEC-promoted discount formulas, S. 3637 was much more acceptable to the broadcasters. But only time would tell if a majority of the Senate and House could be persuaded to back his alternative proposals.

Having placed his bill on the calendar, Pastore next had to arrange for floor debate. Getting a bill to the floor, once it has been placed on the calendar, is the primary concern of the majority-party leadership in the Senate. The Majority Leader, as chairman of the Democratic Policy Committee, sets the date on which bills will be called up out of their numerical order for consideration by the Senate. The scheduling of debate by the Majority Leader is not made arbitrarily. The Minority Leader and other interested Senators are frequently consulted so that debate can be arranged at a mutually convenient time for all. Such prior accommodation is sought because a single Senator can stall the entire legislative process by objecting to the unanimous-consent agreements by which the Senate undertakes most of its business. Of course, Senator Pastore's membership on the Democratic Policy Committee helped to insure that floor action would take place at a time convenient for the Senator from Rhode Island and his committee associates.

On the afternoon of April 13, 1970, debate on S.3637 began when Senator Pastore's motion to consider the bill was agreed to in a voice vote by the scattering of members present.[14] [*Doc. 4-13*]

---

[13] See Appendix B for a more detailed comparison of the original NCEC bill and S.3637 as it passed the Senate.

[14] Debate in Congress is not the sort of adversary contest one might imagine it to be. Rather, it more closely resembles short talks or discussions, as the selections that follow from the *Congressional Record* reveal. The unwritten rules of comity—such as addressing a Senator as the "distinguished Senator from _____"—reduce the possibility of invective entering into a Senator's comments, which in any event is a strict violation of the Senate rules. Donald R. Matthews described these norms well:

> "The Senate of the United States exists to solve problems, to grapple with conflicts. Sooner or later, the hot, emotion-laden issues of our time come before it. Senators as a group are ambitious and egocentric men, chosen through an electoral battle in which a talent for invective, righteous indignation, "mud-slinging," and "engaging in personalities" are often assets. Under these circumstances one might reasonably expect a great deal of manifest conflict and competition in the Senate. Such conflict does exist, but its sharp edges are blunted by the felt need—expressed in the Senate folkways—for courtesy.
>
> "A cardinal rule of Senate behavior is that political disagreements should not

DOCUMENT **4-13**: Consideration of S.3637

In the following extract from the Congressional Record, *Senator Pastore moves that the chamber consider S.3637. Senator Saxbe, then a freshman Republican Senator from Ohio, is presiding officer—a task usually allocated to junior members. All extracts of Senate floor debates are taken from the* Congressional Record *(daily edition) of April 13 and 14, 1970.*

EQUAL-TIME REQUIREMENTS FOR CANDIDATES FOR PUBLIC OFFICE

Mr. PASTORE. Mr. President, I move that the Senate proceed to the consideration of Calendar No. 747, S.3637.

The PRESIDING OFFICER (Mr. SAXBE). The bill will be stated by title.

THE ASSISTANT LEGISLATIVE CLERK. S.3637, to amend section 315 of the Communications Act of 1934 with respect to equal-time require-ments for candidates for public office, and for other purposes.

The PRESIDING OFFICER. The question is on agreeing to the motion of the Senator from Rhode Island.

The motion was agreed to, and the Senate proceeded to consider the bill.

Mr. PASTORE. Mr. President, I think that the pending bill is of in-tense interest to everyone in this Chamber and I would very much appreciate their indulgence and their attention so that they will understand what the pending measure really is and what it really does.

Early in his opening statement, Pastore indicated the reason for the considerable change in the pending legislation.

Mr. President, the amendments recommended in S.3637 are the result of extensive hearings and deliberations by the Commerce Committee.

The committee unanimously agreed that they are the minimum steps necessary if the public is to receive the full benefit of the dynamic media of radio and television in the arena of political broadcasting. And, after all, this is the fundamental purpose of section 315—to insure that the electorate is fully informed on the issues and the candidates.

Senator Norris Cotton (R., N.H.), the ranking minority member of the Committee on Commerce, corroborated Pastore's remarks and indicated the general bipartisan strategy behind most of the bill. But

---

influence personal feelings. This is not an easy task; for as one Senator said, 'It's hard not to call a man a liar when you know that he is one.' "

Donald R. Matthews, *U.S. Senators and Their World* (Chapel Hill: University of North Carolina Press, 1960), p. 97.

he also gave explicit warning that a forthcoming Pastore amendment proposing ceilings on television expenditures would be opposed. [*Doc. 4-14*]

DOCUMENT **4-14**: Senator Cotton's Statement

Mr. COTTON. I agree with the distinguished Senator, but it is important that we make this legislative history, I think.

Mr. President, may I simply say this: The Committee, at least all those who were present when the bill was reported out, were in agreement on the first part of the suspension of rule 315. We were in agreement on the second step—namely, the step that broadcasters must not charge political advertisers—that is, bona fide legal candidates—more than the low unit rate which they give to their regular business advertisers who advertise all year round. We felt that that was a perfectly just enactment because, after all, political candidates are not running all the year round. So it is in a sense a discrimination against them and against the people who want to hear them if they are not given the same rate that the regular advertisers on the particular broadcasting station

are given for the same time. . . . On those two points, the committee was in agreement.

As to the rest of the bill we were considering, there was disagreement. There was some disagreement—about the advisability of the limit that is in the amendment of the distinguished Senator from Rhode Island which he was about to offer. . . . To some of us who were in opposition, he said, "We agree. Let us report to the floor of the Senate the bill with just the two points in it, and then these other points—namely, the restriction on limiting of expenditures for advertising, possibly the matter of discounts and a lower rate of advertising for candidates—and any of the other points that were in the original bill can be offered in the form of amendments. If the Senate chooses to take them, the Senate will do so. But we will report that portion of the bill on which we are in agreement."

And, indeed, Pastore then announced that he planned to offer such an amendment. Cosponsored by Senator Pearson, the amendment would establish a limit on the amount of money spent by a candidate for radio and television advertising. According to the Pastore-Pearson amendment, a candidate's limit would be determined by multiplying by five cents the total number of votes cast in the previous election for the office sought. If the five-cent-per-vote formula should fall below $20,000, then $20,000 would be the spending limit. When Senator Pearson attempted to arrive at a unanimous-consent agreement to facilitate a vote on the Pastore-Pearson amendment, another Senator objected and further action was put off until the following day.

The Pastore-Pearson Amendment

The Pastore-Pearson amendment setting limits on the amount of money a candidate could spend on radio and television advertising was the pending business as the Senate entered the second day of debate on S.3637. As initially conceived, the limit was to be five cents per vote, but, as he offered the amendment on the floor, Pastore raised the figure to seven cents per vote.[15] The new figure was a compromise between the five cents per vote suggested by Pastore and the ten cents per vote urged by several Senators from large states who felt they needed more leeway. Some observers believe Pastore arrived at the five-cent figure by examining his own campaign expenditures in Rhode Island and then computing a figure from these. As one legislative assistant put it, "Pastore's figure was a 'guestimate.' Hell, you can spit from one end of Rhode Island to the other. But what about Texas or Pennsylvania? No two campaigns are alike. And his bill didn't allow for that."[16]

How would the spending limit be enforced? Pastore tried to assuage doubts about that concern. [*Doc. 4-15*]

DOCUMENT **4-15**: Senator Pastore Comments on the Amendment

Mr. PASTORE. In this particular case, the rules and the regulations inaugurated by the amendment will compel the FCC to make a record of expenditure. In turn, of course, they have the way and the method and the means and power to discover the amount very easily.

I think this is as airtight as anything can be. Of course, we can begin to conjure up and imagine many outlandish situations in which someone possibly could work out some small subterfuge. After all, I do not pretend to be the man who can write the perfect law. I do not think we have ever done that.

I think this is a sensible rule. It is very simple and plain. It speaks out very clearly as to what we intend to

[15] According to one staff assistant, "The amendment was written at Pastore's desk on the Senate floor—it had so many holes it looked like a Swiss cheese. For one thing, you couldn't tell whether it covered primaries or not. You could read it about four different ways." Of course, the main thrust of the language of the Pastore amendment had been available to other Senators for at least five days.

[16] One of Pastore's aides put the matter quite differently: "Sure, we considered our own experiences in Rhode Island. But we also made spot checks around and talked informally with other Senators." One important by-product of Pastore's inquiries was more detailed collection and reporting of broadcast spending data. The stations, themselves, must report this information directly to the Federal Communications Commission.

Doc. 4-15 (cont.)

do. We have the mandate that the FCC shall watch it. The broadcaster will have to keep a log. A coordinator can be selected by the candidate. Each broadcaster can contact him.

In my State there are three television stations, and observation is the easiest thing in the world, because the fellow who will raise the question will be your opponent. The man who will raise the question that you were on there too much and spent too much money is your opponent. He is your best detective. I think this is easy to find.

As it is today, the sky is the limit.

Anybody who has the money can buy all the time he wants. All he needs to do is form a little committee, and that committee can buy $2 million or $3 million worth of time, and there is no way to stop it.

We are getting to the point where this thing is getting out of hand, and it verges on the scandalous. The time is now and the place is here to do something about it. That is my only motive. If the Senate wants to go along with it, fine. On the other hand, if the Senate wants to reject it, I have done my best. I will have to wait and try again the next time.

As Pastore finished his remarks, Senator Robert C. Byrd (D., W.Va.) questioned the existence of a quorum, thereby necessitating a quorum call. A quorum is the minimum number of members who must be present if a vote is to be taken and held binding on the chamber. Hence, a quorum call—or head count—is made on challenge before the vote is taken. [Doc. 4-16]

DOCUMENT 4-16: The Quorum Call

The PRESIDING OFFICER. The question is on agreeing to the amendment.

Mr. BYRD of West Virginia. Mr. President, I suggest the absence of a quorum.

The PRESIDING OFFICER. The clerk will call the roll.

The assistant legislative clerk proceeded to call the roll.

Mr. BYRD of West Virginia. Mr. President, I ask unanimous consent that the order for the quorum call be rescinded.*

The PRESIDING OFFICER (Mr. HOLLINGS). Without objection, it is so ordered.

RECESS UNTIL 1:45 P.M.

Mr. BYRD of West Virginia. Mr. President, I ask unanimous consent that the Senate stand in recess until 1:45 o'clock p.m. today.

The PRESIDING OFFICER. Is there objection to the request of the Senator from West Virginia?

There being no objection, the Senate (at 1 o'clock and 3 minutes p.m.) took a recess until 1:45 p.m., the same day.

* Senators attempting to arrive at an agreement on legislation will frequently utilize a call of the roll to gain time. Once they have accomplished their objective, they will request that the call be rescinded or stopped. Such a procedural device may consume only a minute or two, or it may run a half-hour or more.

During the quorum call, the Republican leadership advised their Democratic counterparts that they wished to convene a short recess in order to explore the thrust of the Pastore-Pearson amendment. They went so far as to call a meeting of the GOP Policy Committee in an effort to hammer out a party position. After some debate, the consensus was to oppose both the amendment and the bill. Many Republican Senators were opposed to ceilings on expenditures of any sort. Others feared any legislation that might alter the ground rules in the forthcoming fall elections. In the meantime, Pastore was using the brief recess to marshal his own forces for the votes ahead. When the Senate reconvened, Pastore asked that the "yeas and nays" be ordered. A roll-call vote was then taken.

Despite substantial Republican opposition, the Pastore-Pearson amendment carried by a vote of 50 to 35.

Vote on the Seven-Cents-Per-Vote Spending Limit
Amendment for Electronic Media

Party	Yes	No	Total
Democrats	42	3	45
Republicans	8	32	40
Total	50	35	85

The vote was finalized when a member (who had voted for the amendment) moved to reconsider the vote. According to the Senate Rules, reconsideration can be done only once within two days following the vote. Since a motion to reconsider is debatable, this leaves open the possibility that opponents may stall Senate action by an extended debate. Thus, immediately after the member has moved to reconsider, another proponent offers an accompanying motion "to lay on the table," that is, put aside the motion to reconsider. This motion is not debatable and takes precedence over reconsideration. In combination, the two motions have the effect of "sealing" or making final the result of the vote.

Since no other amendments had been offered, the Senate then proceeded to consider S.3637 as amended. As the final vote approached, the debate began to take on a more acerbic, partisan quality. Senator George Murphy (R., Calif.) engaged in a somewhat heated exchange with Senator Pastore. [*Doc. 4-17*]

In the meantime, a Republican theme was emerging. As debate continued, they began to stress the need for comprehensive legislation. They argued against trying to tackle just one part of the problem, such as television spots, and in favor of drafting a thorough bill. Senator John G. Tower (R., Tex.), the chairman of the GOP Senate Campaign Committee, raised this point, which was later to be restated in the

DOCUMENT **4-17**: The Pastore-Murphy Exchange

Mr. MURPHY. Mr. President, will the Senator yield?

Mr. PASTORE. I yield.

Mr. MURPHY. My distinguished colleague has asked a question about an infraction of the rule with respect to expenditures and the blame falling on the candidate. My colleague stated a case in which someone wanted to buy the time, break the rule, and attack the candidate, and this would be blamed on the candidate. Suppose somebody bought the time and spoke for the candidate, in order to bring the candidate under an infraction of the rule. This is possible.

Mr. PASTORE. The question is getting a little complicated.

Mr. MURPHY. This is a complicated matter.

Mr. PASTORE. If this group is acting with the acquiescence and consent of your opponent and that would be their only motive, that time perhaps could be charged to the opponent.

Mr. MURPHY. When do you prove this—during the campaign, afterward, the Saturday night before?

Mr. PASTORE. You prove it if your opponent should win and try to take his seat in Congress. Your colleagues will stand up———

Mr. MURPHY. This is after the election is over.

Mr. PASTORE. That is correct.

Mr. MURPHY. That is a very dangerous situation.

Mr. PASTORE. Will the Senator permit me to finish my statement? You are subject to denial of your seat if you violate the law.

Mr. MURPHY. I understand that.

Mr. PASTORE. In your particular case, if your opponent is not involved and any group speaks against your candidacy or speaks against you, you have a perfect right, over and beyond what is in this bill, to ask for time under the fairness doctrine.

Mr. MURPHY. I said suppose he speaks for me. Suppose a group comes in and they find that I have already spent the permitted 7 cents a vote, and they buy extra time, and they do not attack me. They speak for me.

Mr. PASTORE. They cannot do it.

Mr. MURPHY. Let me finish.

Suppose someone says, "Wait a minute. This fellow broke the rule." Now there is a headline that says he broke the rule; he broke the rule of the good Senator from Rhode Island which has been laid down today. Now you go into litigation—there are charges and countercharges. By the time you have any proof one way or the other, the election is over, the damage has been done, and I do not know how it can be repaired.

This is a very complicated matter. I understand the situation, and I congratulate my distinguished colleague for trying to take it on and unravel it. But I am afraid that parts of this bill could react in ways that even he has not perceived. I am sure there are possible problems that I have not perceived.

Mr. PASTORE. If we sit around long enough, we can even stir up a nightmare. The point is that in your particular case———

Mr. MURPHY. I wish the Senator would not refer to my particular case. I stated that earlier.

Mr. PASTORE. All right; in the case that the Senator has cited.

Mr. MURPHY. Yes.

Mr. PASTORE. We have already

Doc. 4-17 *(cont.)*

adopted an amendment here that the FCC must make rules and regulations and a broadcaster must keep a log. While all this is going on, the Senator still has it within his right to pick up the phone and have the FCC make an investigation, even while the campaign is going on.

President's veto message. [*Doc. 4-18*]

Minority Leader Hugh Scott and the ranking Republican on the Commerce Committee, Norris Cotton, intensified the fight against the bill. Both Scott and Cotton had opposed the spending limitation that was now a part of the bill. Scott was concerned about the effect of the limit on certain individual candidates, especially moderate-to-liberal Republicans from his own wing of the party. Cotton was opposed to any changes in the bill as reported; in his judgment, the original bill was the best legislation possible. "I regret to say," he concluded, "I cannot vote for final passage of the bill with this [Pastore-Pearson] amendment included in it."

Because the motion to reconsider the amendment had been laid on the table, it was, in effect, frozen into the bill. The only way to strike the amendment would be to recommit the entire bill to committee. This is exactly what Senator James B. Allen, a conservative Democrat from Alabama, attempted. Moving to recommit S.3637, Allen's motion was quickly endorsed by the Republican leadership, by then firmly opposed to the legislation as amended.

DOCUMENT **4-18**: Senator Tower Challenges the Bill

Mr. TOWER. Mr. President, will the Senator yield at that point?

Mr. COTTON. I yield.

Mr. TOWER. Is there not a committee in the Senate that would be competent to deal with campaign practices and procedures on a comprehensive basis, to include all media?

Mr. COTTON. Yes, of course.

Mr. TOWER. Why can we not submit comprehensive legislation to that committee for consideration rather than attacking the problem piecemeal?

If the bill were recommitted, Pastore would be faced with reworking it again in committee—and with the strong possibility it would die. Pastore's final floor defense of his legislation played upon the prestige of his chairmanship and the respect he felt was owed him for fulfilling his professional obligation in the Senate, then and in the past. His mock apprehension about Senator Tower's criticism was calculated to maintain the kind of tolerant climate on the floor that would hold on to some needed Republican support. [*Doc. 4-19*]

DOCUMENT **4-19**: Pastore Sums Up

Mr. PASTORE. Many Senators prodded me every time I came to the floor, saying, "When are you going to do something about that bill?" I was being prodded by Republicans and by Democrats—"When are you going to do something about the bill?"

We sat down patiently, constantly, and consistently, and we held very exhaustive hearings. As for myself, I worked on this day and night, and finally we came forth with this recommendation.

The Senator from Texas is arguing as to why we do not have a comprehensive bill. Perhaps we should have had a comprehensive bill. But this was within our jurisdiction, this was our authority and was our responsibility—and this forward step is the product we bring to the floor.

Let me conclude by saying this: This bill is neither a help nor a hindrance to me personally.

This bill in its import does not mean a row of beans to me in my situation. It makes no difference to me this afternoon whether we pass it or not. All I said from the committee was that I had a responsibility. I carried it out. I said let us go on the floor and see what they want to do. I am not trying to help incumbents, nor am I trying to hurt those outside. I am not trying to help Democrats or hurt Republicans. I have no such motive in my mind. I do not care a row of beans what the Senate does with the bill this afternoon, whether we send it back to the committee or kill it. I say, the best thing is, if we want to send it back to committee is, please stop it. Stop giving me this bother-some, burdensome responsibility—this nuisance. Just stop giving me this nuisance. Just say you do not want it. I think we have brought out a bill that makes sense. What we are trying to do is to eliminate—not create abuses. I have been told by every member of the committee that they were for the limitation. Now I am surprised to see that we are picking at this sentence and that sentence. It does not make sense. It is a simple formula. Either agree with it or disagree with it. You either want the bill or you do not want the bill. If you want to spend $18 million to run a presidential campaign, go ahead and do it. If you want the sky to be the limit because you have the money, then do it. I do not care. If you have the idea that you will send it back to committee, it is as dead as a doornail if it goes back there. I say, let us have the courage to stand up and vote.

Mr. TOWER. Mr. President, will the Senator from Rhode Island yield?

Mr. PASTORE. I yield.

Mr. TOWER. I should simply like to say that I did not mean to imply, in any event, that there was a personal motive on the part of the Senator from Rhode Island. I have great confidence that the Senator from Rhode Island is absolutely right when he says it makes no difference to him personally. I am confident, as chairman of the senatorial campaign committee for the Republican Party, that we cannot beat the distinguished Senator from Rhode Island in that State this fall. We are not even going to try. The Senator is home free.*

Mr. PASTORE. The Senator's statement is now in the CONGRESSIONAL

*Senator Tower's predictions were easily borne out: Senator Pastore won re-election by better than 67 per cent of the vote.

Doc. 4-19 *(cont.)*

RECORD. It is in the CONGRESSIONAL RECORD. Do not go into the Official Reporters' room to knock it out. [Laughter.]

Mr. TOWER. I am not. We will leave it in there. It will be there.

Mr. PASTORE. Leave it right in there. [Laughter.]

At the conclusion of debate, Pastore moved to lay the recommittal motion on the table so as to avoid a vote on sending S.3637 back to committee. As before, the yeas and nays were ordered, and Pastore's position prevailed by a vote of 48 to 37.[17]

Vote on the Motion to Table the Recommittal Motion

Party	Yes	No	Total
Democratic	41	5	46
Republican	7	32	39
Total	48	37	85

Following the successful tabling of the recommittal motion, Pastore moved to consider the final passage of the bill. As is frequently the pattern, the final margin of victory, 58 to 27, was more substantial than the vote on the recommittal motion. The losing side had made its main thrust; now minority Senators were free to follow their personal inclinations. The final result was thus a more muted partisan alignment.

Final Vote on S.3637

Party	Yes	No	Total
Democratic	45	1	46
Republican	13	26	39
Total	58	27	85

[17] Senator Lee Metcalf (D., Mont.) agreed to a "pair" with Senator Vance Hartke (D., Ind.). Pairing is a procedure by which a Senator who supports a measure but who is absent for a roll-call vote enters into an agreement with a Senator opposing a measure such that neither of the parties will vote. Since Metcalf was present for the vote, and Hartke was absent, Metcalf was recorded as entering a "live pair." Thus, the net result here was to subtract one vote from the winning side. On close decisions, a paired vote of this type could be crucial. Whether or not one or both Senators are present, pairs are not counted in the official roll call for the purpose of accepting or rejecting a proposal.

DOCUMENT **4-20**: Comparison of Three Roll-Call Votes

Although the Congressional Record *does not identify votes by party membership, in the following roll calls Republicans are set apart by italicized type.*

The Pastore-Pearson 7¢-Per-Vote Amendment

The result was announced—yeas 50, nays 35, as follows:

[No. 130 Leg.]

YEAS—50

Allen	Gore	Long	Proxmire
Bayh	Gravel	*Mathias*	Ribicoff
Burdick	Harris	McGee	Sparkman
Byrd, Va.	Hart	McGovern	Spong
Byrd, W.Va.	Hartke	McIntyre	Symington
Cannon	Holland	Metcalf	Talmadge
Case	Hollings	Mondale	Tydings
Cooper	Hughes	Montoya	Williams, N.J.
Cranston	Inouye	Moss	*Williams, Del.*
Eagleton	Jackson	Muskie	Yarborough
Ellender	*Javits*	*Packwood*	Young, Ohio
Fulbright	Jordan, N.C.	Pastore	
Goodell	Kennedy	*Pearson*	

NAYS—35

Aiken	*Dole*	*Hatfield*	*Scott*
Allott	*Dominick*	*Hruska*	*Smith, Maine*
Baker	Ervin	*Jordan, Idaho*	*Smith, Ill.*
Bellmon	*Fannin*	McClellan	Stennis
Boggs	*Fong*	*Miller*	*Stevens*
Brooke	*Goldwater*	*Percy*	*Thurmond*
Cook	*Griffin*	*Prouty*	*Tower*
Cotton	*Gurney*	*Saxbe*	*Young, N. Dak.*
Curtis	*Hansen*	*Schweiker*	

ANSWERED "PRESENT"—1
Murphy

NOT VOTING—14

Anderson	Dodd	McCarthy	Pell
Bennett	Eastland	*Mundt*	Randolph
Bible	Magnuson	Nelson	Russell
Church	Mansfield		

So Mr. Pastore's amendment was agreed to.

Doc. 4-20 *(cont.)*

Motion to Table Recommittal Motion

The result was announced—yeas 48, nays 37, as follows:

[No. 131 Leg.]

YEAS—48

Bayh	Gore	*Mathias*	Proxmire
Burdick	Gravel	McGee	Ribicoff
Byrd, Va.	Harris	McGovern	*Saxbe*
Byrd, W.Va.	Hart	McIntyre	*Schweiker*
Cannon	Holland	Mondale	Spong
Case	Hollings	Montoya	Stennis
Church	Hughes	Moss	Symington
Cranston	Inouye	Muskie	Talmadge
Eagleton	Jackson	Nelson	Tydings
Ellender	Jordan, N.C.	*Packwood*	Williams, N.J.
Fulbright	Kennedy	Pastore	Yarborough
Goodell	Long	*Pearson*	Young, Ohio

NAYS—37

Aiken	*Curtis*	*Hatfield*	*Scott*
Allen	*Dole*	*Hruska*	*Smith, Maine*
Allott	*Dominick*	*Javits*	*Smith, Ill.*
Baker	Ervin	*Jordan, Idaho*	Sparkman
Bellmon	*Fannin*	McCarthy	*Stevens*
Boggs	*Fong*	McClellan	*Thurmond*
Brooke		*Miller*	*Tower*
Cook	*Griffin*	*Murphy*	*Williams, Del.*
Cooper	*Gurney*	*Prouty*	*Young, N. Dak.*
Cotton	*Hansen*		

PRESENT AND GIVING A LIVE PAIR, AS PREVIOUSLY RECORDED—1
Metcalf, against

NOT VOTING—14

Anderson	Eastland	Mansfield	*Percy*
Bennett	*Goldwater*	*Mundt*	Randolph
Bible	Hartke		
Dodd	Magnuson	Pell	Russell

So Mr. PASTORE'S motion to lay Mr. ALLEN'S motion to recommit on the table was agreed to.

Doc. 4-20 (*cont.*)

Final Vote on S.3637

The result was announced—yeas 58, nays 27, as follows:

[No. 132 Leg.]

YEAS—58

Aiken	*Goodell*	McGee	Ribicoff
Allen	Gore	McGovern	*Saxbe*
Bayh	Gravel	McIntyre	*Schweiker*
Burdick	Harris	Metcalf	*Smith, Maine*
Byrd, Va.	Hart	Mondale	Sparkman
Byrd, W. Va.	Holland	Montoya	Spong
Cannon	Hollings	Moss	Stennis
Case	Hughes	Muskie	*Stevens*
Church	Inouye	Nelson	Symington
Cooper	Jackson	*Packwood*	Talmadge
Cranston	*Javits*	Pastore	Tydings
Eagleton	Jordan, N.C.	*Pearson*	Williams, N.J.
Ellender	Kennedy	*Prouty*	Yarborough
Ervin	Long	Proxmire	Young, Ohio
Fulbright	*Mathias*		

NAYS—27

Allott	*Curtis*	*Hansen*	*Scott*
Baker	*Dole*	*Hatfield*	*Smith, Ill.*
Bellmon	*Dominick*	*Hruska*	*Thurmond*
Boggs	*Fannin*	*Jordan, Idaho*	*Tower*
Brooke	*Fong*	McClellan	*Williams, Del.*
Cook	*Griffin*	*Miller*	*Young, N. Dak.*
Cotton	*Gurney*	*Murphy*	

NOT VOTING—15

Anderson	Eastland	Mansfield	*Percy*
Bennett	*Goldwater*	McCarthy	Randolph
Bible	Hartke	*Mundt*	Russell
Dodd	Magnuson	Pell	

So the bill (S.3637) was passed.

As Document 4-20 reveals, on final passage there was much greater unanimity among the Democrats than on any prior vote. [*Doc. 4-20*] Even Senator Sam J. Ervin, Jr. (D., N.C.), who had opposed both the spending limit and Pastore's motion to table the recommittal motion, now voted with his party brethren. Senator John L. McClellan (D., Ark.) was the lone, yet consistent, Democratic maverick, voting against limits, against the tabling motion, and finally, against the bill itself.

Across the aisle, there was greater Republican unity on the previous votes than on final passage. Senators Aiken (Vt.), Prouty (Vt.), Smith (Me.), and Stevens (Alas.) had voted against limits and against tabling the recommittal motion. But they seemed willing to endorse the whole bill as better than no legislation at all. With the Democrats practically certain of winning on final passage, the need for Republicans to maintain a partisan position was less critical.

For all practical purposes, the change in the NCEC-sponsored bill had been metamorphic. Much of the hectic staff work—some done externally, a good part of it by Senate and House assistants—would have to be scrapped. As one Senate legislative aide reported, "All the high principles we had fought for were junked. We wound up saying 'I don't care what it looks like; I'll take anything that will pass.'"[18] Still, the first major hurdle had been overcome. From this point on, the NCEC would assume a more pragmatic stance, intent on getting something on the books and willing to put off worrying about how to improve it.

One intriguing facet of the legislation remained submerged throughout the Senate hearings and the floor debate. The effective date of the spending limitation was set at thirty days following the enactment of S.3637. If the House of Representatives could move with some pace, it still might be possible for the bill to become law before the 1970 elections. In that event, all of the House members and one-third of the Senate would have to operate under the new spending limitations. Surprisingly, there was no recorded discussion of the effective date either in the Senate hearings or on the floor. Soon, however, this issue would emerge, and it was to play a crucial role in both the House enactment and the subsequent Presidential veto of S.3637.

[18] A Pastore aide would later counter: "What is so 'high principled' about discount formulas on spot commercials? In this business of legislating you don't go after everything at once; you start with a smaller chunk and work at it."

FURTHER READING

Ralph K. Huitt's articles are an invaluable source of information on the United States Senate. They are collected in Ralph K. Huitt and Robert L. Peabody, *Congress: Two Decades of Analysis* (New York: Harper & Row, 1969).

Donald Matthews, *U.S. Senators and Their World* (Chapel Hill: University of North Carolina Press, 1960), remains the standard, most comprehensive book on the Senate. In a more recent analysis, *Power in the Senate* (New York: St. Martin's Press, 1969), Randall B. Ripley explores the internal distribution of power in the Senate and some of its consequences.

The rules, procedures, and legislative strategies governing both the Senate and the House are set forth by Lewis A. Froman, Jr., in his *The Congressional Process* (Boston: Little, Brown, 1967).

Journalists have also provided us with some excellent analyses of the Senate. Notable is William S. White's *Citadel: The Story of the United States Senate* (New York: Harper & Row, 1956). The Senate leadership of Democrat Lyndon B. Johnson is dissected by Rowland Evans and Robert Novak in *Lyndon B. Johnson: The Exercise of Power* (New York: New American Library, 1966). A behind-the-scenes account of the fight over the Senate confirmation of Supreme Court nominee G. Harrold Carswell is given by Richard Harris in *Decision* (New York: E. P. Dutton, 1971).

The House of
Representatives Responds

THE LEGISLATIVE PROCESS IN THE HOUSE

The Structure of the House

The United States House of Representatives is a large, complex legislature made up of 435 members and a supporting staff approaching nearly 10,000.[1] In only a handful of national legislatures are there more members—the British House of Commons has 630 and the French National Assembly has 482—but none has the elaborate base of personal assistants, committee staff, and support personnel. Most national assemblies in Western democracies are characterized by multiparty systems. In contrast, the House is organized by a dual-party hierarchy: currently, a Democratic majority and a Republican minority. Not since the 83d Congress (1953–54) have Republicans controlled more than 218 seats and thus earned the right to choose the Speaker and select the committee chairmen. But, the one factor that sets the United States Congress apart from every other national legislature is the complexity of its committee system. Other representative bodies make use of ad hoc committees, some even have committees that continue from one session to the next, but none has developed such a powerful set of standing committees—twenty-one in the House, seventeen in the Senate. And in no other national legislatures throughout the world has so much authority devolved into the hands of the senior committee chairmen.

---

[1] The supporting staff of the typical House member begins with his clerk-hire allowance—up to fifteen (sixteen for districts with populations of over 500,000) employees and approximately $141,000–$148,000 per year. Not every Representative takes full advantage of his allowance, but, as of 1970, members were employing nearly 5,000 people in their Capitol Hill and district offices. In addition, the standing committees of the House employ some 230 professional and clerical personnel, and joint, select, and special investigating staffs account for more than 300 employees. A complete inventory of Hill staffs would also include majority- and minority-leadership employees; the Parliamentarian's staff; and the offices of the Clerk, Doorkeeper, Postmaster, and Sergeant-at-Arms. These offices would add nearly 1,000 more employees, including 250 policemen and numerous doormen, elevator operators, pages, mail-room and folding-room employees. To this accumulative figure of 6,500, one would also have to add the staffs of such agencies as the Capitol Architect, the Congressional Reference Service of the Library of Congress (more than 300 employees), and the General Accounting Office, all of which are accountable to Congress. Even allocating but half of these staffs to the House of Representatives, a figure approximating 10,000 employees is easily approached. In contrast, the Executive Office of the President employs over 4,600 people; the total civilian employment of the executive branch is almost 3 million.

The Constitution of the United States requires that seats in the House of Representatives be apportioned to the states on the basis of population, with each state entitled to at least one seat. The Constitution further provides that following the national Census—taken every decennial year—the number of seats allotted to each state is to be reapportioned to reflect its population movement and growth. For example, following the 1970 Census, the size of the California Congressional delegation will be increased from thirty-eight to forty-three. The same Census will cause nine states to lose one or more seats. The total number of House seats is fixed by federal legislation at 435. With the 1970 Census showing a resident population of 203,184,772, the ideal Congressional district population should approximate 467,000.

Elections for all 435 seats in the House of Representatives are held every two years. When the newly elected House members convene for the first time, they must organize and adopt their rules and procedures anew, since the House is not a continuing legislative body.[2] The convening of the new House of Representatives in January designates a new Congress, that is, the beginning of the two-year term of office.

The first Congress met from 1789 to 1791, and the 91st Congress, from 1969 to 1971. Congressional sessions, which used to amble on for a leisurely six months or so, now extend for ten months or longer. For example, the first session of the 91st Congress convened on January 3, 1969, and did not adjourn until December 23, 1969. The second session got underway on January 19, 1970, and lasted until the constitutional limit—January 2, 1971.

Leadership in the House. The *dual* and *decentralized* nature of Congressional leadership distinguishes it from most other forms of organizational leadership. Before a new Congress convenes, the two parties, majority and minority, meet in caucuses or conferences to select their nominees for Speaker of the House. When the House convenes, the majority's nominee is automatically elected, since this vote is *strictly* along party lines. The majority party also chooses the committee chairmen. The minority-party nominee becomes the Minority Leader, and the minority party's most senior members on the twenty-one standing committees are known as ranking minority members. This duality of the party and committee structure contributes to the decentralized nature of decision-making in the House. The fact that every Representative, be he chairman or lowly freshman, is ultimately responsible only to a majority of his constituents, makes for

---

[2] The adopted rules are seldom modified from Congress to Congress. Almost a quarter of a century elapsed between the major reforms of the Legislative Reorganization Act of 1946 and the more modest, incremental changes of the Legislative Reorganization Act of 1970.

further independence from centralized party pressures. Hence, the Speaker must continually confer and cooperate with other party leaders and with committee chairmen and their minority counterparts if he expects to pass his party's legislative program.

Leadership of his party is one of the Speaker's main responsibilities; the other is service as presiding officer of the House. In the latter capacity, he must avoid partisanship and strive instead for objectivity and neutrality in his rulings. His formal powers are rather restricted: deciding upon the admissibility of motions (whether they are in order); recognizing members who wish to speak or offer motions; appointing members to boards, commissions, select and conference committees; counting for quorums and votes; maintaining "order and decorum" in the chamber; and controlling the legislative schedule to a substantial degree. But, when these formal responsibilities are combined with the considerable personal and political favors that can be dispensed, such as appearances at fund-raising dinners and the wide range of legislative assistance that a Speaker can offer, then the total power exercised can be very great indeed.

How does one get to be the Speaker, the Minority Leader, or a committee chairman? Elected House leaders, majority or minority, are generally senior Representatives from safe districts who have demonstrated leadership capacity in lesser-ranked party positions—such as chairman of the Caucus (for the Democrats) or Conference (for the Republicans), chairman of the Republican (or Democratic) Campaign Committee, or party Whips. Majority and minority leaders are generally men in their fifties who have served a minimum of six to eight terms. Typically, they represent districts located in party strongholds—southern and big-city districts for Democrats; midwestern and rural or suburban districts for Republicans. The main responsibilities of the leaders include overseeing the passage of their own party's legislation, frustrating their opponent's objectives, and, on occasion, working in harmony with their counterparts on bipartisan measures.

Obviously, in order to be Speaker or Majority Leader, one must be part of the majority party—the party that elects more than 218 of the 435 members of the House. Since 1930, the Democratic Party has controlled every Congress save two, the 80th (1947–48) and the 83d (1953–54).

To become a committee chairman one must not only be a member of the majority, but also have served longer for a consecutive period on a given committee than any other majority member. This means one must come from a safe seat. This in turn means that most committee chairmen (and their minority counterparts) represent their respective party heartlands. Of the twenty-one Democratic chairmen serving in the 91st Congress (see Document 5-1), eight are from southern states; seven represent northern or western big-city districts. As a

DOCUMENT 5-1: Major House Party Leaders

Democratic Majority*	91st Congress (1969–70)	92d Congress (1971–72)
Speaker	John W. McCormack (Mass.)	Albert
Majority Leader	Carl Albert (Okla.)	Boggs
Majority Whip	Hale Boggs (La.)	Thomas P. O'Neill (Mass.)
Chairman of Caucus	Dan Rostenkowski (Ill.)	Olin E. Teague (Tex.)
Republican Minority†		
Minority Leader	Gerald R. Ford (Mich.)	Ford
Minority Whip	Leslie C. Arends (Ill.)	Arends
Chairman of Conference	John B. Anderson (Ill.)	Anderson
Chairman, Policy Committee	John J. Rhodes (Ariz.)	Rhodes

* After McCormack decided to retire (at seventy-eight), Albert moved up to become Speaker with only token opposition. Boggs won a five-man race for Majority Leader at the same opening caucus on January 19, 1971.

† There was no change in the Republican leadership, although Conference Chairman Anderson narrowly withstood a challenge from Rep. Samuel Devine of Ohio (89–81) at the opening Republican Conference on January 20, 1971.

result of this seniority system, chairmen tend to be much older and generally more conservative than rank-and-file members.

As the Congressional parties have become more institutionalized, other party leaders have taken on added responsibilities. Generally, the party Whip is third in the hierarchy of the Democratic Party, while the Whip in the Republican Party is second in the line of succession.[3] Whips have two prime functions in both parties: to ascertain in person or by telephone just how their fellow members are leaning on important legislation or amendments scheduled for floor debate, and to help obtain maximum attendance on the floor when key votes are being

[3] This is not a rigid rule. When Secretary of Defense Melvin Laird served in the House of Representatives as chairman of the Republican Conference during 1965–68, he was widely viewed as the most likely heir to Minority Leader Gerald Ford.

taken. Both parties have a set of "regional" or Assistant Whips to help party leaders in obtaining information and maintaining maximum floor participation.

Conference or Caucus chairmen are mainly preoccupied at the opening organizational meeting of a new Congress. The position has taken on added importance in the Democratic Party with the institutionalization of monthly caucuses. Both parties also have lesser party positions, such as chairmen of Policy (Republican) or Steering (Democratic) committees, and the chairmen of Congressional Campaign committees. In recent years, these positions have generally meant some control over staff and sometimes other resources, including campaign contributions. Hence, they are beginning to be sought for their own right and not just as possible stepping-stones to higher Congressional office. [*Doc. 5-1*]

The Stages of Legislation

What happens to a bill from the time it is introduced until the time it reaches the floor of the House? Much of the description of pre-floor activity in the Senate is easily transferable to the House. The step-by-step process of hearings, subcommittee mark-up or perfecting sessions, approval by the full committee, reporting out, and assignment to a calendar—all of these stages are duplicated in both houses. Perhaps the major difference at the committee stage is one of numbers. As Document 5-2 indicates, House committees tend to be large, averaging thirty-five members as compared to a typical Senate committee of about fifteen or so members. Another important difference is that Senators are spread thinner in committee work. Most Senators will serve on three committees; the average House member, only one or two.

In the 91st Congress (1969–70), there were twenty-one standing committees, that is, "permanent" committees continuing from one Congress to the next. As in the Senate, each committee has its jurisdiction specified in the House Rules. Furthermore, the size of each committee is generally prescribed by the Rules, although from time to time the House leadership will increase or decrease the size of a particular committee, usually to accommodate the committee-assignment needs of a favored member.

The ratio of Democrats to Republicans on a given committee is flexible, in most instances an approximation of all Democrats to all Republicans in a given Congress. Thus, in the 91st Congress, with 246 Democrats to 189 Republicans, the majority party maintained a rough 57-to-43 split on almost every committee. [*Doc. 5-2*]

DOCUMENT **5-2**: Standing House Committees, 91st Congress (1969–70)

Committee	Number of Members	Ratio of Dem:Rep	Chairman	Number of Subcommittees
Agriculture	34	19:15	Poage, Tex.	10
Appropriations	51	30:21	Mahon, Tex.	13
Armed Services	41	24:17	Rivers, S.C.*	15
Banking and Currency	36	21:15	Patman, Tex.	7
District of Columbia	25	14:11	McMillan, S.C.	5
Education and Labor	35	20:15	Perkins, Ky.	6
Foreign Affairs	38	21:17	Morgan, Pa.	9
Government Operations	35	20:15	Dawson, Ill.*	8
House Administration	25	14:11	Friedel, Md.*	4
Interior and Insular Affairs	34	19:15	Aspinall, Colo.	6
Internal Security	9	5:4	Ichord, Mo.	0
Interstate and Foreign Commerce	37	21:16	Staggers, W.Va.	4
Judiciary	35	21:16	Celler, N.Y.	7
Merchant Marine and Fisheries	37	21:16	Garmatz, Md.	7
Post Office and Civil Service	26	15:11	Dulski, N.Y.	7
Public Works	34	19:15	Fallon, Md.*	5
Rules	15	10:5	Colmer, Miss.	0
Science and Astronautics	32	18:14	Miller, Calif.	6
Standards of Official Conduct	12	6:6	Price, Ill.	0
Veterans' Affairs	25	14:11	Teague, Tex.	5
Ways and Means	25	15:10	Mills, Ark.	0

* The 92d Congress (1971–72) began with four new chairmen: Hebert, La., Armed Services; Holifield, Calif., Government Operations; Hays, Ohio, House Administration; and Blatnik, Minn., Public Works. Two of their predecessors had died in office (Rivers, Dawson); two had been upset in 1970 primaries (Friedel, Fallon).

Ways and Means, Appropriations, and Rules Committee assignments are notable exceptions to this ratio, for control of these committees is deemed so important that more fixed distributions of 3:2 or 2:1 are maintained. Appointment to these "big three" committees is usually exclusive—that is, a member cannot serve on other, less prestigious committees as well.

Senior members of the House with considerable committee seniority will sometimes request an appointment to one of these high-prestige committees if there is a vacancy. For example, Omar Burleson of Texas gave up the chairmanship of House Administration to become a member of the Ways and Means Committee at the opening of the 91st Congress. The acceptance of such an assignment meant a loss of his other committee assignments, but for him membership on a committee that controls tax legislation and monitors the oil industry was more than worth the cost in seniority.

In the House, even more than in the Senate, the committee chairman holds a life-and-death grip over most legislation. His many powers include: (1) calling meetings; (2) presiding over meetings; (3) determining the subcommittees, if any, within his committee's jurisdiction; (4) appointing subcommittee chairmen and subcommittee members; and (5) developing a staff, freeing or restraining its discretion, and determining its size. With the passage of the Legislative Reorganization Act of 1970, however, the actual or potential dangers of an overly arbitrary chairman have been substantially curtailed.

The Workload of the House. The legislative workload of the House is considerable, with more than 10,000 bills introduced in a single session of Congress. Part of its heavy workload is due to the size of its membership (over four times larger than the Senate); part stems from a hesitancy of the members to exploit the Senate practice of cosponsorship. Until April, 1967, every bill introduced in the House, even if it was identical to another, would receive a new number. Since 1967, a bill may be sponsored by up to twenty-five members. The following document indicates the workload for a typical Congress, the 91st. [*Doc. 5-3*]

DOCUMENT **5-3**: Workload of the House*

91st Congress (1969–71)

Measure†	House Designation	Number Introduced	Number Passed
Bill	H. R. + number	20,015	762
Joint resolution	H. J. Res. + number	1,421	61
Concurrent resolution	H. Con. Res. + number	799	72
Resolution	H. Res. + number	1,340	412

* House-introduced measures only.

† For definitions of these measures, see Document 4-1.

The most striking generalization from this workload pattern is how few bills that are introduced ever become law—seldom more than one out of twenty. Most bills perish in committee. Still, more than a thousand bills and resolutions will reach the floor in any one session. In order to handle this load, the bills are separated into classes and placed upon one of five different House calendars.

Calendars of the House, which are printed lists of the bills in the order in which they have been reported, are separated according to certain standards:

All measures raising, spending, or involving money are placed on the *Union Calendar*.

All measures providing relief for individuals are placed on the *Private Calendar*.

All public, non-money measures are placed on the *House Calendar*.

Measures of a noncontroversial character on the House or Union calendars may be placed, by request and House approval, on the *Consent Calendar*.

By a petition of a majority of the House, a bill not reported by a committee may be placed on the *Discharge Calendar*.[4]

Most legislation reaches the floor by way of the Private and Consent calendars. This is not surprising since these measures are the least controversial. Special legislative days are established to permit the consideration of bills involving the District of Columbia and certain noncontroversial issues. For example, on the first and third Mondays of each month, the Speaker may entertain a motion to suspend the operation of the regular rules of the House in order to pass a bill or resolution. It requires a two-thirds vote in the affirmative to suspend the rules. These various devices—calendars and special legislative days—permit the House to act more efficiently on the numerous essentially noncontroversial measures. [*Doc. 5-4*]

Important legislation—numbering perhaps as many as 100 to 125 bills and resolutions per session—will reach the House floor for consideration in two alternative ways. Several committees, most notably Appropriations and Ways and Means, may bring privileged reports directly to the floor. The right of these committees to report at any time is confined, rather narrowly, to general appropriations bills or, in the case of Ways and Means, to bills raising revenue. The other alternative, resorted to on almost all legislation of substantial controversy, is the request of a "special order" or "rule" from the Committee on Rules.

---

[4] A majority of the House members (218) must sign a Discharge Petition in order to place a bill on the Discharge Calendar. This procedure is rarely used.

DOCUMENT **5-4**: The Calendars of the House

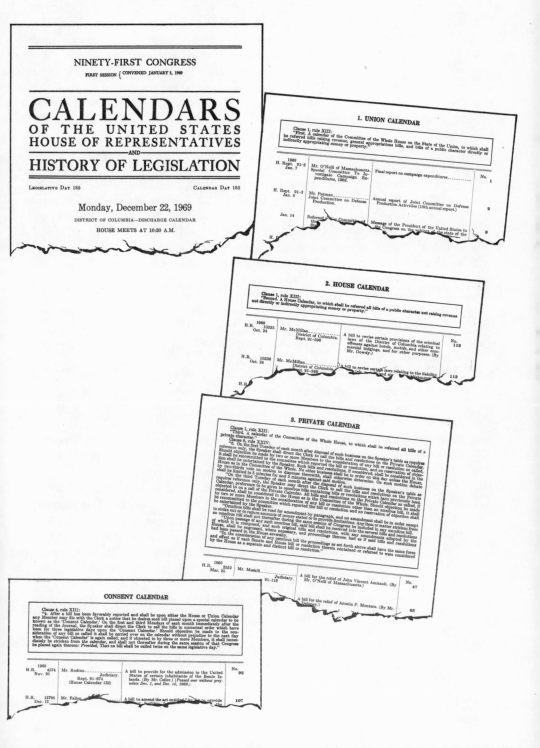

The House Committee on Rules. The Senate has no close counterpart to the House Committee on Rules. The Senate Committee on Rules and Administration operates more like the House Administration Committee, which is charged with matters of internal operations, office space, and travel. The two Rules committees do resemble each other in the sense that each has jurisdiction over modification of the rules of its respective chambers. What makes the House Committee on Rules unique is its vital role in the scheduling of bills for floor debate. The closest approximate body in the Senate would be the Democratic Policy Committee, but that body seldom meets; most Senate scheduling matters are resolved by the Majority Leader's working out unanimous-consent agreements.

When a committee chairman reports out a bill on which there is any controversy, the first thing he does is to file a report and a copy of the bill with the House Clerk. Depending on the kind of legislation —for example, whether it involves money—his bill will be assigned a position at the bottom of the appropriate calendar. If the measure is at all controversial, the chairman will generally request a hearing from the Committee on Rules.

The Rules Committee is composed of fifteen members—ten Democrats and five Republicans. Before the Rules Committee was enlarged (from twelve members) in January, 1961, a coalition of four Republicans and two southern Democrats dominated it. One of these conservative southerners was the legendary Judge Howard W. Smith of Virginia; the other was William M. Colmer of Mississippi, who is now chairman. Since the committee "packing," the more liberal House Democratic leadership has enjoyed, first, an eight-to-seven majority, and, in the past several Congresses, a nine-to-six favorable ratio. On most legislation that comes before the committee, these harsh "liberal-conservative," or more accurately, pro- and anti-leadership lines are seldom drawn.

After Rules Committee Chairman Colmer receives a request for a hearing, he will, in most instances, call his committee together at 10:30 a.m. in Room H-313, located off the House chambers on the third, or gallery, floor of the Capitol. Democrats sit to the chairman's right, in order of seniority; Republicans sit on his left. The chairman of the committee requesting a rule (or perhaps the subcommittee chairman) will be first to testify. He will be followed by the ranking minority member (or subcommittee ranking member). Other interested members of Congress may speak for or against the proposed legislation and the requested rule. No other witnesses may testify, but representatives of affected interest groups are usually in attendance.

Hearings may take as little as a minute or two, or they may proceed for several weeks, as they did for the Civil Rights Act of 1964. Typically, they are over in about thirty minutes to an hour. If the Rules Committee chairman is obliging, and Colmer is a courtly southern gentleman on most occasions, an executive or closed-door session of the committee may be held that same day. The end product of the deliberations of the Rules Committee is a special order or rule.

The special order takes the form of a House Resolution (H. Res.) specifying the ground rules under which the legislation will be considered. It sets forth the amount of debate that will be allowed—one hour, two hours, or more—and the kinds of amendments that can be offered from the floor. If the special order is adopted in the House, consideration of the measure can proceed outside of the sequential order of the calendars.

Day after day, month after month, the Committee on Rules typically works in close harmony with the House majority leadership. Sometimes the leadership will ask it to hold up legislation. Perhaps it is a bill the leadership opposes outright, perhaps the timing is not ripe for floor passage, for "If they can't be certain of winning, they don't want to go."[5]

On rare occasions, which make for newspaper headlines, the chairman, or a majority of the Rules Committee will thwart the leadership. If it is only the chairman, or only a minority of the committee, then devices exist to hold meetings and pry a special order out. In some Congresses, such as the 81st and 89th, strong Democratic majorities were able to adopt "21-day rules," a device for by-passing the Rules Committee altogether if it holds a bill for more than twenty-one calendar days after request for a rule has been made.[6] But in each of those Congresses, after two years of use, election changes and more conservative House majorities forced repeal of this procedure for by-passing the Rules Committee.

The relationships between the majority leadership, the Committee on Rules, and the members as a whole are almost continuously shifting. Their ebb and flow crucially affect the legislative process in the House of Representatives.

Floor Consideration

Decisions about which measures will come before the House, and when, are made by the Speaker in close consultation with the Majority Leader and the affected committee chairmen. Once a bill

[5] Clem Miller, *Member of the House,* John W. Baker, ed. (New York: Charles Scribner's Sons, 1962), p. 91.

[6] Robert L. Peabody, "The Enlarged Rules Committee," in *New Perspectives on the House of Representatives,* 1st ed. (Chicago: Rand McNally, 1963), pp. 129–64.

DOCUMENT 5-5: Whip Notice

THOMAS P. O'NEILL, JR.
Massachusetts
DEMOCRATIC WHIP

FLOOR WHIPS
JOHN J. McFALL
California

JOHN BRADEMAS
Indiana

Congress of the United States
House of Representatives
Office of the Democratic Whip
Washington, D.C. 20515

ASSISTANT WHIPS
1. TORBERT H. MACDONALD
2. HUGH L. CAREY
3. SAMUEL S. STRATTON
4. WILLIAM S. MOORHEAD
5. PETER W. RODINO
6. DAVID E. SATTERFIELD
7. JOHN J. FLYNT
8. CLEMENT J. ZABLOCKI
9. LEE H. HAMILTON
10. HARLEY O. STAGGERS
11. RICHARD H. FULTON
12. G. V. MONTGOMERY
13. TOM BEVILL
14. LEONOR K. SULLIVAN
15. DAN ROSTENKOWSKI
16. JIM WRIGHT
17. ED EDMONDSON
18. MORRIS K. UDALL
19. EDITH GREEN
20. GEORGE E. DANIELSON

September 23, 1971

WHIP NOTICE INFORMATION
55605   TELEPHONES   55606

My dear Colleague:

The program for the House of Representatives for the week of September 27, 1971, is as follows:

MONDAY

DISTRICT DAY
(FOUR BILLS)

1.	H.R. 10383	–	To Enable Individuals and Firms to Incorporate
2.	H.R. 10784	–	To Amend D.C. Election Laws
3.	H.R. 456	–	Tax Exempt Reserve Officers Association
4.	H.R. 10738	–	Regulate practice of Dentistry

SUSPENSIONS

1.	H.R. 9212	–	Black Lung Benefits
2.	S. 1253	–	Patents Study Program
3.	H.R. 10203	–	Water Resources Act Amendment
4.	H. Con. Res. 374	–	Humane Treatment of Prisoners of War
5.	H.R. 8817	–	Cooperative Forestry Programs
6.	H.R. 10538	–	To extend the Authority for Insuring Loans Under the Consolidated Farmers Home Administration Act.
7.	H.R. 3304	–	Fisherman's Protective Act Amendment

TUESDAY

H.R. 10351	–	Economic Opportunity Act Amendments (Consideration of Rule Only)
H.R. 6893	–	Weather Modification Reporting (OPEN RULE – ONE HOUR OF DEBATE)

WEDNESDAY

H.R. 10351	–	Economic Opportunity Act Amendments (OPEN RULE – TWO HOURS OF DEBATE) (GENERAL DEBATE ONLY)

THURSDAY AND BALANCE OF WEEK

H.R. 10351	–	Economic Opportunity Act Amendments (CONCLUDE CONSIDERATION)
H.R. 8085	–	Executive Agencies Age Requirements (OPEN RULE – ONE HOUR OF DEBATE)

****CONFERENCE REPORTS MAY BE BROUGHT UP AT ANY TIME****
ANY FURTHER PROGRAM WILL BE ANNOUNCED LATER

Sincerely,

Thomas P. O'Neill Jr.

Thomas P. O'Neill, Jr., M.C.
Democratic Whip

has been granted a special order (and sometimes just operating on a promise from the Rules Committee that it will report out legislation), the Majority Leader will make up a Whip notice outlining the schedule for the next week. [*Doc. 5-5*] Each member receives a copy of this notice on Thursday so he can plan his schedule, including possible trips home, for the following week.

On the day on which the bill is scheduled—usually a Tuesday, Wednesday, or Thursday[7]—the Speaker will first recognize a member of the Committee on Rules to present the special order. Routinely, he will make a brief presentation, yield half an hour to a member of the Rules Committee minority, and then reserve the balance of his time. Debate on the special order will seldom take up the full hour. Once the special order is adopted, sometimes by a voice vote but more often by a roll call, the House may proceed to consider the legislation under a device called the Committee of the Whole House on the State of the Union.

Committee of the Whole House. All measures on the Union Calendar (and most measures on the House Calendar requiring special orders) are considered by the House sitting in this committee. After the approval of a motion to consider a measure according to a special order, the Speaker appoints a chairman to preside over the Committee of the Whole. The only visible signs of the change from the House to the Committee of the Whole are the absence of the Speaker from the rostrum and the removal of the mace, symbol of authority in the House, from its stand.[8]

Deliberations usually begin with statements from the major proponents and opponents of the legislation. Such debate may take as little as a few minutes or as long as several days. When general debate has concluded, the members of the House typically enter into a section-by-section analysis of the bill under the so-called five-minute rule. Alternatively, the entire bill may be considered as read and opened up for amendment at any part.

The Committee of the Whole permits the House to expedite its business by less restrictive requirements. These requirements include:

---

[7] Monday is usually given over to District of Columbia bills or less controversial legislation. Members prefer to hold Friday open to begin trips home over the weekend. So routinized has this legislative and travel pattern become that Representatives living east of the Mississippi frequently keep their principal residences at home and join the "Tuesday to Thursday" club.

[8] The mace is forty-six inches tall. Its eagle and globe surmount rods representing the first thirteen states. In the event of extreme disorder on the House floor, the Speaker will direct the Sergeant-at-Arms to enforce order by displaying the mace.

(1) a quorum[9] of 100 in the Committee of the Whole, instead of the required House quorum of 218 members; (2) the absence of time-consuming roll-call votes in the Committee of the Whole; and (3) a five-minute time limit for each member debating an amendment. When debate has concluded and amendments, if any, have been considered, the Committee of the Whole reverts back into the House. Again, the only visible signs of the change are the return of the Speaker to the rostrum and the return of the mace to its stand. The chairman reports to the Speaker what has happened in the Committee of the Whole. The House then proceeds to adopt or reject the report of the Committee of the Whole, more likely than not through a roll-call vote.

Voting. There are four ways to vote for amendments or bills in the House when it sits as the Committee of the Whole:

1. Voting can be done by *voice*, with the chair asking for "ayes" then "nays," and with no record of how individual members voted.

2. Voting can be done by *division*, in which the members stand and the chairman counts. A division vote can be requested by a single member, and again, no record is kept.

3. Voting can be done by *tellers*, which must be considered upon the demand of a single member, but cannot be used unless seconded by at least twenty members. In a teller vote, those in favor of the bill or amendment line up on one side of the center aisle and those opposed line up on the other side. Each line files past its own teller, who counts the number of votes and reports to the presiding officer. When both tallies are in, he announces the result. Once again, such votes are unrecorded. The great advantage of an unrecorded vote from the member's viewpoint is that he can vote with little or no accountability to his constituents. Sometimes the leadership will ask a member who is opposed to a bill to "take a walk," that is, just not show up for a teller vote. Most of these methods of maneuvering have been fore-shortened by a newly adopted voting procedure, not yet available when the political broadcast legislation was considered in the House in 1970—the *recorded* teller vote.

4. Voting can be done by *recorded tellers*. This new procedure enables a minimum of one-fifth of a quorum (twenty members) to request a *record* vote in the Committee of the Whole. The record vote indicates the names of members voting for, voting against, or not voting on a measure. Members pick up either a small red (nay) or a green (yea) card, sign it, indicate their state and district number, and then deposit the ballot in one of two boxes watched by the tellers. The adoption of recorded tellers was part of the Legislative Reorganization Act of 1970, and the method was first used in the 92d Congress.

[9] The minimum number of members who must be present in order to conduct business.

Amendments rejected in the Committee of the Whole may not be considered by the House. When the chairman reports the bill back to the Speaker, the approved amendments may be voted on again. Reported amendments are often voted as a bloc. If no member contests the amendments, they need not be ratified in the full House.

The voting in the House can proceed in the same manner as in the Committee of the Whole, with the exception that the roll-call vote replaces a simple or recorded teller vote. A *roll-call vote* is a public record of a Representative's position on a measure. A roll call on a measure may force a Representative to vote differently in the House than he would have voted in the Committee of the Whole. One of the principal benefits of the recorded teller vote is that it makes such maneuvering much less likely.

Each of these stages of a bill—from introduction to subcommittee, full committee, consideration by the Committee on Rules and floor action—will come into sharper perspective through the examination of an actual piece of legislation, the Political Broadcast Act of 1970.

POLITICAL BROADCAST LEGISLATION

Representative Torbert Macdonald (D., Mass.) introduced the NCEC-sponsored campaign broadcast bill in the House of Representatives on the same date the Senate bill was being introduced —September 10, 1969. Although the bill was supported by thirty-four cosponsors, nothing much was to happen on the House side until after Senate passage. Over the following seven weeks, five more bills duplicating the NCEC proposals were introduced, bringing the total number of cosponsors to thirty-nine (thirty-one Democrats and eight Republicans).

Unlike the Senate, the introduction of bills in the House requires neither the member's presence nor formal recognition by the Speaker. The member introducing the measure, or someone delegated by him, may place it directly in the hopper—a box at the Speaker's desk—or hand it directly to the House Parliamentarian or to the Bill Clerk. If the measure is placed in the hopper, it is removed for examination by the Parliamentarian, Lewis Deschler, who designates the committee to which the measure will be referred, under the authority of the Speaker. Most referral of legislation is routine, but occasionally the Speaker may use his discretionary powers to refer a bill to a more favorable forum. After being numbered, it is forwarded to the Government Printing Office to be duplicated; copies are then sent to the

House documents rooms and to the committee to which the measure was referred.

The NCEC bill was designated H.R.13721 and was referred to the Committee on Interstate and Foreign Commerce. The decision to send political broadcasting legislation to this committee was routine; the bill clearly fell within the committee's jurisdiction over the "regulation of interstate and foreign communications."

Representative Harley O. Staggers (D., W. Va.), chairman of the committee, referred H.R.13721 to his Subcommittee on Communications and Power, chaired by Representative Torbert Macdonald, the bill's chief sponsor. For over nine months, almost nothing would happen. Even after Pastore's version replaced the NCEC bill in the Senate, the subcommittee did not move to consider the proposals to amend Section 315 of the Communications Act immediately; the strategy behind the legislation was to get a bill through the Senate first. Should legislation be forthcoming from the Senate, then Macdonald's subcommittee could be used to improve the legislation, if need be, and to work toward successful House passage.

S.3637 was approved in the Senate on April 14, 1970. The act[10] was sent to the House on April 15, where it was routinely taken from the Speaker's Table and referred, first, to the Committee on Interstate and Foreign Commerce and, subsequently, to the Macdonald subcommittee. [*Doc. 5-6*]

DOCUMENT **5-6**: Membership of the Subcommittee on
Communications and Power

Democrats	*Republicans*
Torbert Macdonald (Mass.), Chairman*	James T. Broyhill (N.C.)
Lionel Van Deerlin (Calif.)	James Harvey (Mich.)*
Fred B. Rooney (Pa.)	Donald G. Brotzman (Colo.)
Richard L. Ottinger (N.Y.)*	Clarence J. Brown (Ohio)
Robert O. Tiernan (R.I.)*	

* Cosponsors of H.R.13721

At fifty-three, "Torby" Macdonald was perhaps a bit better educated and a little more disgruntled with the House than the typical third-ranking member of one of the House's middle-prestige workhorse committees. As an undergraduate at Harvard, he had been one of John F. Kennedy's roommates. A graduate of Harvard Law School,

---

[10] Once a bill is approved by either the House or the Senate, it is referred to as an act, even though it still has many stages to go before it becomes the law of the land.

Macdonald had first been elected to the House in 1954. His suburban district north of Boston has returned him to Congress ever since. A close friend of Speaker McCormack, Macdonald also served as Assistant Whip for the New England area and was twelfth-ranking member on the Government Operations Committee.

Now that the subcommittee had before it both the Senate measure and the original bill sponsored by Macdonald and three subcommittee members, chances for House passage were looking up. A meeting was scheduled in early May by the subcommittee's legal staff. Among those present were Susan King of the NCEC, Robert Nordhaus of the House Legislative Counsel's office, F. Martin Kuhn of Representative Macdonald's staff, and several senior specialists from the Federal Communications Commission and the Legislative Reference Service of the Library of Congress. The meeting served as a general planning session because, as one participant argued, "the Senate's legislation was so shoddy." The result was a general critique of S.3637 establishing its deficiencies in coverage as well as making recommendations for improved legislation.

On May 20, at a caucus of House Democrats, other House members began laying the groundwork for possible partisan support for political broadcast legislation. The key members behind this drive for Democratic support were Representative Ed Edmondson (Okla.), cochairman of the House Congressional Campaign Committee, and Representative Morris Udall (Ariz.), a young party activist who later ran unsuccessfully for his party's majority-leadership post. The transformation of political broadcast legislation into a partisan controversy could be traced back to the votes on passage of the Senate bill on April 14. Several votes taken in the Senate had begun to split sharply along party lines. The partisan character of the legislation became even clearer when the Democratic Party leadership came out in support of House passage of the spending limits on radio and television time. Such controls on spending would very likely work to the advantage of Democratic candidates; if they could be passed in time to be operative for the November, 1970, elections, Democratic incumbents would be more likely to hold, and perhaps extend, their three-to-two working majorities in the House and Senate.

In early June, Speaker McCormack called a meeting in his office to see if an agreement could be reached on which strategy to pursue: support for the Senate version or the stronger House bill that was in the process of being drafted by Representative Macdonald and his staff. Senator Pastore and Senator Daniel Inouye of Hawaii, the chairman of the Senate Campaign Committee, argued for immediate House acceptance of S.3637 so that spending limitations would apply in the fall elections. Representative Macdonald, backed by Committee Chairman Harley Staggers, refused to go along. He preferred a stronger bill,

DOCUMENT **5-7**: Title Page of the House Subcommittee Hearings

POLITICAL BROADCASTING—1970

HEARINGS

BEFORE THE

SUBCOMMITTEE ON
COMMUNICATIONS AND POWER

OF THE

COMMITTEE ON
INTERSTATE AND FOREIGN COMMERCE
HOUSE OF REPRESENTATIVES

NINETY-FIRST CONGRESS

SECOND SESSION

ON

H.R. 13721, H.R. 13722, H.R. 13751, H.R. 13752,
H.R. 13935, H.R. 14047, and H.R. 14511

BILLS TO AMEND THE COMMUNICATIONS ACT OF 1934 TO
PROVIDE CANDIDATES FOR CONGRESIONAL OFFICES WITH
CERTAIN OPPORTUNITIES TO PURCHASE BROADCAST TIME
FROM TELEVISION BROADCAST STATIONS

AND

S. 3637

AN ACT TO AMEND SECTION 315 OF THE COMMUNICATIONS ACT
OF 1934 WITH RESPECT TO EQUAL-TIME REQUIREMENTS
FOR CANDIDATES FOR PUBLIC OFFICE, AND FOR OTHER
PURPOSES

JUNE 2, 3, AND 4, 1970

Serial No. 91–57

Printed for the use of the Committee on Interstate and Foreign Commerce

U.S. GOVERNMENT PRINTING OFFICE

46–491　　　　　　　　WASHINGTON : 1970

even if it would not become operative until January, 1971. Majority Leader Albert and Representative Edmondson also urged support for a bill that would be in effect by fall. The meeting broke up with Macdonald promising to expedite his hearings, but still planning to bring out a tougher House version. Senator Pastore left threatening that if the Senate version were not accepted, there would be no legislation at all.

House Hearings

Hearings were scheduled before Macdonald's Subcommittee on Communications and Power for June 2–4, 1970. [*Doc. 5-7*] In his opening remarks, Chairman Macdonald voiced his misgivings about both the original NCEC bill and the Senate-passed legislation:

> What is covered by these bills immediately suggests what is not covered. Primary campaigns are not covered. Perhaps consideration should be given to including them. In certain states and obviously some districts nomination in the primary is tantamount to election to office.[11]

The implication was clear: He and his subcommittee would move to correct this and other deficiencies.

A total of eleven witnesses testified before the subcommittee, and Macdonald, in his questioning of them, left little doubt about his dissatisfaction with the Senate bill. In his exchange with FCC Chairman Dean Burch, Macdonald pushed the need to incorporate primaries in the legislation and also indicated his concern over production costs. [*Doc. 5-8*]

DOCUMENT **5-8**: Macdonald and Burch*

Mr. MACDONALD. . . . but my point is, what is your opinion as to whether this should be extended to include primaries?

Mr. BURCH. As to spending limit?

Mr. MACDONALD. Yes.

Mr. BURCH. I suspect that it should. If it is to be meaningful, certainly it should.

Mr. MACDONALD. And second, a problem I thought was not covered in the Senate bill is something which should be in any campaign budget. Of course, many Congressmen of modest

* *House Hearings*, pp., 21–22.

---

[11] House Committee on Interstate and Foreign Commerce, *Hearings on Political Broadcasting—1970*, 91st Congress, 2d session (Washington, D.C.: Government Printing Office, 1970), p. 1. [Hereinafter cited as *House Hearings.*]

means take their wife and dog and kids and sit down in front of the camera and discuss issues, whereas others to my own personal knowledge, will go to some rather hot shot advertising agency and say, "okay, here is *x* number of dollars. Make me a public figure."

And in some campaigns that I know of the candidate himself never spoke. I think it was strictly production. Don't you think that should be curbed? Don't you think if this is to

be in the public interest, we don't want the voters merely to find out who has the best advertising agency?

I am speaking of the member of the public who would like to find out who has the best brains, and who has the most to say and the most to offer. The way it is going, whoever gets the best advertising agency first has a better spot than the other candidates. Don't you think this should be curbed?

The inclusion of primaries and production costs in the legislation was raised again as Macdonald questioned Russell Hemenway. [*Doc. 5-9*]

DOCUMENT **5-9**: Macdonald and Hemenway*

Mr. MACDONALD. Mr. Hemenway, I know that you support wholeheartedly the Senate version. I also saw you here in the audience and I was wondering if you had any remarks to make concerning the new things in the bill, or concerning proposals to add production costs and extending the bill to cover primaries.

If you have any ideas, I would be happy to hear them. . . .

Mr. HEMENWAY. . . . We think as you do that the primary election in America is not only an integral part, but a very important part of our political process. Sometimes the primary election is even more important than the general election. There are parts of the country still where, if you

are elected in the primary, you are practically guaranteed election in the general.

And in the development of this bill, obviously, it was considered that the bill should be extended to cover primary elections. . . .

Mr. MACDONALD. If I could interrupt, Mr. Hemenway, you say it was considered. Do you mean it was considered in the Senate? Because I did not read anything about that.

Mr. HEMENWAY. It was discussed among the 38 Senate sponsors as to whether the primary should be included. Like many other aspects of the bill, that part was dropped during the exchange in the development of that bill.

* *House Hearings*, pp. 46, 47, 48.

Throughout the hearings, Macdonald sought to maintain a bipartisan approach to the legislation. He summed up his approach:

I think the people here on the committee who are for the bill can count themselves either in the public interest or not in the public interest. As I tried to say yesterday, this bill is not a Republican bill or a Democratic bill; it is a bill in the public interest.[12]

Two of the three major television networks sent executives to testify at the subcommittee hearings. In general, all three networks were in favor of repeal of the equal-time provisions of Section 315 for Presidential and Vice-Presidential races. Two network spokesmen objected to the lowest-unit-cost provision in S.3637; and all three were opposed to a limitation on media spending.

The testimony of Everett H. Erlick, group vice-president and general counsel for the American Broadcasting Company, third largest of the networks, focused upon repeal of Section 315. Both the Senate version and the draft of the bill that Chairman Macdonald was developing would limit the repeal to the general election and then only for contenders for the office of President and Vice-President. But as Macdonald's probings brought out, ABC was not opposed to broadening the repeal to include other political offices—though Macdonald was. [*Doc. 5-10*]

DOCUMENT **5-10**: Macdonald and Erlick on Section 315*

Mr. MACDONALD. You also indicated you were for the bill because it repeals 315 as far as the Presidency goes, and, therefore, while you did not say it, I gather you would like to then progress with the repeal to the Senate and then to the House; am I correct?

Mr. ERLICK. Yes sir. We took the position——

Mr. MACDONALD. And you figure this is the first step?

Mr. ERLICK (continuing). On a trial basis.

Mr. MACDONALD. This is the first step?

Mr. ERLICK. We hope so.

Mr. MACDONALD. Today, Germany; tomorrow, the world.

Mr. ERLICK. That is the chairman's characterization; not mine.

* *House Hearings*, p. 80.

Later in the hearings, the chairman referred to the trial suspension of Section 315(a) that led to the Kennedy-Nixon debates in 1960. But he made it clear that he did not favor broadening the repeal beyond the top two executive offices of the land: "I hope you never get it [an extension to all federal offices] either. I can say flatly, as long as I am

[12] *Ibid.*, p. 49.

here they have one vote against it anyway."[13] It would not take pre-science to realize that as long as Macdonald occupies the highly strategic position of chairman of the subcommittee that holds jurisdiction over Section 315, the repeal of the equal opportunities requirements with respect to broadcasters is not likely to occur. Critical to such a decision is the general reluctance on the part of most Congressmen to turn over to local broadcast stations the power to control who gets access to free television time.

Sometimes Congressmen are at a disadvantage in questioning experts about highly technical subjects such as nuclear physics or even the mechanics of television advertising. But the subcommittee had an expert, Representative Lionel Van Deerlin, who was fully conversant with the television industry as a communications medium. The four-term Congressman from San Diego had served as a radio and television news editor and analyst before becoming a member of the House. Note how skillfully he takes Mr. Erlick of ABC through a series of questions dealing with the rates candidates would pay under the lowest-unit-cost formula. [*Doc. 5-11*]

DOCUMENT **5-11**: Van Deerlin and Erlick on the Lowest Unit Cost*

Mr. VAN DEERLIN. What would be your estimate as to the maximum reductions that would be achieved under the present legislation?

What kind of rates would candidates be getting?

Mr. ERLICK. It would depend entirely upon the time period involved and upon the price spread in that particular time period, and it would vary greatly. I could not give you any general answer.

Mr. VAN DEERLIN. Generally, we would be talking about prime time, I think.

Mr. ERLICK. Yes.

Mr. VAN DEERLIN. What would be a typical rate-card reduction for, say, a 360-spot campaign by Campbell Soup as compared to what the candidate would get if he wanted a 12-spot purchase?

Mr. ERLICK. It is difficult to say. I would have to refer to one of our rate cards to say. Perhaps, something on the order of 25 or 30 percent. Probably less than ABC is willing, voluntarily, to grant, incidentally.

* *House Hearings*, p. 82.

In short, were the lowest-unit-cost formula to apply, a candidate using twelve prime-time spots would benefit from the same low rate as a major advertiser such as Campbell Soup, for a net saving to the candidate of 25–30 per cent.

[13] *Ibid.*, p. 80.

Van Deerlin, the ranking Democrat on the subcommittee, also tried to obtain an estimate on whether the $20,000 over-all limit or seven cents per vote—whichever was greater—was enough to cover the television broadcast costs of most House races. Erlick was not anxious to commit himself, but he went on to point up the great variations in television costs, from New York City at one extreme to the hinterlands at the other. [*Doc. 5-12*]

DOCUMENT **5-12**: Van Deerlin and Erlick on the Spending Limit*

Mr. VAN DEERLIN. The question of whether 7 cents per vote at the last previous election is adequate, is one you have asked yourself without answering. Of course, with this 25 or 30 percent additional break that would be achieved through the reduction in rates, do you not think that this $20,000 outside or 7 cents a vote, whichever is greater, would more than blanket the vast majority of present campaigns for public office?

Mr. ERLICK. Congressman, we are just not in a position to say. We have not seen any studies of maximums and minimums and with the amount of advertising it would buy in various localities from, say, Wyoming and including New York City, we really are not in a position to say. We have no opinion on it. We agree in principle with limitations. We think it should be up to Congress to decide precisely what those limitations will be.

Mr. VAN DEERLIN. I think the gist of your recommendation is that we should take a little longer to decide.

Mr. ERLICK. Yes, sir.

* *House Hearings,* p. 83.

Paul B. Comstock, vice-president and general counsel of the National Association of Broadcasters, was the last witness to testify before the subcommittee. Comstock was speaking for a majority of the radio and television stations who are members of the Association. He urged repeal of the equal-opportunities requirement of Section 315 for Presidential and Vice-Presidential races. But he was opposed to the lowest-unit-cost provision and to the radio and television spending limitation because he felt that these features of S.3637 discriminated against the electronic media. Macdonald was quick to reply. [*Doc. 5-13*]

Still, this problem of limited applicability—that the bill dealt only with television costs and not with other media—was to be raised against the bill when it reached the floor. Later it was to become a central element in President Nixon's veto message.

Once the hearings were concluded, the subcommittee began its closed-door executive sessions on June 9, 1970. Comments made throughout the hearings by Democrats and Republicans alike gave

DOCUMENT 5-13: Macdonald on Media*

Mr. MACDONALD. When you say that, how can you say all of the media should be treated alike?

We have no control over billboards.

We have no control over newspapers.

We have no control over magazines.

So, how can you say we should treat them as we do you, who we do have control over?

It seems to me rather an absurd statement. . . .

The whole point of this—I am going back and forth like a ping-pong ball, and you are not giving me answers that impress me. I am really curious why you come in here and represent the broadcasters and indicate you feel you are being discriminated against when you admit yourself that the Congress has, according to your words—that Congress should not have any further control over the other branches of the media. The two things are not comparable.

* *House Hearings*, pp. 102, 103.

---

indications that substantial changes would be made in S.3637. Indeed, more than three weeks later, a clean bill—one substantially revised, reprinted, and given a new number—was reported out.

During these executive sessions, open only to members and staff, the bill was read, section by section. This activity—called marking-up a bill—is at the heart of the legislative process. Typically, the legislative clerk will read the bill until some member offers an amendment. Debate will go on, back and forth, until conflicts are resolved, either through consensus, or, if necessary, by an actual vote. Sometimes whole paragraphs will be disposed of without a pause. On other occasions, the subcommittee may debate the exact language of a single phrase for an entire morning or more. Majority and minority staff members may be asked to meet together to work out a suitable compromise. When amendments are extensive, as they were with S.3637, the introduction of a clean bill for consideration by the full committee is almost routine. Among other reasons, such a procedure also avoids the time-consuming task of considering each change, one at a time, on the House floor. Occasionally, however, strategic considerations may dictate an alternative procedure—bringing the Senate bill to the floor and adopting the House proposals, one by one.

Negotiations in Executive Session

In executive session, acting very much in accord with his earlier statements, Macdonald urged that S.3637 be broadened to cover primary elections and all statewide races. Representative James T. Broyhill of North Carolina, the ranking Republican, was at first opposed to the inclusion of statewide offices. A compromise was reached so that gubernatorial races (and, later, races for Lieutenant Governor) would be included in any legislation reported by the subcommittee. In addition, Representative Van Deerlin developed the idea of a triggering device by which lesser state offices would come within the framework of the federal legislation when a state, by legislative enactment, established spending limits for designated state offices, if these limits did not exceed the cost-per-vote limitations imposed on Congressional and gubernatorial races.

With the cooperation of the subcommittee staff, headed by Robert F. Guthrie, and the House Legislative Counsel's staff, a clean bill was drafted incorporating provisions of S.3637 and the changes recommended in the executive session. On July 7, the subcommittee ordered its final product reported for consideration by the full committee, and, on July 13, 1970, the clean bill was introduced in the House by Representative Macdonald and was cosponsored by every member of the subcommittee. The bill was designated H.R.18434 and was, of course, routinely referred back to the Committee on Interstate and Foreign Commerce.

Why was the subcommittee unanimous in support of the clean bill? It is especially surprising because H.R.18434 incorporated stronger, more extensive, and thereby more controversial provisions than the Senate version. The answer is complicated, but a number of factors combined to produce the unanimity. First and most important was the bipartisan relationship skillfully cultivated by Chairman Macdonald and ably supported by the ranking minority member, James Broyhill. These men had served together on the Commerce Committee for several terms; each respected the other's integrity and competence, and both treated the other members of the subcommittee with fairness. Throughout the mark-up sessions, Macdonald had sought ways to placate the objections of other subcommittee members. In his own words, "Guys would come up with a good thought, we'd kick it around, and if it was a good idea, I'd take it."

In line with this, Macdonald, measuring the mood of the subcommittee and the House, believed he would have a better chance for successful passage if the potential partisan differences within the legislation were muted. To this end, and following Van Deerlin's urgings, he opted for a January 1, 1971, effective date. In short, though a stronger bill, it was in some ways a more neutral one because it would not apply to the upcoming elections.

A final reason for unanimity at the subcommittee level has to do with the nature of most House Congressional campaigns. They rarely involve large-scale media use; fewer than one-sixth of House candidates running for office in 1970 spent more than $10,000 on television campaigning. Furthermore, following a general practice of comity between the two Houses, the subcommittee members were prone not to tamper with the main provisions of S.3637 that affected Senate campaigns, which, in contrast to most House races, rely heavily on television.

On July 16, the clean bill, which had been referred back to the Committee on Interstate and Foreign Commerce after it had been introduced in the House, was brought before the full committee, which, for the first and only time, met and considered it. The bill was approved with only one dissenting vote—that of a midwestern Republican who complained he "just didn't like the feel of it." A key staff man later commented, "It surprised me that it [the bill] was considered and ordered reported in the same day." Generally, a bill of such potential controversy might undergo days of further discussion and amendments before being reported out. [*Doc. 5-14*] H.R.18434 was placed on the Union Calendar. [*Doc. 5-15*]

After the Commerce Committee acted, Chairman Staggers followed the usual procedure when reporting out important measures—he sent a letter to the chairman of the Committee on Rules requesting a hearing and a special rule for floor consideration. Thus far, all was routine. But shortly after Staggers requested this hearing, at a closed-door meeting of the Democratic Whips on July 23, the House leadership abandoned Macdonald's bipartisan approach and decided to push for quick enactment of political broadcast legislation so that it would be effective in the 1970 elections. Majority Leader Carl Albert and party Whip Hale Boggs reached agreement with thirteen of the party's nineteen Assistant Whips that H.R.18434 should reach the floor as soon as possible. On August 14, the House was set to recess for a three-week holiday. Time was critical. As soon as the House measure was on the floor, the new plan called for the substitution and adoption of the Senate version. This would make a conference committee unnecessary, which meant the act could then go directly to the President for his consideration. The Senate version that was to be substituted for Macdonald's was to be effective thirty days following enactment (as contrasted with the House bill, which would not have become effective until January 1, 1971); it would apply to the November elections. The plan also called for a special party caucus to be held on August 5 so that the leadership could mobilize support for its strategy.

DOCUMENT **5-14**: Excerpts from the Report of the Committee on Interstate and Foreign Commerce

---

91st Congress } HOUSE OF REPRESENTATIVES { Report
2d Session } { No. 91–1347

POLITICAL BROADCASTING

July 29, 1970.—Committed to the Committee of the Whole House on the State
of the Union and ordered to be printed

Mr. STAGGERS, from the Committee on Interstate and Foreign
Commerce, submitted the following

REPORT

[To accompany H.R. 18434]

The Committee on Interstate and Foreign Commerce, to whom
was referred the bill (H.R. 18434) to revise the provisions of the
Communications Act of 1934 which relate to political broadcasting,
having considered the same, report favorably thereon without amendment and recommend that the bill do pass.

PURPOSE OF THE LEGISLATION

The legislation (H.R. 18434) has a four-fold purpose.
First, to repeal the equal opportunities provisions of the Communications Act of 1934 (hereafter "the Act") with respect to candidates
for the office of President and Vice President of the United States,
thus permitting the broadcast networks to donate free broadcast time
for the presentation of the significant candidates for President and
Vice President.
Second, to reduce the rate which broadcast stations may charge
legally qualified candidates for public office for the use of broadcast
time.
Third, to establish reasonable limits on the amounts which may be
spent for broadcast time by candidates for President and Vice President for general elections and by other candidates for major elective
office (United States Senator, United States Representative, Governor,
and Lieutenant Governor) for primary and general elections.
Fourth, to permit the several States, by law, to place candidates
for State and local office under the provisions of the legislation.
The legislation will take effect on January 1, 1971. . . .

48–006

DOCUMENT **5-15**: First Page of H.R.18434

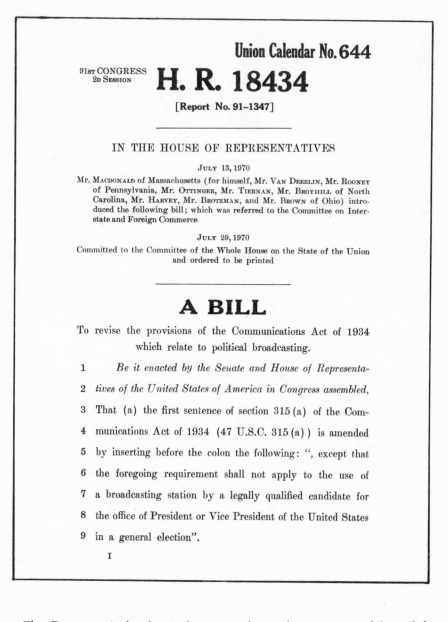

Union Calendar No. 644

91st CONGRESS
2D SESSION

H. R. 18434

[Report No. 91–1347]

IN THE HOUSE OF REPRESENTATIVES

JULY 13, 1970

Mr. MACDONALD of Massachusetts (for himself, Mr. VAN DEERLIN, Mr. ROONEY of Pennsylvania, Mr. OTTINGER, Mr. TIERNAN, Mr. BROYHILL of North Carolina, Mr. HARVEY, Mr. BROTZMAN, and Mr. BROWN of Ohio) introduced the following bill; which was referred to the Committee on Interstate and Foreign Commerce

JULY 29, 1970

Committed to the Committee of the Whole House on the State of the Union and ordered to be printed

A BILL

To revise the provisions of the Communications Act of 1934 which relate to political broadcasting.

1   *Be it enacted by the Senate and House of Representa-*

2   *tives of the United States of America in Congress assembled,*

3   That (a) the first sentence of section 315 (a) of the Com-

4   munications Act of 1934 (47 U.S.C. 315 (a)) is amended

5   by inserting before the colon the following: ", except that

6   the foregoing requirement shall not apply to the use of

7   a broadcasting station by a legally qualified candidate for

8   the office of President or Vice President of the United States

9   in a general election".

I

The Democratic leaders' plan to seek quick enactment faltered for two reasons: The chairman of the party caucus, Dan Rostenkowski of Illinois, refused to call a caucus for August 5, because he would of necessity be absent that week. More important, Torbert Macdonald and other members were prepared to oppose with all the force they could marshal the dumping of the subcommittee's stronger bill. Inability to implement the leadership strategy meant that passage of the legislation before the three-week recess could not be assured. But, even if action could be taken, the House did not appear likely to substitute the Senate version for Macdonald's. Hence, two different versions would necessitate a conference between the House and Senate. In the process of ironing out the differences, more time would be lost.

Request for a Rule

With the failure of the new strategy, much of the drive for rapid enactment collapsed. This meant a return to more routine procedures. Ordinarily, the committee or subcommittee chairman would make the presentation before the Rules Committee. But, on the day of the hearing, both Staggers and Macdonald were out of town. The task fell to the ranking majority subcommittee member, Representative Van Deerlin. He was selected, as he later recalled, "by a process of elimination."

Ten of the fifteen Rules Committee members were present when the meeting was called to order at 10:30 on the morning of August 4. Representative Van Deerlin made his presentation a short time later. His request for an open rule[14] and two hours of debate followed his remarks, which focused on the shortcomings of the Senate measure and the improvements to be found in H.R.18434. The effect of the House bill on House races was noted by Van Deerlin, who also illuminated the need for reform by recalling recent primary campaigns, particularly those in New York and Tennessee, involving considerable media use. Representative James T. Broyhill buttressed Van Deerlin's request for a rule by stressing the bipartisan support behind the House bill. The Rules Committee meeting ended when the absence of a quorum was noted. But the hearing on H.R.18434 had concluded, and the bill was one step closer to consideration by the full House. Six days later, on August 10, the Committee on Rules met again, this time in executive session, to report out H.R.18434.

The scheduling of legislation for consideration by the House is the special concern of the Majority Leader. On August 6, Majority Leader Albert listed the items on the legislative program for the week of August 10. Among the bills to be considered was H.R.18434, subject to a rule being granted from the Rules Committee.

On August 10, Representative Richard Bolling (D., Mo.) of the Committee on Rules introduced H.Res.1177, the special rule under which

---

[14] A rule permitting amendments is known as an open rule. A rule preventing amendments is known as a closed, or "gag," rule.

the political broadcast bill would be considered by the full House. [*Doc. 5-16*] The resolution was accompanied by the committee report urging the adoption of the rule.

DOCUMENT **5-16**: H.Res.1177

House Calendar No. **254**

91st CONGRESS
2D SESSION

H. RES. 1177

[Report No. 91–1388]

IN THE HOUSE OF REPRESENTATIVES

AUGUST 10, 1970

Mr. BOLLING, from the Committee on Rules, reported the following resolution; which was referred to the House Calendar and ordered to be printed

---

RESOLUTION

1   *Resolved,* That upon the adoption of this resolution it

2   shall be in order to move that the House resolve itself into

3   the Committee of the Whole House on the State of the

4   Union for the consideration of the bill (H.R. 18434) to

5   revise the provisions of the Communications Act of 1934

6   which relate to political broadcasting. After general debate,

7   which shall be confined to the bill and shall continue not to

8   exceed two hours, to be equally divided and controlled by

9   the chairman and ranking minority member of the Com-

10   mittee on Interstate and Foreign Commerce, the bill shall

11   be read for amendment under the five-minute rule. At the

12   conclusion of the consideration of the bill for amendment,

V

The rule, if adopted by the House, would do the following:

1. It would make it in order to move to resolve the House into the Committee of the Whole for consideration of the bill and any amendments that might be made.

Doc. 5-16 *(cont.)*

2

1 the Committee shall rise and report the bill to the House

2 with such amendments as may have been adopted, and the

3 previous question shall be considered as ordered on the bill

4 and amendments thereto to final passage without intervening

5 motion except one motion to recommit. After the passage of

6 H.R. 18434, the Committee on Interstate and Foreign Com-

7 merce shall be discharged from the further consideration of

8 the bill S. 3637, and it shall then be in order in the House to

9 move to strike out all after the enacting clause of the said

10 Senate bill and insert in lieu thereof the provisions contained

11 in H.R. 18434 as passed by the House.

2. It would provide for two hours of debate to be divided equally between the majority and the minority.

3. It would provide time for amendments according to the five-minute rule, which means that a member proposing an amendment would have five minutes to speak for the amendment he has offered.

4. It would permit one motion to recommit the bill back to committee.

5. It would provide that if the bill passed the House, the Committee on Interstate and Foreign Commerce would be discharged from consideration of S.3637 (still technically in the committee). Then a motion would be in order to strike out everything after the enacting clause[15] of S.3637 and replace the Senate provisions with the provisions of the House bill (H.R.18434).

None of the rule's provisions was extraordinary, but number 5 may be confusing. The purpose of this provision is to enable the House to substitute the language of its amended version under the title of the Senate measure. This would require either that the difference between the two bills (S.3637 as it passed the Senate and S.3637 as it passed the House) be resolved in a conference between the House and the Senate, or that the Senate accept the House version in total. Without the substitution of number and title, the House bill (H.R.18434) would be sent to the Senate, where it would follow the same course as a newly introduced measure; that, clearly, would increase the possibility of further alteration or even actual defeat.

Floor Action

H.Res.1177 was taken up by the House on August 11, when Representative Richard Bolling of the Committee on Rules rose and secured recognition from the Speaker. Under the rules, Bolling was granted one hour's time, half of which was allotted by custom to a minority member of the committee, in this case Representative David T. Martin (R., Neb.). Bolling confined his remarks to the rule. Martin's comments were addressed more to a description of the bill itself. But, much less than an hour passed before the resolution was agreed to by a voice vote. It was then in order to consider H.R.18434 on the floor.

Shortly thereafter, Representative Torbert Macdonald began the debate on H.R.18434. [*Doc. 5-17*]

The House was now sitting as the Committee of the Whole, where the rules concerning quorums and voting set less rigorous requirements. The Sergeant-at-Arms removed the mace from its stand at the

[15] This clause is required on all legislation: "Be it enacted by the Senate and House of Representatives of the United States of America in Congress assembled . . . "

DOCUMENT **5-17**: Introduction on the Floor

All extracts of the House floor debate are taken from the Congressional Record *(daily edition) of August 11, 1970.*

POLITICAL BROADCASTING

Mr. MACDONALD of Massachusetts. Mr. Speaker, I move that the House resolve itself into the Committee of the Whole House on the State of the Union for the consideration of the bill (H.R.18434) to revise the provisions of the Communications Act of 1934 which relate to political broadcasting.

The motion was agreed to.

IN THE COMMITTEE OF THE WHOLE

Accordingly the House resolved itself into the Committee of the Whole House on the State of the Union for the consideration of the bill H.R. 18434, with Mr. STRATTON in the chair.

Speaker's rostrum. Speaker McCormack retired from the dais after appointing Representative Samuel S. Stratton (D., N.Y.) to preside over the Committee of the Whole.

Chairman Stratton noted that the two hours of debate[16] would be controlled, one hour apiece, by Representative Torbert Macdonald for the Democrats and Representative William L. Springer[17] for the Republicans. Macdonald spoke first, detailing the need for legislation to control rising campaign spending, pointing out the inadequacies of the Senate's legislation and elaborating upon the provisions of H.R.18434. The prudential concerns of House members were not overlooked in Macdonald's remarks. [*Doc. 5-18*]

Representative Springer's comments were along similar lines to Macdonald's, but the ranking Republican on Commerce was careful to place special emphasis on the effective date provision in the House version. [*Doc. 5-19*]

Van Deerlin then rose to support the bill. His comments also touched upon the effective date provision and the attempt by some Democrats to seek an effective date before the November elections. [*Doc. 5-20*]

Further comments by members of the subcommittee and other Representatives centered on the need for legislation and praise for the Interstate and Foreign Commerce Committee as well as its Communications and Power Subcommittee. No further requests for time were

---

[16] Debate in the House, as in the Senate, is more in the order of discussion or dialogue. The Rules of the House generally prevent the heated invective typical of such legislative bodies as Britain's House of Commons.

[17] Springer was the ranking Republican on the Interstate and Foreign Commerce Committee.

DOCUMENT **5-18**: Macdonald's Defense of Bill

Mr. MACDONALD. Before closing, Mr. Chairman, I would like to review for the Members of the House how this legislation would work in their case.

First, I think that in almost every instance they will be limited to $10,000 for broadcast time for a primary election and $20,000 for a general election, as will their opponents. Let me emphasize that this is only for broadcast time. It does not cover production costs, promotional ads in newspapers, or any other expenditures.

But it does cover all purchases of broadcast time by the candidate or on his behalf. The old committee ploy will not work here.

When the candidate wishes to purchase broadcast time for his campaign, he or someone specifically authorized by him in writing must certify that the payment of the charges for that time will not cause him to exceed his limit under the legislation. No committee or other group may purchase time on behalf of the candidate without the station receiving such a certification from the candidate or his agent. If the candidate or his agent makes a false certification he, of course, would be subject to criminal penalties.

Mr. Chairman, today campaign costs and expenditures have reached crisis proportions. If our American political processes are not to be dominated by special moneyed interests there must be effective regulation and reduction of campaign expenditures. The bill before the House is a major step in that direction. I earnestly hope that it will be passed by the House.

DOCUMENT **5-19**: Springer's Defense of the Bill

Mr. SPRINGER. This bill is hardly a cure-all for the many problems involving campaign practices and campaign spending. It is, however, the most practical piece of legislation thus far proposed to make progress in the right direction. For one thing, the electronic media is gaining more and more attention from candidates as the best means to reach the voter. No doubt it is. If, therefore, we can successfully curb the amounts which can thus be spent, it is bound to put some restraints on excessive overall campaign spending.

One issue which will become of importance once this bill is passed regards the effective date. The Senate bill would put the new limitations in effect at once. The House bill delays implementation until next year. I think we should be clear here and now that a serious attempt to force immediate effect will probably result in no legislation. It is entirely too late in the year and too near election time for the administrative details to be worked out before campaigns are underway. No doubt much of the available air time has already been contracted for. Licensees need to look forward to election time with full knowledge of these new limitations and requirements. The Federal Com-

Doc. 5-19 (*cont.*)

munications Commission must also make preparations to carry out its new responsibilities and this cannot be done in a few weeks. The provisions of the House bill in this regard make sense and should be upheld in conference between the two bodies.

With these observations and recommendations, I endorse the proposed legislation and recommend its passage.

DOCUMENT 5-20: Van Deerlin's Defense of the Bill

Mr. VAN DEERLIN. Mr. Chairman, this legislation is needed, and it is timely. It comes at a juncture in our history when I perceive, and I think most Members do, that the American public is becoming quite cynical about this matter of campaign spending.

The question has been raised whether we as a nation are not pricing ourselves out of democracy. This legislation addresses itself to the most sensitive area of runaway campaign spending.

It came out of the subcommittee unanimously. Indeed, with one dissenting vote, it came out of the full Committee on Interstate and Foreign Commerce as a truly bipartisan measure. This is essentially a reform bill. Reform legislation can and should be bipartisan.

Some persons in the White House have not jumped with joy at the prospect of this legislation. It portends a really basic change in the matter of equal time provisions, leading to a fuller public discussion of campaign issues in the very next and in future presidential campaigns.

By the same token, as has been noted in the debate thus far, there are those on our side of the aisle who feel that they represent the poor man's party, who would have hoped that the legislation could take effect in time to protect Democrats for this year's campaign.

But the bill which we have come up with in our committee is much better in all respects than the measure which the other body sent to us some months ago. The delayed effective date seems a small price to pay for getting good, permanent, ongoing legislation that will truly reform the American elective process.

---

made, and Stratton was about to proceed further under the special rule when Representative J. J. "Jake" Pickle (D., Tex.) made a point of order that a quorum was not present. [*Doc. 5-21*] His motion was a routine device to alert absent House members that the bill was about to enter the critical amendment phase of floor consideration.

The full reading of the bill was dispensed with by unanimous consent, and amendments under the five-minute rule were then in order. A total of six amendments were offered, but in each case Macdonald was opposed to any changes. All six amendments were defeated. Representative Richard Ottinger (D., N.Y.), who had spent over $1 million to win the Democratic senatorial *primary* nomination in New York, offered two amendments. One would have provided free television time for all candidates; the other would have eliminated the primary election spending limits from the House bill. These changes were opposed by Macdonald and other Representatives, partly for substantive reasons and partly because they wished to discourage a flood of additional amendments. Both amendments were easily defeated by voice votes.

Another amendment was offered by Representative Andrew Jacobs,

DOCUMENT 5-21: Pickle and the Quorum Call

The CHAIRMAN. There being no further requests for time, the Clerk will read.

Mr. PICKLE. Mr. Chairman, I make the point of order that a quorum is not present.

The CHAIRMAN. The Chair will count. [After counting.] Seventy-five Members are present, not a quorum.

The Clerk will call the roll.

The Clerk called the roll, and the following Members failed to answer to their names:

[Roll No. 270]

Alexander	Cramer	McCarthy	Rogers, Colo.
Anderson, Tenn.	Cunningham	McClory	Rooney, N.Y.
Arends	Daddario	McClure	Rostenkowski
Ashley	Dawson	McCulloch	Roudebush
Aspinall	Diggs	McKneally	Ryan
Baring	Edwards, La.	Mailliard	Scherle
Berry	Evins, Tenn.	Meskill	Scheuer
Bray	Fallon	Moorhead	Schwengel
Brock	Flynt	Nedzi	Staggers
Buchanan	Gilbert	O'Hara	Sullivan
Burleson, Tex.	Hébert	O'Neal, Ga.	Symington
Caffery	Hull	Passman	Teague, Tex.
Celler	Jonas	Pollock	Tunney
Clay	Jones, Ala.	Powell	Weicker
Conyers	Keith	Price, Tex.	Whitten
Corman	King	Rarick	Wright
Cowger	Long, La.	Reifel	

Accordingly the Committee rose; and the Speaker having resumed the chair, Mr. STRATTON, Chairman of the Committee of the Whole House on the State of the Union, reported that the Committee having had under consideration the bill H.R.18434, and finding itself without a quorum, he had directed the roll to be called, when 362 Members responded to their names, a quorum, and he submitted herewith the names of the absentees to be spread upon the Journal.

The Committee resumed its sitting.

Jr. (D., Ind.), to extend the spending limitations to all media—print as well as electronic. According to the Rules, amendments in the House must be relevant, or germane, to the bill under consideration. Macdonald objected to the Jacobs amendment on this parliamentary ground. The presiding officer concurred. [*Doc. 5-22*]

DOCUMENT **5-22**: Non-Germane Inquiry

The CHAIRMAN (Mr. STRATTON). The Chair is ready to rule.

The gentleman from Massachusetts has made a point of order against the amendment offered by the gentleman from Indiana on the grounds that it is not germane. The gentleman from Indiana has shown the Chair the amendment, and the Chair has had an opportunity to study it.

The bill pertains solely to radio and television.

The amendment offered by the gentleman from Indiana, however, introduces another subject: Expenditures for newspaper and periodical advertising.

The effect of the amendment is to significantly broaden the scope of the bill. While both the bill, in part, and the amendment have a common purpose—limiting campaign expenditures

—this fact alone does not insure the germaneness of the amendment. The Chair has examined a ruling made by Chairman Cannon, of Missouri, in the 77th Congress which stands for the following proposition:

The fact that an amendment and the provision in the bill to which the amendment is offered have a common purpose and are directed toward the same objective is not conclusive, and an amendment dealing with a subject to which there is no reference in the text to which offered is not germane to the bill (Cong. Rec. pp. 875–78, Feb. 10, 1941).

Since there is no mention in the pending bill of an expenditure control on any campaign costs except radio and television, the Chair finds that the amendment is not germane and sustains the point of order.

Additional amendments were defeated, with Macdonald rising each time to voice opposition to them. In all, no amendment warranted sufficient support to merit other than a voice vote. Finally, the presiding chairman announced that there were no further amendments pending. The following document details the routine steps by which the Committee of the Whole returns to the House and the Speaker resumes the chair. [*Doc. 5-23*] It would be at this point that a *recommittal motion*, either to send the bill back to committee or to attempt a major modification in the measure, would have been in order. Opposition to the bill, however, had not sufficiently crystallized around any one feature; hence, no recommittal motion was forthcoming. Instead, the Speaker merely called for the question on the passage of the bill— that is, for the vote. [*Doc. 5-24*]

DOCUMENT 5-23: The Committee of the Whole Rises

As noted earlier, when the committee rises, the Speaker resumes the chair and the former presiding officer, in this case, Mr. Stratton, reports what has occurred in the Committee of the Whole. The motion for the previous question has the effect of cutting off all debate and bringing the House to an immediate vote on the bill before it. An order for engrossment directs the enrolling clerk to receive all of the official papers, including amendments offered on the floor, and prepare a final copy of the bill on blue paper to be sent to the other body. It will be accompanied by a certificate signed by the Clerk of the House that the bill has passed the House. Third reading is by title only, following a rules change in 1965 abolishing the complete re-reading—theretofore usually used as a dilatory tactic by opponents.

The CHAIRMAN. There being no further amendments, under the rule, the Committee rises.

Accordingly the Committee rose; and the Speaker having resumed the chair (Mr. STRATTON), Chairman of the Committee of the Whole House on the State of the Union, reported that that committee having had under consideration the bill (H.R. 18434) to revise the provisions of the Communications Act of 1934 which relate to political broadcasting, pursuant to House Resolution 1177, he reported the bill back to the House.

The SPEAKER. Under the rule, the previous question is ordered.

The question is on the engrossment and third reading of the bill.

The bill was ordered to be engrossed and read a third time and was read the third time.

DOCUMENT 5-24: Final Passage

The SPEAKER. The question is on the passage of the bill.

Mr. MACDONALD of Massachusetts. Mr. Speaker, on that I demand the yeas and nays.

The yeas and nays were refused.

The SPEAKER. The question is on the passage of the bill.

The question was taken; and the Speaker announced that the ayes appeared to have it.

Mr. MACDONALD of Massachusetts. Mr. Speaker, I object to the vote on the ground that a quorum is not present and make the point of order that a quorum is not present.

The SPEAKER. Evidently a quorum is not present. The Doorkeeper will close the doors, the Sergeant at Arms will notify absent Members, and the Clerk will call the roll.

As floor manager, Macdonald's first response to the Speaker's call for the passage of the bill was to "demand the yeas and nays." If he could have obtained the assent of one-fifth of the members present, this would have resulted in a formal roll call. However, by late afternoon, and in late August just prior to a recess, members are prone to skip roll calls; not enough members stood up to support Macdonald's request. After the Speaker called for a voice vote and announced that "the ayes appear to have it," Macdonald had one further recourse under the House rules, and he took advantage of it. He made a point of order that a quorum—218 members—was not present.

Why was the floor manager so insistent upon a record vote? The answer is that Macdonald hoped to demonstrate strong bipartisan House support for his bill, so that if and when a conference committee met, he would be in the best possible bargaining position.

H.R.18434 passed by a vote of 272 to 97. An analysis of the roll-call vote revealed the following division:

Party	Yeas	Nays	Total
Democratic	174	31	205
Republican	99	67	166
Total	273	98	371

Democrats overwhelmingly supported the legislation; still, Republicans backed it by a ratio of three to two. In addition, there were fifty-six pairs, that is, fifty-six Representatives absent from the vote entered into twenty-eight recorded agreements such that a member for and a member against the proposal could indicate their respective positions. Pairs are not counted in the actual calculation of the vote on the bill.

Following passage of the bill, Macdonald moved to strike out all the language of S.3637 following the enacting clause and replace it with

DOCUMENT 5-25: Appointment of Conferees*

APPOINTMENT OF CONFEREES ON S.3637

Mr. MACDONALD of Massachusetts. Mr. Speaker, I ask unanimous consent that the House insist on its amendment to the bill S.3637 and request a conference with the Senate.

The SPEAKER. Is there objection to the request of the gentleman from Massachusetts?

The Chair hears none, and appoints the following conferees: Messrs. STAGGERS, MACDONALD of Massachusetts, VAN DEERLIN, SPRINGER, and BROYHILL of North Carolina.

* Three Democrats and two Republicans were appointed to represent the House. Notice the importance of a Representative's position in the selection of conferees. For the Democrats, the chairman of the full committee and the chairman and ranking majority member of the subcommittee were chosen; Republicans appointed their ranking minority members on the full and subcommittee.

the text of H.R.18434 as passed. The motion was agreed to by a voice vote; the effect was to change the designation of H.R.18434 to S.3637. Of course, the Senate version of S.3637 was substantially different from the new House version. These differences had to be reconciled before the legislation could be sent to the President for his approval or disapproval. Unless the Senate agreed to accept the House version, a conference with members from each body would have to meet to resolve the differences. [*Doc. 5-25*]

Of all the differences between the two versions of S.3637 to be resolved in the conference, none would be more fraught with politics and personal differences than the effective-date provision.

FURTHER READING

What do Congressmen do? Perhaps the best description of the day-to-day activities of a Representative is captured by the late Clem Miller in *Member of the House: Letters of a Congressman* (New York: Charles Scribner's Sons, 1962). How members carry out their tasks is detailed by Donald G. Tacheron and Morris K. Udall in their comprehensive book *The Job of a Congressman*, 2d ed. (Indianapolis: Bobbs-Merrill, 1970).

How a Representative perceives his job is explored by Roger Davidson in *The Role of a Congressman* (New York: Pegasus, 1969). Lewis Anthony Dexter's "The Representative and His District," *Human Organization* XVI (Spring, 1957): 2–13, is a classic discussion of Congressmen and their relationships with constituents. This article and others by Dexter are collected in *The Sociology and Politics of Congress* (Chicago: Rand McNally, 1969).

A highly readable history of the House is offered in Neil MacNeil's *Forge of Democracy: The House of Representatives* (New York: David McKay, 1963).

Randall B. Ripley analyzes House leadership in *Party Leaders in the House of Representatives* (Washington, D.C.: The Brookings Institution, 1967). James A. Robinson's *The House Rules Committee* (Indianapolis: Bobbs-Merrill, 1963) is a useful study of one of the most important committees in Congress.

Richard F. Fenno's *The Power of the Purse: Appropriations Politics in Congress* (Boston: Little, Brown, 1966) has stimulated much committee-centered research on Congress. Another outstanding analysis is John F. Manley's *The Politics of Finance: The House Ways and Means Committee* (Boston: Little, Brown, 1970).

The most comprehensive compilation of articles focusing on the workings of the House is Robert L. Peabody and Nelson W. Polsby's *New Perspectives on the House of Representatives*, 2d ed. (Chicago: Rand McNally, 1969).

From Conference Committee to Enactment

THE PROCESS OF COMPROMISE

A bill must pass the House and the Senate in identical form before the measure can be sent to the President for his approval or disapproval. If legislation passes the House and the Senate in differing forms and neither body will accept the changes offered by the other, then a conference committee composed of members of both chambers must meet to work out the differences in the legislation. Complete agreement must be reached if a bill is to become law.

Who selects the conferees? By long tradition, codified since 1890 by Rule X, Clause 2, of the House Rules, the Speaker appoints the House members. Senate conferees are appointed by the Vice-President or the President Pro Tempore. Only on rare occasions will the appointing officers break with the customary practice of accepting the names suggested by the chairman of the committee in charge of the bill. The conferees (or managers, as they are called) usually include the committee and subcommittee chairmen plus the ranking minority member from both the House and Senate. Sometimes the selection is altered or enlarged to include other ranking majority and minority members or perhaps even the entire subcommittee. Several practices are always followed: Appointments are always bipartisan; the majority party in each House will always be represented by a majority of the conferees. It is in conference committees that the seniority system has its most sustained and pervasive impact. The size of a chamber's delegation can vary widely—as few as three, as many as fifteen or more. Size in itself is not a significant factor since decisions made by House and Senate conferees must have the approval of a majority *within* each delegation. However, on closely fought, important legislation such as the Voting Rights Act of 1965, a chairman may request the Speaker to increase the number of conferees in order to insure a favorable majority—in that case, to include more northern than southern Democrats.

Most conferences used to be held on the Senate side, a practice House members sometimes resented. When the east front of the Capitol was extended in 1963, a special conference room was created, EF-100, which exactly straddles the House and Senate sides of the Capitol. All conference meetings are held in executive (closed-door, secret) sessions.

House conferees do not allow proxy voting (the practice of indicating to the chairman or another member how you wish to vote and allowing him to cast your vote if you are not present), but the Senate condones more flexibility.

The two delegations operate under certain broad constraints. They are free to compromise on the differences between the House and Senate versions; they may trade off some House provisions for some Senate provisions and vice versa. What they cannot do, at least in theory, is advance beyond the differences between the two chambers. New legislation cannot be added, and identical provisions already approved by both chambers cannot be altered. Occasionally, conferees may be instructed to insist on their own provisions or to refuse to accept provisions passed by the other chamber. If agreement by a majority of each delegation cannot be reached, then the delegations can report to their respective chambers for further instructions. In the event that a conference committee cannot resolve its disagreements, the legislation in conference is dead.

Conference committees operate with great flexibility. As former Senator Albert Gore of Tennessee, an adept conferee in his own right, describes the process:

> It is here, in secret meetings often not even announced until the last minute, that a few men can sit down and undo in one hour the most painstaking work of months of effort by several standing committees and the full membership of both Houses.[1]

On rare occasions, a conference committee will draft a new bill almost from scratch. Still, certain protections exist. The Speaker may rule out a conference report if it can be demonstrated that the managers exceeded their authority. The ultimate determiners of what is permissible are working majorities in the two bodies.

When a majority of the conferees from the House and the Senate agree on the language of a measure, their decisions are embodied in a report, drafted in duplicate, and signed by at least a majority of each delegation. The product of the conference is explained by a statement of the managers, which is often central to later statutory interpretation. Minority reports are not permitted, but members may express their dissatisfaction by refusing to sign the conference report. The report is sent to each chamber, where it may not be amended when called up for consideration. The power of these conferees is considerable since the decisions reached in conference cannot be modified by the House or the Senate—they can only be accepted or rejected.[2] In both houses, conference reports are matters of high privilege and can be considered by the full chamber almost immediately.

---

[1] Albert Gore, "The Conference Committee: Congress' Final Filter," *The Washington Monthly*, June, 1971, p. 43.

[2] Appropriations measures coming from conference provide somewhat more flexibility, since they may allow for separate votes on items in disagreement between the two houses.

S.3637 GOES TO CONFERENCE

Representative Macdonald's request for a conference following the passage of the House bill on Tuesday, August 11, was made to assure immediate appointment of the House managers. Though both houses were slated to be in a three-week recess by August 15, the Democratic leadership still had hopes of bringing the conference report back for final passage by the end of the week. The Senate responded on August 12 by appointing its managers to the conference. [*Doc. 6-1*]

Shortly after the Senate conferees were appointed, Senator Pastore and Chairman Staggers arranged for a 4:30 meeting on Wednesday afternoon, August 12, in Room EF-100 in the Capitol. The success of

DOCUMENT **6-1**: Conferees on S.3637

House Managers	*Position*
Harley O. Staggers, D., W. Va.	Chairman, Interstate and Foreign Commerce Committee
Torbert Macdonald, D., Mass.	Chairman, Communications and Power Subcommittee
Lionel Van Deerlin, D., Calif.	Ranking Democrat, Communications and Power Subcommittee
William L. Springer, R., Ill.	Ranking Republican, Interstate and Foreign Commerce Committee
James T. Broyhill, R., N.C.	Ranking Republican, Communications and Power Subcommittee
Senate Managers	*Position*
Warren Magnuson, D., Wash.	Chairman, Commerce Committee
John Pastore, D., R.I.	Chairman, Communications Subcommittee
Vance Hartke, D., Ind.	Ranking Democrat, Communications Subcommittee
Hugh Scott, R., Pa.	Senate Minority Leader and Ranking Republican, Communications Subcommittee
Howard H. Baker, Jr., R., Tenn.	Third-ranking Republican, Communications Subcommittee

the conference was threatened from the start by two problems: First, Scott and Baker, though opposed to the original Senate legislation, were even more unhappy with the provisions of the stronger House measure. There was little likelihood that Baker would agree to whatever provisions might be worked out in conference. Scott, although a little more open to compromise than the junior Senator from Tennessee, generally favored disclosure rather than limitations on expenditures. Second, Pastore, the proxy votes of his two Democratic Senate colleagues in hand, was in no mood to brook opposition. With only one exception, he had no strong objections to the language of the House bill; the exception, however, was the effective-date provision. Here he was adamant—the Senate language must prevail. He felt that the bill should become law thirty days following enactment and not on January 1, 1971, as the House version had it. Implicit in his position was the understanding that the new law would then apply to the rapidly approaching fall elections—providing, of course, that it passed both Houses almost immediately and that President Nixon did not veto it. If the House conferees did not agree to the thirty-day provision, the temperamental Rhode Islander threatened to walk out of the conference and not return.

When the conferees met again the next morning, Senator Pastore agreed to concur in all but one of the House provisions, much to the approval of all of the House managers. In return, the Democratic House managers accepted a modified thirty-day effective-date provision as promoted by Pastore. Overnight, a compromise had been worked out by Senate and House staff members—Zapple, Guthrie, and Nordhaus—to overcome some of the objections raised by the conferees. [*Doc. 6-2*] The staff-drafted language inserted into the bill

DOCUMENT **6-2**: The Agreement

Provision	Accepted by
Modified 30-day enactment	All 3 House Democratic managers
	All 3 Senate Democratic managers
All other provisions	All 5 House managers of both parties
	All 3 Senate Democratic managers

would exempt media time purchased up until August 12 from the spending limitations of the legislation. The compromise won the support of the Democratic managers of each chamber, but the Republican conferees from both the Senate and the House refused to sign the conference report, transforming the compromised political broadcast bill into a sharply defined partisan measure. The failure of Scott and Baker to concur was not surprising; but the loss of Springer and Broyhill from a theretofore strongly bipartisan bill served only to exacerbate the partisan split implicit in the original Senate vote and explicit in House Democratic leadership maneuvering and support. Would the House and Senate Republicans who voted for the original measures now support a compromised bill with clear partisan overtones?

The conference report was filed in the House by Representative Staggers on the afternoon of Thursday, August 13. [*Doc. 6-3*] Appended to it was the required Statement of the Managers. In this, the Democratic House managers explained the problems they had encountered in reaching the conference compromise:

> Although they accepted all other provisions of the legislation as passed by the House, the managers on the part of the Senate were adamant in their refusal to accept the House effective date. The managers on the part of the House reluctantly acceded believing that the legislation is much more important than the date it becomes effective.

House rules require that all committee reports must lie over at least one day before they may be called up for a vote. That same day, however, Majority Leader Carl Albert indicated that the conference report might be called up on Friday, the last day before the three-week recess was to commence. By this time, many Representatives had made plans to leave Washington either late Thursday or early Friday. Even before the leadership announced its plans for Friday, the NCEC began alerting "friendly" Representatives to the possible forthcoming vote. Four members were enticed to return from New York, one of them just as he was about to board an airplane for Europe.

Response to the initial quorum call on Friday indicated that passage of the conference report was by no means assured. Rumors circulated that Republicans were keeping a number of opposing members in the cloakroom to convey a distorted impression of possible support for the bill. Rather than risk the defeat, the Democratic leadership, at Macdonald's urging, called off its attempt to pass the conference report. Final consideration was thus pushed off until after Labor Day, when the House was due to reconvene.

Although the House began meeting on September 9, 1970, it was not until September 16 that Representative Macdonald finally called up the conference report on S.3637. The rules limit debate on such measures to one hour, customarily divided equally between majority and minority. In his remarks, Macdonald stressed that the three-week delay had made the effective-date issue moot since the bill, if enacted, would probably not take effect until after the November elections or so close to election day that the provisions of S.3637 could not be enforced.

Springer once again indicated his support for the bill in spite of his failure to sign the conference report. He, too, noted that the effective-date issue was no longer relevant.

DOCUMENT **6-3**: Excerpts from the Conference Report

91ST CONGRESS ⎱ HOUSE OF REPRESENTATIVES ⎰   REPORT
   2d Session ⎰   ⎱ No. 91–1420

POLITICAL BROADCASTING

AUGUST 13, 1970.—Ordered to be printed

Mr. STAGGERS, from the committee of conference,
submitted the following

CONFERENCE REPORT

[To accompany S. 3637]

The committee of conference on the disagreeing votes of the two Houses on the amendments of the House to the bill (S. 3637) to amend section 315 of the Communications Act of 1934 with respect to equal-time requirements for candidates for public office, and for other purposes, having met, after full and free conference, have agreed to recommend and do recommend to their respective Houses as follows:

That the Senate recede from its disagreement to the amendment of the House to the text of the bill and agree to the same with an amendment as follows:

In lieu of the matter proposed to be inserted by the House amendment insert the following:

That (a) the first sentence of section 315(a) of the Communications Act of 1934 (47 U.S.C. 315(a)) is amended by inserting before the colon the following: ", except that the foregoing requirement shall not apply to the use of a broadcasting station by a legally qualified candidate for the office of President or Vice President of the United States in a general election".

(b) Section 315(b) of such Act is amended to read as follows:

"(b) The charges made for the use of any broadcasting station by any person who is a legally qualified candidate for any public office shall not exceed the lowest unit charge of the station for the same amount of time in the same time period."

SEC. 2. Section 315 of the Communications Act of 1934 is further amended by redesignating subsection (c) as subsection (f) and by inserting immediately before such subsection the following new subsections:

"(c)(1) For purposes of this subsection, the term 'major elective office' means the office of President, United States Senator or Representative, or Governor or Lieutenant Governor of a State. . . .

48–006

Doc. 6-3 (cont.)

SEC. 3. (a) The amendment made by subsection (b) of the first section of this Act shall take effect on the thirtieth day after the date of its enactment.

(b)(1) The amendments made by section 2 of this Act, insofar as they relate to primary elections, shall take effect on January 1, 1971. Except as provided in paragraph (2), the amendments made by section 2, insofar as they relate to general elections, shall apply with respect to amounts paid for broadcast time used after the thirtieth day after the date of enactment of this Act.

(2) If the Federal Communications Commission determines that—

(A) on August 12, 1970, a person is a legally qualified candidate for major elective office (or nomination thereto),

(B) there are in effect on such date one or more written agreements with station licensees for the purchase of broadcast time to be used after such thirtieth day on behalf of his candidacy for such office (or nomination thereto), and

(C) such agreements specify amounts to be paid for the purchase of such time to be used after such thirtieth day which, in the aggregate, exceed the limitation imposed by section 315(c)(2) of the Communications Act of 1934 with respect to the general election for such office,

then such amendments shall not apply to any of the candidates for election to such office in an election held before January 1, 1971.

And the House agree to the same.

That the Senate recede from its disagreement to the amendment of the House to the title of the bill, and agree to the same.

HARLEY O. STAGGERS,
TORBERT H. MACDONALD,
LIONEL VAN DEERLIN,
Managers on the Part of the House.

WARREN G. MAGNUSON,
JOHN O. PASTORE,
VANCE HARTKE,
Managers on the Part of the Senate.

As the vote neared, Macdonald again urged his colleagues to support the legislation. [*Doc. 6-4*]

DOCUMENT **6-4**: Excerpts from Macdonald's Speech*

Mr. MACDONALD. The House, on August 11, concurred in the committee's work and concurred in the bipartisan spirit of the committee, passing the measure, without amendment, by a record vote of 272 to 97. The measure then went to conference. And the agreement that emerged from the conference is now before us today.

That agreement—and I cannot stress this too strongly—that agreement accepts every change the House has made in the bill. Every word the House approved stands intact here. The Senate majority conferees, adamant that an attempt be made to apply the legislation to at least a part of the fall campaigns, acceded to the entire House bill in all particulars except the effective date.

As the House knows, the majority conferees agreed to a complex compromise on the effective date and a bonafide effort was made to seek adoption of that compromise in both bodies before the House last recessed. But the minority conferees would not sign the conference report because of the change in the effective date, and for my part I had great reluctance to proceed in a partisan spirit on what had been so sensibly a nonpartisan matter. Nevertheless, careful language was drafted that would have brought some limited control of campaign spending for at least the closing weeks of this fall's elections. That language would have proved workable, as the Federal Communications Commission has observed in correspondence with the minority leader of this body. But the need for a speedup in the enactment caused by the plans of the House to go into recess further increased attempts to have the report adopted in both the Senate and the House before or during the House recess were not successful.

That being the situation, I would hope that the House can proceed with its consideration of this important matter, in the light of the long-range problem and in terms of the workable reforms the House has already approved. On August 11 the House passed landmark legislation—the most thoroughgoing reform of the political uses of the broadcasting media since the enactment of the original Communications Act in 1934. It was a good bill in August; it remains a good and necessary bill in September. In fact, because of the passage of these last few weeks, the conference report before us today is in effect identical to the bill we passed last month. In actuality, nothing has been subtracted, and nothing has been changed. It remains only for the House to finish its work with a final formality.

Mr. Speaker, I urge the adoption of that report.

* *Congressional Record* (daily edition), September 16, 1970.

A roll call was ordered. The terse language of the *Congressional Record* reveals the result: "So the conference report was agreed to."

Party	Yeas	Nays	Total
Democratic	166	43	209
Republican	81	69	150
Total	247	112	359

This time, however, the Republicans were more evenly split on the issue, and the Democrats had lost some support. Of the members present for both the original vote on H.R.18434 and the vote on the conference report, ten Republicans and eight Democrats switched their votes from yea on H.R.18434 to nay on the conference report.

The Senate was left to complete the Congressional process; it took up the conference report on the afternoon of September 23. By unanimous consent, debate preceding the vote was limited to thirty minutes, to be equally divided between Senator Pastore and Senator Scott, or Scott's designee.

Pastore and Senator Baker (Scott's designee) both addressed themselves to the effective-date question. [*Doc. 6-5; Doc. 6-6*] Senator Pearson, who was the original cosponsor of the NCEC bill in the Senate, offered his final comments supporting the legislation, in the main avoiding the partisan character of the conference committee action. [*Doc. 6-7*]

Senator John Tower then voiced strong opposition to the bill. [*Doc. 6-8*]

DOCUMENT 6-5: Excerpts from Senator Pastore's Speech

All excerpts of the Senate floor debate that follow are taken from the Congressional Record *(daily edition) of September 23, 1970.*

Mr. PASTORE. We passed this bill in April, and included a provision that it would not take effect until 30 days after its enactment, to give the FCC an opportunity to write rules and regulations to govern the structure. It went over to the House of Representatives, and the House did not see fit to pass it until August. They passed it 3 or 4 days before they took their 3-week vacation. Right now, with the provision that it shall not become effective until 30 days after enactment, and this being September 23, and by the time the President receives it and takes his 10 days, it will not apply to this election.

This grieves me, because I was very much insistent that as far as the limitation is concerned, it should apply to

Doc. 6-5 (cont.)

the 1970 election. The House of Representatives changed that provision, and made it effective as of January 1, 1971. I was much opposed to that, and insisted on its becoming effective for this election—so much so that I shall live up to it even on a voluntary basis.

DOCUMENT 6-6: Excerpts from Senator Baker's Speech

Mr. BAKER. Mr. President, I yield myself such time as I may require.

I think it is fortunate that this bill is not to take effect, or probably will not take effect in time for this election. That was one of the heated issues in conference, and was one of the heated issues, as a matter of fact, in committee.

It strikes me as singularly unfair that we would change the rules in the middle of the ball game and allow this to take effect in this campaign.

There is every likelihood that candidates would have committed certain amounts to radio and television advertising that they suddenly would find they were unable to use. It is entirely possible that some candidates would find themselves in violation of contracts that had already been entered into and paid for. To make a long story short, it seems to me that if we are going to take this sort of action, it ought not to be taken in the middle of a political season.

DOCUMENT 6-7: Excerpts from Senator Pearson's Speech

Mr. PEARSON. Mr. President, we have come a long way since Abraham Lincoln spent 75 cents on his first congressional campaign and many of the changes wrought in the election process since then are perhaps inevitable, but in need of constant adjustment lest they so dominate the system that it loses all meaning. As our population has expanded it has become increasingly difficult for an elected official to maintain close contact with the constituency he has been elected to represent. Heavy use of the mails is expensive and a rather impersonal method of contact. A face to face meeting with constituents is the most effective way to communicate, of course. But, as everyone in this chamber realizes, it is impossible to ever personally meet with a large enough percentage of our constituents to do the job they expect us to do of keeping them informed of our activities. Even in the course of a long and vigorous campaign only a small portion of the electorate are ever personally contacted by the candidate. Yet, the votes we cast for our elected officials are among the most important decisions we make during our lives. They determine who will bear the heavy responsibility of shaping the future of our communities and our Nation. Whenever talented men and women are barred from successfully offering their services simply because they lack great wealth or whenever the voter makes his crucial decisions on the basis of misleading images artfully

Doc. 6-7 (cont.)

contrived and marketed by public relations specialists, the interests of the entire community suffer.

How then to effectively communicate with a continually expanding electorate while preserving the equality of access that is so essential for keeping the political process open to all points of view? The answer, of course, is television. Television has become the most vital ingredient in every major can.paign today. It has also become the most expensive. The result has been to price many worthwhile candidates out of the election market simply because they lack the means to buy enough television time to compete effectively. . . .

Mr. President, these spiraling costs are gravely distorting the election process and simply must be curbed. The bill we consider today may not offer the perfect formula, but it at least represents a positive start and because of the overwhelming need for reform it demands our support.

DOCUMENT 6-8: Excerpts from Senator Tower's Speech

Mr. TOWER. Mr. President. I am strongly opposed to S. 3637. In my opinion this legislation would impose a campaign spending limitation which is unrealistic, even if the Congress decides it should impose a limitation, and I am still not convinced that a dollar limitation should be imposed at all.

It may be that this bill will actually subvert its own intent. The actual result of legislation designed to limit political broadcasts and reduce campaign costs may be only to inhibit the use of a most economical method of explaining to the voters the positions of the candidate on significant issues.

This legislation favors incumbents, discriminates against broadcasters, and contains what I believe to be serious legal deficiencies which may only throw candidates and broadcasters into a quandary and subject them to the judgment of the courts.

Finally, Charles Goodell, freshman Senator from New York, rose to offer supporting comments before the vote on the conference report began. Already embroiled in the crucial campaign of his career, Goodell was subsequently to run third in the November election. In that campaign, his opponents, Representative Richard L. Ottinger (Democrat) and James L. Buckley (Conservative), the eventual winner, were to wage expensive media campaigns considerably above the standards set by the proposed legislation. [*Doc. 6-9*]

DOCUMENT 6-9: Excerpts from Senator Goodell's Speech

Mr. GOODELL. Mr. President, the Political Broadcasting Act of 1970 should really be called the Public Protection Act of 1970.

When enacted, it will limit the amount of money a political candidate

Doc. 6-9 (cont.)

can spend on radio and television advertising to 7 cents a vote. It will protect the public against candidates who attempt to buy their way to elective office, simply by taking over the airwaves with catchy 30-second commercials. By putting an end to the campaign "TV blitz," it will encourage candidates to participate in substantive debates on the issues—rather than run away from them.

Unlimited broadcast advertising in political campaigns does a gross injustice to the television media's potential for educating the public on a candidate's qualifications. Television is the single-most important element of a political campaign, and the people expect a great deal from this medium. The people expect, through television, that they will learn the views, qualifications, and positions of opposing candidates on the crucial issues.

This is not possible when nearly all that is seen of a candidate is a facade —a slick packaging of his image and a vague presentation of his views on his choice of the issues. A candidate with limited qualifications but an unlimited budget can easily circumvent "communicating with the public" and choose instead an alternative of "mesmerizing the public."

To place limitations on TV spending will encourage better qualified people to run for office. Too often today, qualified individuals cannot enter a race because they do not have personal or family fortunes to finance prohibitively expensive campaigns. . . .

Mr. President, our democratic society rests on the trust which the people place in their elected officials. The people must be able to choose the most qualified representatives through an open and fair process. By limiting the use of massive TV spending sprees in political campaigns, we have strengthened the foundation on which our Government stands. I urge my colleagues to pass this conference report.

When the conference report was finally called to a vote, the Senate roll call revealed the following partisan distribution. [*Doc. 6-10*]

DOCUMENT **6-10**: The Final Vote

Party	Yeas	Nays	Total
Democratic	43	1	44
Republican	17	18	35
Total	60	19	79

The Democrats retained almost total unanimity, while the Republicans were almost equally divided. Of the members present at the original vote on S.3637 and at the vote on the conference report, five Republicans and one Democrat switched from opposition to support. Only one Republican and one Democrat voted against the conference after having voted for the original bill.

Although the conference report was agreed to, S.3637 was not yet a law. Now, it was to evolve into an executive branch decision. Would President Nixon sign the legislation?

FURTHER READING

Conference committee activities, conducted in secret sessions, remain among the least understood and researched activities of Congress. The classic historical analysis is Ada C. McCown, *The Congressional Conference Committee* (New York: Columbia University Press, 1927). Gilbert Y. Steiner substantially updated this understanding in his monograph *The Congressional Conference Committee: Seventieth to Eightieth Congresses* (Urbana: University of Illinois Press, 1951). With the important exceptions of isolated chapters in such studies of the Appropriations and Finance–Ways and Means committees as those of Fenno and Manley (see the bibliography for Chapter 5), we know little more about conference committee activity today than we did two decades ago.

The President
Vetoes

After passage of a bill by both houses of Congress, it must be presented to the President of the United States.[*Doc. 7-1*] Whether or not the bill becomes a law depends at this stage on the President's official response, which may take any of four forms. First, he can approve the bill with his signature, in which case it becomes a law. Second, if the President does not approve the bill, he can return it together with a statement of his objections to the house in which it originated; in so doing, he vetoes the bill. If the President vetoes a bill by returning it to Congress, it cannot become law unless it is passed again in identical form by two-thirds of the members present and voting in each chamber, provided they constitute a quorum. If the vetoed bill receives the required two-thirds vote in both houses, the President's veto is overridden and the bill becomes a law. Third, the President can, in addition to approving or vetoing the bill, take no action at all upon it. If ten days pass (excluding Sundays) after the day the President receives a bill from Congress and he has neither approved the bill nor vetoed it, the bill becomes a law just as though the Presi-

DOCUMENT **7-1**: U.S. Constitution, Article I, Section 7,
Clauses 2 and 3

Every Bill which shall have passed the House of Representatives and the Senate, shall, before it become a Law, be presented to the President of the United States; If he approve he shall sign it, but if not he shall return it, with his Objections to that House in which it shall have originated, who shall enter the Objections at large on their Journal, and proceed to reconsider it. If after such Reconsideration two thirds of that House shall agree to pass the Bill, it shall be sent, together with the Objections, to the other House, by which it shall likewise be reconsidered, and if approved by two thirds of that House, it shall become a Law. But in all such Cases the Votes of both Houses shall be determined by yeas and Nays, and the Names of the Persons voting for and against the Bill shall be entered on the Journal of each House respectively. If any Bill shall not be returned by the President within ten Days (Sundays excepted) after it shall have been presented to him, the Same shall be a Law, in like Manner as if he had signed it, unless the Congress by their Adjournment prevent its Return, in which Case it shall not be a Law.

Every Order, Resolution, or Vote to which the Concurrence of the Senate and House of Representatives may be necessary (except on a question of Adjournment) shall be presented to the President of the United States; and before the Same shall take Effect, shall be approved by him, or being disapproved by him, shall be repassed by two thirds of the Senate and House of Representatives, according to the Rules and Limitations prescribed in the Case of a Bill.

dent had signed it with his approval. A fourth possibility, known as a pocket veto, occurs when the President takes no action on a bill after receiving it, but Congress adjourns before the expiration of the ten days. When that happens, the bill does not become a law and Congress has no opportunity to override the pocket veto. On the other hand, even though Congress may have adjourned in the meantime, the President still has the opportunity to sign the bill into law during the ten-day period.

After passage by both houses of Congress, and before going to the President, a bill is painstakingly checked for accuracy and punctuation by clerks of both houses and put into *enrolled* form, which means that it is printed on fine parchment paper and certified. The enrolled bill must be signed by the Speaker of the House (who is always the first to sign) and the President or President Pro Tempore of the Senate. The bill is then delivered to the White House by a clerk of the house in which the bill was first passed, and he is given a receipt for it. This can all be done within a day or two, or it can be delayed. The ten-day period allotted to the President for consideration of a bill does not begin until the day after he receives it, and there is no requirement as to when a bill must be delivered to the White House. President Wilson left Washington to attend the Paris Peace Conference in 1919 while Congress was still in session. By pre-arrangement with the President, the required signatures of the presiding officers of both houses were withheld from bills passed by Congress until Wilson returned, thus affording him the full ten days to consider the bills and preventing them from becoming law without his signature while he was absent.[1]

The President's basic option in dealing with any bill presented to him by Congress is either to approve the bill in its entirety or to veto it. The President does not have the power to exercise an item veto— that is, to excise parts of a bill while allowing the remainder to become law. Most modern Presidents have wished that they could use the item veto. The option to eliminate only certain sections or provisions would presumably make it easier for a President to deal with complex and controversial legislation, particularly those bills making multiple appropriations. Sometimes one house will add a non-germane "rider," an amendment or provision tacked onto a bill that has no relationship to the main purpose of the legislation. If the other house can be persuaded to go along, perhaps because it fears loss of the major sections of the bill, then the amendment has "had a free ride." Hence the label. But, Congress has all along refused to provide the President with the freedom to excise parts of legislation; therefore, his basic choice is limited to all or nothing.

[1] Joseph E. Kallenbach, *The American Chief Executive: The Presidency and the Governorship* (New York: Harper & Row, 1966), p. 352.

FACTORS CONDITIONING A PRESIDENT'S DECISION

The actual process of deciding whether to approve or veto a bill varies, of course, from one President to another and from bill to bill. Every President has his own style and his own set of priorities; each faces a temporally unique political situation. There are, however, some general similarities in the factors that contribute to any President's decision to approve or veto a bill.

All bills introduced of any importance go through a process of agency clearance. As soon as a bill is introduced, copies of it are obtained by the Legislative Reference Division of the Office of Management and Budget (OMB)—formerly the Office of Legislative Clearance in the Bureau of the Budget. The Office of Management and Budget decides which agencies will examine the bill. Usually the choice is obvious, but in any case the OMB tries to be an "honest broker" by submitting the bill to all the agencies with a relevant and meaningful interest in the legislation. An OMB official noted, however, that "because this government is like a sieve," the OMB will not send a draft of legislation proposed by the Administration to all relevant agencies if the bill is "really sensitive and the Administration doesn't want it to get leaked." A decision to exclude one or more agencies from this review process would not be made at the level of OMB, however, but by the more politically sensitive White House staff. The Legislative Reference Division is also responsible for clearing drafts of Administration bills, overseeing preparation of Administration testimony on pending legislation, and offering primary analysis of enacted legislation.

At OMB, every enrolled bill is put through a review process that was described by one agency official as akin to "the whole legislative process compressed into five days." First, the bill is sent from OMB to all the departments and agencies that may have any concern with its provisions. Of course, in most instances the same agencies have been "living with the legislation," sometimes acting as sponsors, often appearing before the relevant committees in hearings, monitoring the floor and conference committee action. Thus, they are likely to be on intimate terms with all aspects of the legislation. The agencies have forty-eight hours to examine the bill and submit to OMB their recommendations as to whether it should be approved or vetoed by the President. After the review of the bill by the agencies, the OMB has three days in which to prepare an "enrolled bill memorandum" for submission to the President. The memorandum contains all the arguments for and against the bill that were presented by the agencies, in addition to OMB's own analysis and recommendation.

Review of a bill by agencies and departments of the executive branch is only the most formal part of the process of Presidential decision concerning legislation passed by Congress. Considerations that influence a President's decisions in his other areas of authority also affect his decision to approve or veto important legislation. Before his election to the Presidency, he will have made many promises to the voters, promises that indicated the kinds of policies he would pursue as President. His campaign speeches and his party's campaign platform rarely bind him to specific actions, but they do create a general framework of public obligation that must weigh heavily in his decisions. Once in office, he continues to amplify this framework of obligations in his messages to Congress, public speeches, press conferences, and, generally, whenever he utters a public word.

The President also has private obligations that crowd in upon his public choices. He will have incurred debts of loyalty to politicians and financial supporters who helped him win Presidential office. During his Presidency, he further obligates himself in the process of bargaining with Congressional leaders, other politicians, and representatives of various private or group interests.

A President's public and private obligations do not, of course, commit him to sign any piece of legislation that comes within the scope of policies he has obligated himself to support. If, for example, a President has publicly and privately pledged to lower taxes, it is unlikely that he would consider himself obligated to approve *any* conceivable tax reduction bill that Congress might pass. Sometimes, on the other hand, a President will take a stand for or against a particular bill long before it is passed by Congress. He would not be expected to veto a bill he had himself submitted to Congress, but since legislation can be radically altered in committee or on the floor of either house, his decision to approve or veto cannot be considered final until the bill is passed and presented to him.

The President's decision is further influenced by the advice he receives from his close associates. Advisers on the President's staff begin discussing important bills while they are still in the early stages of the legislative process. These men, in the words of one who has worked closely with two Presidents, are expected to be "politically sensitive guys who watch for blips on the political radar and can spot the red-tinged ones early." At this point, a few close associates may hold an informal exploratory session with the President to get his initial reaction to the problem and to obtain direction for further efforts. The more major the bill or the more politically acute the issue, the greater the amount of top-level staff time allocated to it. Gradually, the informal discussions among the White House staff broaden to include members of Congress, Cabinet officers, and others whose interests may be involved or whose advice may be thought useful. As the time for a

Presidential response of some kind draws near, the process will grow somewhat more formal and begin to focus on the preparation of a paper analyzing the issue confronting the President and outlining the options available to him. A small group of advisers may meet with the President to go over the issue when it nears a decision point, or the President may retire to his own study to make up his mind in "splendid isolation."

More than most of his predecessors, President Nixon has tended to make his major policy decisions alone. After listening to his counselors at length, he often retires to his Executive Office Building hideaway or to an upstairs den in the White House to make his final decision. It may take the form of a comment written on a government memorandum or a draft of a message outlined in large, clear script on yellow legal pads. Once the President has made up his mind, the entire White House staff and beyond are on tap to see that the decision is implemented.

The political considerations a President must take into account are usually quite different from those that influence a member of the Senate or House of Representatives. To begin with, the nature of the President's constituency is not at all similar to the typical House or Senate constituency. He alone speaks for *all* the nation. The way representation in the House and Senate is apportioned among the states makes Congress, relative to the President, more responsive to pressures from small states and rural voters. The Electoral College system of Presidential election makes it necessary for any candidate running for President to win several large states with many electoral votes. In order to carry the large industrial states, the candidate must do well in urban areas that have heavy concentrations of labor and minority-group voters. The dichotomy of a conservative, rurally based Congressional constituency opposed to a liberal, urban-based Presidential constituency is oversimplified, but it is often sufficiently operative to be of importance.

The President's perspective is also different from that of most members of Congress in that he is the head of his party. Most Presidents are aware that when they speak or act upon an issue, their position is likely to be regarded by the public as the *party* position. Few members of the House or Senate carry anything like a similar responsibility for their party. Only when exceptional leaders—like the late Speaker Sam Rayburn or Senate Minority Leader Everett Dirksen—speak out are the words of a Congressman likely to be given partisan impact approximate to the words of a President.

A President may also be influenced by his awareness of the limitation on his tenure of office. All Presidents have concern for their place in history. As his remaining time in office grows shorter, his opportunity to leave his mark in any area of national policy diminishes. A

Congressman, particularly one whose seat is relatively secure, can lose a battle and still know that he will have multiple opportunities in future Congresses to fight it again.

The period of Presidential action on a bill can promote a time of lobbying as intense, if not more intense, than the period of the bill's passage through Congress. The lobbying techniques used to influence a President's decision are not substantially different from those employed in attempts to persuade Congress, except that in this instance they are focused upon one man and his close circle of friends and advisers.

When, in 1947, the 80th Congress passed the Taft-Hartley Act—an act that severely curbed the power of labor unions—a determined effort was made by opponents of the bill to insure President Truman's veto.[2] He had already indicated his strong dissatisfaction with the bill and had threatened a veto. Within a few days after the bill's passage, the White House received hundreds of thousands of letters, postcards, and telegrams urging him to reject the bill. Many representatives of labor had been in Washington to oppose the bill actively while it was going through Congress; even more came to the city after it had passed to indicate their strong opposition. Across the country, rallies were held and petitions were signed. The President was also subject to intense pressure from his party's northern urban wing, although most southern Democrats in Congress supported the bill. Still other pressures operated *against* the veto. During and after World War II, public opinion turned against the growing power of labor unions. The 1948 elections were little more than a year away and Republican strength seemed to be mounting. Truman hoped to maintain as united a Democratic Party as possible, but Democratic southerners in both Houses of Congress had voted for the bill's passage and would surely vote again to override a veto.

Truman vetoed the bill even though the majority of public opinion was against such an action. His veto was quickly overridden in both houses of Congress, and the bill was thus enacted into law. By vetoing the bill, however, Truman acted in accordance not only with his convictions, but with the wishes of a majority of Democratic politicians and the important urban labor-oriented segment of the electorate.

Pointing out the political considerations that may influence a President's decision should not obscure the fact that he also relies on his own judgment of what is best for the country. In this consideration, too, the President's perspective is different from that of a Congressman. His responsibility is wider than a typical Congressman's, and he has access to a far wider range of more specialized advisers. Thus, a Presi-

[2] R. Alton Lee, *Truman and Taft-Hartley: A Question of Mandate* (Lexington: University of Kentucky Press, 1966), pp. 80–105.

dent is usually in a better position to relate one issue to several others and to consider them in terms of the broadest national interest. This does not necessarily mean that a President is more likely to be right than the collective wisdom of Congress or even a single Congressman. Although, as President, he is in a stronger position than most Congressmen to further his concept of the national interest, the very factors that contribute to this potential also give him more power to act out of partisan motivation or even, in rare instances, on behalf of strictly private interests.

When a President signs a bill, he can use the occasion to accomplish more than simply creating a law. Most bills that a President approves are signed routinely by him with little or no fanfare. Occasionally, in order to reward a bill's proponents or to draw attention to a major piece of legislation, the signing will take place publicly, accompanied by a more or less elaborate ceremony. President Lyndon Johnson frequently signed important bills using a number of pens, which he then presented to the Congressmen, agency officials, and lobbyists gathered around him. In 1965, Johnson signed a major aid-to-education bill in the small Texas schoolhouse where his own education began. The Voting Act of 1965 was signed before hundreds of dignitaries in the Capitol Rotunda near a large statue of Abraham Lincoln. President Nixon has not been averse to similar appeals to a broader public in his bill-signing ceremonies.

The President can also register disapproval of a bill he feels he is unable to veto by allowing it to become a law without his signature after ten days have passed. Occasionally, a President will reluctantly sign a bill into law but at the same time point up his strong reservations. Usually his statement will call for remedial legislation as soon as possible. President Nixon, for example, signed into law an extension of the Voting Rights Act of 1965 that also lowered the minimum voting age to eighteen, even though he issued a statement at the same time emphasizing his misgivings about the bill's constitutionality.[3]

The President's power to veto legislation also allows him to accomplish more than just preventing bills from becoming law. The *threat* of a veto is often used to influence the shape of legislation in Congress More rarely, the veto can be used to remind the Congress of the President's power. According to Richard Neustadt, "Franklin Roosevelt sometimes asked his aides for 'something I can veto' as a lesson and reminder to Congressmen."[4] The veto power can be used to discipline individual legislators who have withheld support for legislation about

[3] A year later, on June 30, 1971, the new 26th Amendment to the U.S. Constitution granting eighteen-year-olds the right to vote was ratified in record time (three months and seven days).

[4] Richard E. Neustadt, *Presidential Power* (New York: John Wiley & Sons, 1960), p. 84.

which the President feels strongly. Roosevelt used the veto in such a way against Senator Pat McCarran of Nevada after he had helped to lead the fight against the President's proposed Supreme Court reorganization bill in 1937.[5] In three sessions of Congress, the crusty Nevada Senator managed to get a particular measure passed that was sought by some of his constituents with the intention of frustrating cattle rustlers; three times Roosevelt vetoed McCarran's bill.

A President may employ the veto to increase his popularity with his constituents or to improve his position with politicians, interest groups, or his party. Truman's veto of the Taft-Hartley Act accomplished some of these objectives. A veto can also serve, as did the Taft-Hartley veto, to give the President an opportunity to emphasize his position on a particular issue; and, if the veto is overridden in Congress, it can become the basis for appeals to the country for electoral support.

Finally, the President's hand is strengthened as the end of a session of Congress approaches by the power to exercise the pocket veto. A pocket veto cannot be overridden; delaying action on a bill until near the end of a session thus works to the advantage of the President and his Congressional allies.

After the President vetoes a bill, it is returned, by constitutional requirement, to the house of Congress in which it originated. Often, if there is no likelihood of enough votes to override the veto, the bill may be tabled or referred to a committee and be allowed to perish there. If the bill is reconsidered, no amendments can be made. A replacement bill can be drafted, of course, but it is a *new bill* and must be dropped into the hopper to begin the legislative process anew. The factors that influenced the final passage vote will, for the most part, continue to bear on the question of overriding the veto: "Shall the bill pass, the objections of the President to the contrary notwithstanding?" Now, however, the President has expressed his disapproval in the most unambiguous means available to him. This usually serves to strengthen the position of the President's side and to realign members of the President's party behind him; those members of his party who supported the bill the first time around will be especially pressed by such a Presidential action.

PRESIDENT NIXON'S VETO OF S.3637

The enrolled copy of the Political Broadcast Act of 1970, which had received final approval by the Senate on September

---

[5] Kallenbach, *op. cit.*, p. 361.

23, was not delivered to the White House until September 30. Thus, President Nixon had until October 12 (ten days, excluding Sundays) to take action on the bill. Away on a European trip, the President did not return to Washington until Sunday, October 4, which meant that he was actually left with about a week to consider the bill. Of course, in the interim, agency and OMB surveillance was well under way.

Any opportunity to veto legislation can be used to foster a President's personal political interests and those of his party because it generally presents an excellent time for bargaining, disciplining, fulfilling obligations, generating publicity, and, more rarely, even statesmanship. The Political Broadcast Act went beyond most legislation in the richness of these opportunities because the substance of the bill itself would have an immediate effect on the political interests of the President, his party, and their opponents. It would go to the heart of campaign financing and the elective process.

Like all bills that have passed Congress, the Political Broadcast Act was submitted to the Legislative Reference Division of the Office of Management and Budget for agency clearance. This clearance process was probably of minimal importance in President Nixon's decision to veto the Political Broadcast Act. The Legislative Reference Division of the OMB is staffed by career professionals, not political appointees. Their expertise lies in analyzing the impact of a bill on existing government programs, primarily from a budgetary point of view. Such considerations were largely irrelevant to Nixon's decision, which was based partly on the merits of the legislation, but more importantly on underlying partisan political considerations.

All during the year the bill was in Congress (from September, 1969, through September, 1970), the President had largely refrained from giving any indication, even to the leadership of his own party, whether he would veto or approve the bill. Now that the bill was passed, he sought advice from his White House staff—John Erhlichman, Robert Haldeman, Bryce Harlow, and others—and from GOP Congressional leaders such as Senators Scott, Tower, and Baker, and Representatives Ford, Arends, Wilson, and Morton. Most of the advice he received was in favor of a veto, and it was generally framed in terms of the bill's impact on the political fortunes of the Republican Party. Representative Rogers Morton of Maryland, by then the Republican National Chairman, gave advice that was typical of most. He argued that the bill's restrictions on spending worked to the advantage of incumbents, and since the Democrats formed a majority in both houses, the bill would increase "the chances of freezing the Republican Party into a permanent minority" in Congress.[6] The strongest argument in favor of signing the bill—advanced by House Minority Leader Ford—was that, with

6 *National Journal*, Nov. 28, 1970, p. 2605.

elections only a month away, a veto would give the Democrats a new campaign issue.

On Monday, October 12, the last day before it would have become a law without his signature, President Nixon vetoed the bill. That same day the President's veto message and the enrolled bill were returned to the Senate, where S.3637 had originated, by one of the President's secretaries. The message was announced both in Stamford, Connecticut, where President Nixon was spending the day campaigning for Republican candidates, and at the White House, where Presidential aide John Erhlichman conducted the briefing.

The President had spent most of the weekend at his retreat on Key Biscayne near Miami, Florida. Members of the press who had accompanied the President to Florida were expecting him to fly from there to Connecticut on Monday morning. On Sunday, however, the press corps was informed that the President would be returning to Washington immediately. They were also alerted that an important announcement would be forthcoming. Some reporters anticipated that the announcement would concern the President's decision on the Political Broadcast Act.

Monday morning, the day of the veto, the President and the press flew to Connecticut. Late in the afternoon, after a hard day of campaigning in Hartford and Stamford, the President made his "important announcement," which turned out to be a statement about further troop withdrawals from Vietnam. In the main, these amounted to but a minor extension of previously announced plans for reductions. In contrast to the President's spoken message, the announcement of the veto was merely handed to reporters in the form of a White House news release.

The timing had been superbly managed. It was too late to allow detailed coverage of the veto on the evening news that night. The troop-withdrawal announcement and the last minute revelation of the veto to the press at a highly inconvenient moment, seemed to one experienced member of the White House press corps to be interrelated. Dismissing the troop-withdrawal announcement as a "smokescreen," he concluded that the events of Sunday and Monday were intended to keep the veto from receiving the priority in the news media it ordinarily would have had. This interpretation, while difficult to substantiate, was regarded by a former high-ranking member of the Nixon Administration as "perfectly plausible." "Presidents can do that," he noted, "they also like to turn the process around to generate news and gain headlines." [Doc. 7-2]

A veto message is seldom framed in terms of overtly partisan political rhetoric. Thus, to whatever extent Nixon's decision to veto the Political Broadcast Act was influenced by apprehension about the bill's potential adverse effect on future Republican showings at the polls, no

DOCUMENT **7-2**: A View of the Veto

EQUAL TIME

Copyright © 1970, the *Denver Post*. Reprinted with the permission of the Los Angeles Times Syndicate.

such considerations were touched upon in the veto message. [*Doc. 7-3*]

The main arguments advanced by President Nixon were, not surprisingly, those made by the bill's opponents in Congress. He complained that the bill limited spending only for television time, while leaving spending on other media unrestricted. This would not result in lower campaign costs, Nixon reasoned, because candidates would simply shift their spending from television to billboards, newspapers, and other means of reaching the voters. The President argued further that the fixed limit on spending, as opposed to a limit on broadcast time, was unfair to candidates in urban areas where broadcast time is relatively expensive. Moreover, the lowest-unit-charge provision of the bill would amount to rate-setting for private industry by Congress, Nixon noted, a "radical departure for the Congress which has traditionally abhorred" any such attempt. Furthermore, the President branded the bill as an "incumbent's measure": Restrictions on television spending would be immeasurably advantageous to incumbent officeholders who are usually better known than their challengers and who, in the conduct of their offices, have a "natural avenue of public attention through the news media." Typically, such channels are unavailable to a little-known opponent.

DOCUMENT **7-3**: The President's Veto Message*

TO THE SENATE OF THE UNITED STATES:

I return herewith, without my approval, S. 3637, a bill to revise the provisions of the Communications Act which relate to political broadcasting.

This legislation is aimed at the highly laudable and widely supported goals of controlling political campaign expenditures and preventing one candidate from having an unfair advantage over another. Its fatal deficiency is that it not only falls far short of achieving these goals but also threatens to make matters worse.

S. 3637 does not limit the overall cost of campaigning. It merely limits the amount that candidates can spend on radio and television. In doing so, it unfairly endangers freedom of discussion, discriminates against the broadcast media, favors the incumbent officeholder over the officeseeker and gives an unfair advantage to the famous. It raises the prospect of more -- rather than less -- campaign spending. It would be difficult, in many instances impossible, to enforce and would tend to penalize most those who conscientiously attempt to abide by the law.

The problem with campaign spending is not radio and television; the problem is spending. This bill plugs only one hole in a sieve.

Candidates who had and wanted to spend large sums of money, could and would simply shift their advertising out of radio and television into other media -- magazines, newspapers, billboards, pamphlets, and direct mail. There would be no restriction on the amount they could spend in these media.

Hence, nothing in this bill would mean less campaign spending.

* If the reader looks closely just to the right of the caption, "TO THE SENATE OF THE UNITED STATES," he will notice a lightly inked hatch mark (#). This mark is made by the Journal Clerk of the Senate on every document that crosses his desk. The time and date of the actual receipt—in this case 4:15 p.m. on Mon-

Doc. 7-3 (cont.)

2

In fact, the bill might tend to increase rather than decrease the total amount that candidates spend in their campaigns. It is a fact of political life that in many Congressional districts and States a candidate can reach more voters per dollar through radio and TV than any other means of communication Severely limiting the use of TV and radio in these areas would only force the candidate to spend more by requiring him to use more expensive techniques.

By restricting the amount of time a candidate can obtain on television and radio, this legislation would severely limit the ability of many candidates to get their message to the greatest number of the electorate. The people deserve to know more, not less, about the candidates and where they stand.

There are other discriminatory features in this legislation. It limits the amount of money candidates for a major elective office may spend for broadcasting in general elections to 7¢ per vote cast for the office in question in the last election or $20,000 whichever is greater. This formula was arrived at through legislative compromise and is not based on any scientific analysis of broadcast markets. It fails to take into account the differing campaign expenditure requirements of candidates in various broadcast areas. In many urban centers, the $20,000 limitation would permit a Congressional candidate to purchase only a few minutes of broadcast time, thus precluding the use of radio or television as an effective instrument of communication. On the other hand, $20,000 spent on television broadcasting in another district would enable a candidate to virtually blanket a large area with campaign advertising spots. For example, 30 seconds of prime television time in New York City costs $3,500; in the Wichita - Hutchinson, Kansas area, it costs $145.

day, October 13, 1970—are logged on large, blue-lined sheets, which are eventually incorporated into the permanent Journal of the Senate. (If the reader re-examines Document 1-6, he will note a similar mark just above the top, right-hand border of the enrolled copy of S.3637.)

Doc. 7-3 (cont.)

3

S. 3637 raises a host of other questions of both principle and practice. It would require that broadcasters charge candidates no more than the lowest unit charge of the station for comparable time. This is tantamount to rate-setting by statute and represents a radical departure for the Congress which has traditionally abhorred any attempt to establish rates by legislation.

Among the other questions raised and left unanswered are these: How would expenditures of various individuals and organizations not directly connected with the candidate be charged? Would they be considered part of a candidate's allowed total expenditure, even if they were beyond the candidate's control? And how would money spent by a committee opposing a candidate be accounted? Would it be included in the total for that candidate's opponent, even though spent without his consent or control? This bill does not effectively limit the purchase of television time to oppose a candidate.

In the end, enforcement of the expenditure limitation would in most cases occur after the election. This raises the possibility of confusion and chaos as elections come to be challenged for violation of S. 3637 and the cases are still unresolved when the day arrives on which the winning candidate should take office.

There is another issue here which is perhaps the most important of all. An honored part of the American political tradition is that any little known but highly qualified citizen has the opportunity to seek and ultimately win elective office. This bill would strike a serious blow at that tradition. The incumbent -- because he has a natural avenue of public attention through the news media in the conduct of his office -- would have an immeasurable advantage over the "out" who was trying to get in. The only others who would share part of this advantage would be those whose names were well-known for some other reason.

What we have in S. 3637 is a good aim, gone amiss. Nearly everyone who is active or interested in the political process wants

Doc. 7-3 *(cont.)*

4

to find some way to limit the crushing and growing cost of political campaigning. But this legislation is worse than no answer to the problem -- it is a wrong answer.

I urge that the Congress continue to analyze and consider ways to reach this goal through legislation which will not restrict freedom of discussion, will not discriminate against any communications medium, will not tend to freeze incumbents in office, will not favor the famed over the worthy but little-known, will not risk confusion and chaos in our election process and will not promote more rather than less campaign spending. Such legislation will have to be far better than S. 3637.

I am as opposed to big spending in campaigns as I am to big spending in government. But before we tamper with something as fundamental as the electoral process, we must be certain that we never give the celebrity an advantage over an unknown, or the officeholder an extra advantage over the challenger.

Richard Nixon

THE WHITE HOUSE,

October 12, 1970.

Strangely, the veto message made no mention of the bill's suspension of the equal-time requirement in general elections for the Presidency. The suspension of the equal-time requirement, with its result of facilitating televised debates between major-party candidates, would, it is generally thought, work to the advantage of the candidate of the "out" party challenging an incumbent President. Some critics of the veto suggested Nixon's actual motive was his apprehension, based on his own experience in the debates of 1960, of being forced into face-to-face debates with his opponent in 1972.

The veto was immediately attacked by supporters of the bill, who denounced it as politically motivated. Congressman Macdonald described it as an "inexplicable partisan political maneuver of the first magnitude." Russell Hemenway called the veto a "flagrant example of partisan interest." "President Nixon successfully subdued his nobler nature . . . and his veto was full, firm and wholly partisan," editorialized the *Baltimore Sun*. There was no doubt that an attempt would be made to override the veto as soon as Congress resumed its work after the elections.

Television dominated the 1970 election campaign. Spending for political broadcast advertising rose to nearly $58 million, almost double that of the last non-Presidential campaign year of 1966. Once again, the press lamented increasing trends toward the packaging and selling of political candidates. Concern over television's role in the elections led one Senator, who had originally voted against the bill—Democrat B. Everett Jordan of North Carolina—to switch his position and vote to override the veto.

Ironically, the campaign ploy that was most generally denounced as unfair and in bad taste was not a television spot but highly misleading newspaper advertisements attacking Democratic senatorial candidates in more than a half-dozen states across the country. Conceivably, this fact could have been used by the bill's opponents to buttress the argument that restrictions on television spending alone would not necessarily result in campaign reform. It is not surprising that such an argument was not made, however, inasmuch as the objectionable advertisements were placed by Republicans against Democratic incumbents. Adding further irony, the newly created group that placed them seized upon the name "Committee for a *Responsible* Congress."

The Override Attempt

Lobbying aimed at the override vote began almost immediately after the veto. The National Association of Broadcasters sent a letter to its more than 4,000 member stations suggesting that they contact their Senators and Representatives and urge them to sustain the veto. Most of the lobbying on behalf of the broadcast industry was undertaken by state associations and owners of local stations. Telegrams from members of the industry poured in to Congressmen.

Within a week after the President acted, the National Committee for an Effective Congress sent material to more than five-hundred newspapers urging them to write editorials critical of the veto. The NCEC also sent information to Democratic candidates and recommended that the veto be used as a campaign issue. Contacts with friendly interest groups, mostly labor, were stepped up in an effort to override the veto.

The White House effort to muster support to sustain the veto had two essential components. One was to play up the attempt to override the veto as a Democratic effort to strengthen the party for the 1972 elections. The temptation to allow the override contest to be fought strictly as a Democrat-versus-Republican issue was resisted by Democratic leaders in the Senate, however, who were aware that without some Republican support they could not hope to win a vote requiring a two-thirds majority. The President's most successful strategy was to announce support for more comprehensive campaign-reform legislation in 1971. After the veto, Senate Minority Leader Scott promised to introduce such legislation. The day before the override vote in the Senate, Scott revealed a letter sent him by Nixon backing the Republican Leader's call for broader-ranging legislation. [*Doc. 7-4*] After the vote, it became clear that Scott's Presidentially endorsed proposal was an important influence on the decision of some Senators to sustain the veto.

Congressional Democrats wanted an early vote on the veto, one that would take place while the negative reaction to televised political advertising in the 1970 elections was still alive. The Democrats caucused on November 16, and Majority Leader Mansfield was persuaded to schedule a vote before the Thanksgiving recess. Rounding up the Republican votes in favor of overriding was primarily to be the responsibility of the NCEC and, secondarily, Common Cause. These forces worked closely with Republican Senators James Pearson of Kansas, Charles Mathias of Maryland, and Charles Goodell of New York. All had been cosponsors of the original bill; Goodell, in particular, was bitter because his unsuccessful re-election attempt had been subverted both by his opponents' heavy television spending and by lack of Presidential support (if not outright opposition).

S.3637 was brought to a final vote on November 23, 1970. The vote was preceded by three hours of debate in which most of the familiar arguments were restated, with the focus upon the pros and cons of the points made in Nixon's veto message. The bill's opponents stressed

DOCUMENT 7-4: Nixon's "Dear Hugh" Letter

THE WHITE HOUSE

WASHINGTON

November 20, 1970

Dear Hugh:

Your proposal to offer a comprehensive campaign reform bill in the 92nd Congress is commendable. The Administration will, of course, work closely with you, other members of the Congress and the Governors in an effort to arrive at a bill which will deal with all problems of political campaigns, including spending limitations, in a direct, effective and enforceable manner. Our aim must be to provide legislation which is consistent with the processes of free elections and the maintenance of an informed electorate.

As I pointed out in my veto message of the Political Broadcast Act, S. 3637, that bill had many shortcomings. These must be corrected. A major deficiency of this legislation is that it singles out only one form of campaign spending. If, indeed, there is merit in limiting campaign expenditures, the problem should be dealt with in its entirety. To merely limit one form of spending could encourage candidates to spend even more in other areas. The result might well be more expensive, rather than less expensive, political campaigns.

Of utmost importance, new legislation must not discriminate against one communication medium. It must also provide a meaningful mechanism for enforcement, as to which S. 3637 is seriously deficient.

Reform is needed in this area. But this issue need not and should not be dealt with in a hurried and contentious fight over a veto. There will be no major elections between now and the time that Congress can consider this legislation in the next session. Your proposal offers an opportunity to do this in a deliberate and cooperative way.

With best personal regards,

Sincerely,

Honorable Hugh Scott
United States Senate
Washington, D. C.

the President's objection that the bill limited only television spending and did nothing about spending on other media. The bill's supporters generally conceded that argument but insisted that it was no reason to reject this legislation, since more comprehensive reform could come later.

The attempt to override the veto failed. But the vote was close—58 to 34 in favor of the bill, or 4 votes short of the 62 needed for a two-thirds majority of the 92 Senators voting. [*Doc. 7-5*]

DOCUMENT **7-5**: Senate Override Vote Fails

Party	Yeas	Nays	Total
Democratic	49	6	55
Republican	9	28	37
Total	58	34	92

This vote, like most votes in the Senate and the House, was not drawn according to strict partisan lines. Five Democrats who had supported the original bill switched and supported the President's veto. With the exception of "lame-duck"[7] Senator Dodd of Connecticut, the other four Democrats who switched were from southern states: Allen of Alabama, Eastland and Stennis of Mississippi, and Ellender of Louisiana all voted against it. They were joined by McClellan of Arkansas, who had consistently opposed the legislation. The bill's restrictions on television spending in primaries, which are often the only elections that matter in the largely one-party South, would have been difficult for the southern Senators to live with. They probably were also influenced by the lobbying campaigns of the state broadcasting industry associations, which are particularly strong in the South. One Democratic partisan concluded, "This was where the bill was gutted—votes lost in Alabama, Georgia, Arkansas, Mississippi, and the border states."

Once the President—who had never commented on the bill before it passed—had exercised the veto, considerations of party loyalty weighed heavier for Republican Senators than on the original vote. Five Republicans who had supported the original bill—Aiken and Prouty of Vermont, Smith of Maine, Williams of Delaware, and Young of North Dakota—switched and voted to uphold the President's veto. Eight Republican Senators—Case of New Jersey, Cooper of Kentucky, Goodell and Javits of New York, Mathias of Maryland, Packwood of Oregon, Pearson of Kansas, and Schweiker of Pennsylvania—who had supported the original bill on passage and in voting on the conference report, were not swayed by appeals for loyalty to the President, and they voted to override the veto. In the main, the dissenting Republicans were East Coast liberals.

With the failure to achieve a two-thirds majority on the override vote, the bill perished irrevocably. A new bill could be introduced, as

---

[7] A "lame duck" politician is one who is nearing the end of his term of office and is certain not to begin another. The term is usually not applied until after the lame duck's successor in office has been elected.

Senator Scott had promised for 1971 with the President's endorsement. The NCEC would maintain its strong interest. Senator Pastore and Representative Macdonald, their interests aroused and their reputations on the line, would certainly play an active role in the 92d Congress. In January, 1971, a new Congress was organized with most of the same cast of characters on hand ready to try once again to deal with the problem of campaign reform.[8] For the Political Broadcast Act of 1970, however, the legislative process had run its course.

FURTHER READING

The classic historical study of the Presidential veto power is Edward Campbell Mason's *The Veto Power: Its Origin, Development and Function in the Government of the United States (1789–1899)* (Boston: Ginn and Co., 1890). More recent is *Presidential Vetoes 1792–1945* by Carlton Jackson (Athens, Ga.: University of Georgia Press, 1967).

A good treatment of the uses of the veto power is in a chapter entitled "Legislator-in-Chief" (part 2) of Joseph E. Kallenbach's *The American Chief Executive: The Presidency and the Governorship* (New York: Harper & Row, 1966). The best discussion of the process of Presidential choice involving the veto power is in chapter 19 of *The Legislative Struggle: A Study in Social Combat* by Bertram M. Gross (New York: McGraw-Hill, 1953).

The standard legal analysis of the powers of the President remains Edwin S. Corwin, *The President: Office and Powers,* 4th ed. (New York: New York University Press, 1957).

For general consideration of the President's role in the legislative process, see *Congress and the Presidency*, 2d ed., by Nelson W. Polsby (Englewood Cliffs, N.J.: Prentice-Hall, 1971). A good short text on the office of the President is Dorothy Buckton James, *The Contemporary Presidency* (New York: Pegasus Books, 1969).

---

[8] For an overview of significant developments in 1971, see the Epilogue.

The Future of
Campaign Finance
Reform

S.3637, the Political Broadcast Act of 1970, failed to become the law of the land. President Richard M. Nixon's October 12, 1970, veto was sustained by the Senate on November 23 of that year. As the 91st Congress droned to a close on January 2, 1971, it had as yet found no solution to the widely affirmed problem of rapidly expanding and relatively uncontrolled expenditures by candidates competing for the most important elective offices in the nation. More and more of this money was being shunted into television advertising. Politics seemed to be in danger of becoming almost exclusively a rich man's game.

Today, several questions remain largely unanswered. First, to what extent was the struggle over the Political Broadcast Act typical of what happens in Congress when strong interests clash? In other words, to what degree is it possible to generalize from this case study to other legislative controversies? Second, what can be conjectured about the strengths and weaknesses of our political system as a whole, based upon a single case study?

LEGISLATIVE CONFLICT

No single piece of legislation, The Political Broadcast Act of 1970 included, can ever be said to be typical except in the broadest sense. Given the myriad problems the House and Senate are called upon to confront in any Congress, it is almost inevitable that every piece of legislation has its unique features. In part, this is because "one cannot step twice into the same river"; no Congress and no one piece of legislation, strictly speaking, can be compared with earlier Congresses or other legislation. Just as every Congress has different personnel and confronts divergent problems under changing conditions, so every bill is introduced under widely varying circumstances. Still, some generalizations can be made, and comparisons, however incomplete, can often prove fruitful.

Legislation can be classified under three broad categories: (1) national legislation, which affects nearly everyone directly, such as a tax bill, or indirectly, such as an act in aid of elementary and secondary education; (2) middle-range legislation, which is generally aimed at a specific set of interests or has a restricted regional impact, such as sugar-quota legislation or irrigation and reclamation projects; and (3) low-level and relatively noncontroversial minor bills. Most of the latter legislation, many of them private bills, are handled on the private and consent calendars or are passed under suspension of the rules or by voice votes. The second category, middle-range legislation, typically requires a special order from the Committee on Rules in the House, but bills in this group seldom generate much debate in either house and are frequently passed with little or no dissent. It is the national-level legislation that preoccupies the Congressional leaders, generates controversy, and, hence, earns coverage from the news media. Such legislation generally requires decision-making by roll-call votes in both the Senate and the House of Representatives. Perhaps not more than one-fifth of the number of public laws that pass Congress in any one session falls into this last category, but much more than a majority of legislative effort as measured by number of hearing days, or time spent in floor debate, centers around these major Congressional confrontations.

By such criteria, the Political Broadcast Act of 1970 is clearly a national-level bill. But, it began as a fairly low order of legislation and only gradually acquired a partisan, highly controversial character as it moved from the Senate to the House, through a joint conference, on to a President's veto, and finally, into an unsuccessful effort to override that veto in the Senate. Despite its national scope and final partisan tenor, however, S.3637 never became a large-scale confrontation of the kind that preoccupies the Congress no more than three or four times in a session—a Voting Rights Act, a major welfare-reform bill, revenue-sharing, or a resolution to terminate the war in Vietnam. Measured, however crudely, in resources expended—number of Congressmen intensely involved, interest-group activity, news-media attention—the Political Broadcast Act must be included among those important national bills that nevertheless do not quite achieve absolutely top priority on the legislative agenda.

Further evidence for this assessment comes from the White House itself. Despite a widely shared concern about the scope of the problem among both Democratic and Republican Congressional leaders, President Nixon made no effort in 1969 to propose an appropriate solution. Perhaps he was content with the status quo, a climate in which the GOP was raising twice as much money for its candidates as were the Democrats. Or perhaps other legislative issues—tax reform, social security amendments, the Haynsworth and Carswell Supreme Court appointment controversies, Voting Rights extension, welfare reform— led to a downgrading of campaign finance reform in the tough question of legislative priorities that every President is called upon to make. In any event, it was left to a relatively small, essentially nonlegislative interest group, the National Committee for an Effective Congress, to launch an initial draft of political broadcast legislation. Not until the late fall of 1969 did their two principal staff associates, Russell Hemenway and Susan King, secure enough Senate sponsors to generate hearings before Senator Pastore's Communications Subcommittee. The counterpart House subcommittee, under the direction of Massachusetts Representative Torbert Macdonald, did not get around to holding hearings until fully nine months later, and then only after the Senate had passed a drastically altered version of the original NCEC bill.

Throughout most of its legislative history, S.3637 was typical of a special kind of national legislation, that which is relatively noncontroversial and generally gains bipartisan support. Interest-group involvement, save for NCEC, was minimal until the time of the attempt to override the Presidential veto. And as Bauer, de Sola Pool, and Dexter, among others, have demonstrated, the relatively low level of lobbying activity was not so unusual either.

In several important ways, however, the legislative fight over the Political Broadcast Act of 1970 was not typical. In recent decades, most major legislation receives its impetus, if not its origins, from being included as part of the President's legislative program.[1] This is not to endorse an overworked cliche—"the President proposes, Congress disposes." In fact, both branches are inextricably involved in both processes. And more often than conventional wisdom would have us believe, the roots of legislation extend back to sources external to the executive and legislative branches. Such was the case with the NCEC-proposed legislation.

What sets this legislation apart much more decisively, of course, is that it brought on a Presidential veto. President Nixon had used this heaviest gun in his legislative arsenal only nine times throughout the 91st Congress. The gingerly way he went about promulgating his veto message did not succeed in eliminating several of the consequences he most feared—unfavorable press reactions to the veto and an eventual attempt by the originating legislative body, the Senate, to override it. Minority Leader Hugh Scott, by promising new and more comprehensive legislation in the next Congress, was able to defuse Democratic arguments calling for passage in the 91st Congress. Intervention of the November, 1970, Congressional elections had, in the meantime, deprived the legislation of much of its required momentum. Why not wait until a new Congress to take a crack at more comprehensive legislation, as Scott and others urged.

Underlying the final debate of the veto as well as each of the prior stages through which the bill had passed was a frequently unspoken but nevertheless fundamental difference of viewpoint on appropriate campaign finance reform. By and large, Democrats favored *restrictions on expenditures* to put them in a more competitive position with prospective Republican opponents. GOP members, in contrast, typically argued for *disclosure*, both of contributions and expenditures, as the best and most realistic means of control. Resolution of this underlying partisan difference would be crucial if campaign finance

[1] Lawrence Chamberlain, *The President, Congress and Legislation* (New York: Columbia University Press, 1946).

and political broadcast legislation were to have a chance of passage in future Congresses.[2]

THE AMERICAN POLITICAL SYSTEM

No single case study can ever begin to reflect all of the rich nuances and variations characteristic of the Congressional legislative process. Furthermore, the legislative arena is only one of many settings where public policy solutions are hammered out. Still, a case study as central to American governing processes as this one—involving partisan decisions about how political candidates spend money as well as touching on ethical considerations about our political and electoral system; and touching on an array of interest groups including most of the broadcasting industry, key Congressmen, committee staffs in both houses, White House personnel, and ultimately, the President and his exercise of a veto—is bound to reveal a great deal about the weaknesses and strengths of our political institutions.

One of the basic questions this case study raises is whether or not the shortcomings can be laid to the institutions or to the *men* who serve within them. The eighteenth-century English poet Alexander Pope put the question rather well (and answered it for himself, at least) when he commented,

> For forms of government
> let fools contest;
> Whate'er is best administer'd
> is best.

This is a tempting solution; in effect, to argue that if the right man were in office, we wouldn't have the problem. For example, one could maintain that if only the House Democratic leadership had pushed more aggressively on campaign finance reform, then the bill might have originated in the House, and an override would have been achieved more readily in the House. And so on. Perhaps.

Granted that who the man is in office does make a difference; if it were not so, most elections would be meaningless. Granted that Congress could stand considerable "ventilation" through some retirements, forced or otherwise; still, the institutions themselves—their organization, traditions, and methods of operation—require continual examination but not necessarily destruction. Only after careful in-depth study are intelligent and plausible reforms likely to be suggested, let alone

[2] For further developments in the first session of the 92d Congress, see the Epilogue.

adopted. In short, solutions are most likely to be a product of good people elected to office and viable institutions open to change.

One weakness of our political system highlighted by this case study is its slowness to react to change. Our leaders and the institutions within which they work have not proved especially effective at anticipating problems and working them through or resolving them in advance. Instead, we seem capable of reacting to problems only after we are in the middle of muddling through them. The crises that have plagued our country in the 1960's—urban decay, racial unrest, environmental pollution, drugs and crime, the war in Vietnam—all seem to be cases in point. Fortunately, campaign finance had not yet reached the intensity or the magnitude of these crises before some people began to act. But, the problems are real and increasing, as the 1970 election campaigns, primary and general, highlighted still further.

Paradoxically, this inability to anticipate also suggests a partially offsetting strength: Government is not likely to intervene unless the need is widely felt and strongly articulated. Public opinion has been turned against too much spending and increasing tendencies for candidates to be merchandized like automobiles, and that opinion is spreading. Hence, comprehensive campaign finance reform may, in fact, come about sooner than this study, ending as it does on defeat, might seem to presage.

Epilogue

Legislation unquestionably generates legislation. Every statute may be said to have a long lineage of statutes behind it; and whether that lineage be honorable or of ill repute is as much a question as to each individual statute as it can be with regard to the ancestry of each individual legislator. Every statute in its turn has a numerous progeny, and only time and opportunity can decide whether its offspring will bring it honor or shame. Once begin the dance of legislation, and you must struggle through its mazes as best you can to its breathless end—if any end there be.

—Woodrow Wilson, *Congressional Government* (1885)

"The Political Broadcast Act of 1970—that was nothing more than the opening bid in a poker game—since then the stakes have gone up and up." The Senate staff member who made this observation came as close as anyone could to an appropriate analogy for the escalation of forces that focused on electoral reform in the 92d Congress (1971–72). With the death of the 1970 act, many more players became involved; investments of time, energy, and other resources multiplied. Ultimately, the form that federal elections would take, the importance that money would have, even the likely outcome of the Presidential elections of 1972 and 1976 and the viability of the two-party system seemed to hang in the balance.

Still, in a most critical sense, what happened or failed to happen in 1971–72 was built upon the issues developed before and during 1970. Without President Nixon's veto of S.3637, without Senate Minority Leader Hugh Scott's promise of more comprehensive legislation, without the substantial groundwork laid in the 91st Congress by Senator John Pastore and Representative Torbert Macdonald, the considerable advances of the 92d Congress could hardly have been initiated, let alone achieved.

Almost no legislation of substantial scope and impact ever begins and passes in a single Congress. Working majorities must be secured in each of a series of potential stumbling blocks—initially, in House or Senate subcommittees and full committees. Should a bill be approved on the floor of one house, major hurdles may still lie ahead—within the appropriate subcommittee and full committee and, during floor consideration, in the other body. Intense activity by organized minorities may still derail legislation either by generating adverse action or by leading to no action on the part of the House Committee on Rules, or by evoking the threat (or actual use) of a filibuster in the Senate. Even when a bill passes both chambers in only slightly different form, unless one house is willing to accede to the other, the legislation must go to conference. Only after a conference report is adopted by both houses will the act be sent to the President for his approval, acquiescence, or rejection.

The Political Broadcast Act of 1970 made its way through all legislative stages only to be vetoed by the President. Nonetheless, in the process of surmounting each hurdle, most of the principal actors were sufficiently encouraged to try again. Their involvement, together with the onrush of the 1972 Presidential election, propelled them to commit even greater resources toward major electoral and campaign finance reform in 1971.

THE SENATE INITIATES

Although numerous proposals calling for comprehensive campaign finance reform were introduced by both House and Senate members in the early months of the new Congress, it was the Senate Communications Subcommittee that seized the initiative in 1971—as it had in 1969. In large part this reflected the character and commitment of Senator John Pastore, the able, aggressive chairman of its Communications Subcommittee. But other forces were at work as well: a strong bipartisan groundswell of support from both the Majority and the Minority leaders and from other Senators. Early Senate hearings and prompt floor consideration were also in accord with the strategy of the previous year, which was fully endorsed by the National Committee for an Effective Congress: Almost all the proponents, including several House activists, believed that a stronger, more comprehensive measure would be achieved if first passed in the Senate and only later considered in the House of Representatives. By and large, this strategy was to prove its worth.

On January 25, 1971, Senator Mike Gravel (D., Alas.) submitted the first comprehensive election reform bill in the 92d Congress. It was promptly designated S.1. Several days later, Senate Majority Leader Mike Mansfield (D., Mont.) introduced S.382, for himself, Senator Pastore, and Senator Howard W. Cannon (D., Nev.). This bill was to become the prime vehicle for electoral campaign reform, although in February Minority Leader Hugh Scott (R., Pa.), living up to the promise he had made during the debate on President Nixon's veto of S.3637, submitted still another comprehensive bill, S.956.

For the participants promoting electoral and campaign finance reform, critical and complicated questions had to be faced. From the beginning, they had to calculate just how comprehensive the legislation could be if it were still to get passed. At every stage, the question "how much will the traffic bear?" would be with them. Immensely complicating their calculations was the problem of multiple committee jurisdiction, which they faced in both the House and the Senate. One strategy was to narrow the focus to political broadcasting and to limits on television and radio broadcast spending (as NCEC had initially urged in 1969) which would put the matter clearly within the jurisdiction of the Senate and House Commerce Committees. But President Nixon had vetoed the 1970 bill at least in part because it was not comprehensive enough. Should the scope be increased to include related aspects of electoral reform, such as the reporting of expenditures, ceilings on contributions, and the like, the legislation would fall within jurisdictions claimed by the Senate Rules and Administration Committee and the House Administration Committee. But what was potentially the most politically explosive matter was the whole question of federal contributions to candidates through tax credits or deductions for contributions—inclusion of such provisions would immediately involve the Senate Finance Committee and the House Ways and Means Committee. At first impression, it might seem that the more committees that became involved, and the more powerful the chairmen who took an active role, the better the chances for floor passage. It seems more probable, however, that in passing controversial legislation, as in writing books or preparing broth, multiple chairmen, authors, or cooks may lead to a greatly watered-down product or to no product at all.

Senate proponents of electoral reform initially resolved the problem of multiple committee jurisdiction through a simple device. On February 11, 1971, they secured a unanimous-consent request on the Senate floor, which made it possible for all bills dealing with electoral reform to be simultaneously referred to the three Senate committees with overlapping jurisdiction—Rules and Administration, Finance, and Commerce.

Senator Pastore began hearings before the Commerce Committee's

Subcommittee on Communications the first week in March, 1971. Of approximately thirty witnesses who appeared before his group, many were familiar faces from the 1969 hearings—Dean Burch, FCC chairman; the presidents of the three major television networks; Joseph A. Califano, general counsel to the Democratic National Committee; Russell Hemenway, NCEC National Director; Senator Robert Dole (R., Kan.), chairman of the Republican National Committee; and a number of other Senators.

Hearings had been concluded when President Nixon, appearing on ABC-TV on March 22, seemed to reverse his position on a television expenditure ceiling:

> We do favor a limitation on expenses. There is no question about that. The point is how can we have one which will do two things: One, it must be comprehensive, and the other point that I should make is that it must not give an advantage to incumbents over challengers.[1]

In response to the President's statement, and at the request of several Republican Senators, the Subcommittee on Communications reconvened to hear several additional witnesses on March 31 and April 1, 1971. Richard D. Kleindienst, the Deputy Attorney General, testified in favor of a complete repeal of Section 315(a), not just one limited to Presidential and Vice-Presidential candidates. He also endorsed the President's statement on spending limitations, provided such limitations could be extended to other media as well as to broadcasting. Finally, the Deputy Attornel General came out in favor of full disclosure and complete reporting of campaign contributions.

The Nixon Administration's endorsement of many of the key provisions of S.382, when combined with Democratic sponsorship of the legislation, cleared the way for prompt and relatively bloodless Commerce Committee approval. On April 23, 1971, the full committee reported out what came to be called the "Federal Election Campaign Act of 1971."

Two months later, on June 21, the Senate Committee on Rules and Administration brought S.382 closer to the views of the Nixon Administration. The Commerce Committee had adopted a limit of five cents per eligible voter for political broadcast advertising, and a limit of five cents per eligible voter for all other media. By a 4-to-3 party-line vote (two Democratic Senators were absent), the Rules and Administration Committee raised the television and radio allowance for Presidential candidates to ten cents per eligible voter. Instead of a limit of $6.9 million, each Presidential candidate could spend up to $13.9 million on electronic media, providing he reduced newspaper and billboard advertising by comparable amounts. The stage was now set for a pro-

---

[1] Transcript of "White House Conversation: The President and Howard K. Smith," ABC-TV, March 22, 1971, p. 16. (Mimeographed.)

tracted floor fight over this and other controversial provisions of S.382.[2]

Formal Senate debate on S.382 got under way on August 2, 1971. On August 3, the Senate approved two Administration-proposed modifications and compromised on a third. First, the Senate created an independent electoral commission to oversee the new campaign spending requirements; and, second, extended the repeal of the equal time requirements to House and Senate elections as well as to Presidential races. (Subsequently, both amendments were to be stricken in House debate.) Finally, and most important to the bill's chances for passage and Presidential approval, a bipartisan compromise was achieved on the ten-cents-per-eligible-voter spending limitation. The compromise, worked out by Pastore and Senator Marlow W. Cook (R., Ky.), would allow each candidate to split the dime on a six-to-four ratio, in whichever way he should decide. In other words, he could spend up to 60 per cent on electronic media or he could put the larger part into print medium. The NCEC National Director called this final provision "a good compromise," one that should smooth the way to greater bipartisan support for the campaign spending reform bill.

And smooth the way it did; on August 5, 1971, the Senate approved a much modified S.382 by a vote of 88-to-2. Only Arizona's two conservative Senators, Barry Goldwater and Paul Fannin, cast negative votes.

HOUSE ACTION ON CAMPAIGN FINANCE REFORM

House members were no less diligent than their Senate counterparts in efforts to launch major campaign finance reform. On February 25, 1971, John B. Anderson (R., Ill.), the chairman of the Republican Conference, and Morris K. Udall (D., Ariz.), a leading spokesman for young, change-oriented Democrats, introduced several bills on behalf of themselves and over sixty cosponsors. One of those cosponsors was Gerald Ford of Michigan, the House Minority Leader. Although Anderson, Udall, and Ford were later to play a major role in House floor debates on electoral reform legislation, their bills (and most of the main provisions) were to languish in committees on which none of them served.

---

[2] Senator Pastore and Senator Russell Long (La.), chairman of the Senate Finance Committee, met with Larry O'Brien, chairman of the Democratic National Committee, and a number of leading Democratic Presidential aspirants. They decided to work toward the public financing of Presidential campaigns at a later date, using another bill as a vehicle. Thus, it was no longer necessary to refer S.382 to the Finance Committee.

The two bills that were to become the basis of major House legislative action were not introduced until mid-May. Wayne Hays (D., Ohio), the chairman of the House Committee on Administration, introduced election reform legislation modeled after the campaign laws of his native state. Moderate-to-conservative in his beliefs, highly competent in behind-the-scenes and floor maneuvering, and one of the most feared debaters in the House, Mr. Hays was in no particular hurry to pass electoral reform legislation.

Representative Torbert Macdonald, the floor manager of the Political Broadcast Act of 1970, submitted an even more comprehensive bill in 1971, which was drafted to meet the objections raised in President Nixon's veto message. Macdonald's Subcommittee on Communications and Power began holding hearings the second week in June; the Subcommittee on Elections of the House Administration Committee then held hearings in late June and mid-July.

Neither the House Commerce Committee nor the House Administration Committee got around to reporting legislation to the House until mid-October. In part, both committees were waiting to see what the Senate would do with its legislative activity. Chairman Hays never appeared to be strongly committed to electoral reform. Chairman Harley Staggers (D., W. Va.) was not about to move rapidly on any legislation desired by the television networks, such as the repeal of Section 315(a): He was still smarting from a setback on the House floor when his colleagues rejected his motion to issue a contempt citation of CBS for that network's failure to cooperate with his Interstate and Foreign Commerce Committee. Thus, not until October 13, 1971, did the House Administration Committee report out its clean bill, H.R.11060. That same day, the Commerce Committee reported out its revised version of the Macdonald bill. In contrast to the near-unanimous approval received the previous year, the Commerce Committee split almost completely along partisan lines in 1971. The vote of 23-to-20 almost guaranteed a partisan fight when the Macdonald bill reached the floor. H.R.11060, which quickly became known as the Hays bill, had relatively smooth passage out of House Administration. The final vote was 20-to-4.

For a time, the House Administration Committee and the House Interstate and Foreign Commerce Committee seemed headed on a collision course; however, the House leadership, stimulated by the NCEC and other interested pressure groups, was able to bring disparate interests together and arrive at a compromise. Under the terms of the agreement, the Macdonald bill would be offered as Title I of the Hays bill, with the various titles of the House Administration bill to be renumbered, II through X. Agreement was also reached on allowing H.R.11280, a substitute bill identical to S.382 as it passed the Senate, to be offered as a substitute to the Macdonald and Hays bills during floor debate.

On October 28, 1971, the House Committee on Rules met in response to Speaker Albert's "emergency" request for a hearing on campaign finance reform legislation.[3] In addition to making it possible to offer the Macdonald bill as an amendment to the Hays bill, the fifteen-member Rules Committee also provided for the possibility of using the Senate bill as a substitute for the entire Hays bill. After extensive testimony from proponents of all three measures, the House Rules Committee unanimously approved a special order on all three bills one week later, November 4, 1971. The stage was thus set for one of the most complicated parliamentary debates in the history of the House of Representatives.[4]

It was not until November 18, 1971, that the House of Representatives took up the rule on H.R.11060. In part, the delay came about because the House had been busy with more pressing measures such as defense appropriations and foreign aid; in part, the leadership had not vigorously pressed for consideration of the campaign finance legislation. Some progress was made on the Thursday before the Thanksgiving recess—the rule was adopted by a voice vote and the two-hour general debate was concluded. Shortly after the Clerk's reading of the enactment clause, *"Be it enacted by the Senate and the House of Representatives of the United States of America in Congress assembled,"* the Committee of the Whole House rose and the House adjourned for the holiday recess.

Federal election reform was the leading item on the agenda issued by the House Majority Whip for the week beginning November 29, 1971. Although there were many items of contention during the two days of House debate on campaign finance reform, the key to successful passage lay in a decision by the reform forces to abandon attempts to repeal Section 315(a). By his veto message the previous October, the President had indicated his opposition to any legislation that limited application of the repeal to the Presidency alone. S.382, the 1971 Senate bill, had extended repeal of the equal-time provision not just

---

[3] By tradition, the House Rules Committee ceases to hold hearings on bills around October 1, or about a month before the end of the session. When the Speaker makes an "emergency" request, the chairman of the Rules Committee will usually cooperate.

[4] The complete scenario as provided under H.Res.694 (the special order from the Rules Committee) was as follows: (1) Consideration of the rule—one hour of debate; (2) general debate—two hours, divided between Mr. Hays (Administration) and Mr. Macdonald (Interstate and Foreign Commerce); (3) amendments to the Macdonald bill; (4) vote on the Macdonald bill; (5) amendments to the Senate substitute; (6) vote on the Senate substitute; (7) amendments to the Hays bill—if the Senate substitute failed; (8) votes on amendments approved in the Committee of the Whole—optional; (9) motion to recommit and final passage.

to the Presidency (as in the Political Broadcast Act of 1970), but also to Senate and House campaigns. In the House, once an amendment to remove House races from the repeal provision had failed, the reform forces (led by Democrat Morris K. Udall of Arizona and Republican John B. Anderson of Illinois) decided to scrap the entire repeal of Section 315(a) provision. The NCEC then joined AFL-CIO forces headed by Kenneth Young to persuade a key House Administration Committee member, Frank Thompson of New Jersey, to prevail upon Torbert Macdonald to go along with the compromise. Excluding repeal eventually resulted in a campaign reform bill that both Democrats and Republicans could live with.

After a number of amendments to the Senate substitute were adopted, including the insertion of the revised Macdonald bill, it was approved by voice vote. Chairman Hays supported the revised Senate substitute in lieu of his own bill. As he summed up his feelings about the legislation:

> We could make a partisan effort to defeat the substitute and go back through all this process with the [House Administration] Committee bill. It does not do everything we desire or would like to see done. But I think it is a start in the right direction and I am going to support the substitute.[5]

Minutes later, the House voted overwhelmingly in favor of the modified legislation, 373-to-23. The next stage would be reconciliation by a conference committee of Senate-House differences.

CONFERENCE COMMITTEE COMPROMISE

Conference committee activity on S.382, The Federal Election Campaign Act, differed from action on S.3637, The Political Broadcast Act, in two major respects. First, the task confronting the conferees was far more complicated. The 1971 measure ran eighty-five pages; its predecessor had run only five pages. A Conference Committee Print comparing the two texts of S.382 as passed by the Senate and the House listed over thirty provisions in disagreement. In contrast, the previous year's conferees had disagreed on just five provisions, and only one—the effective date language—caused any discord.

The second major difference was the involvement of two additional sets of conferees, senior members from the Senate Committee on Rules and Administration and the House Committee on House Administra-

---

[5] *Congressional Record* (daily edition), November 30, 1971, p. H.11509.

tion. As finally constituted, the Conference Committee on S.382 consisted of ten members from each house:

DEMOCRATS	REPUBLICANS

House Interstate and Foreign Commerce Committee

Staggers, W. Va.	Devine, Ohio
Macdonald, Mass.	Nelsen, Minn.
Van Deerlin, Cal.	

Senate Commerce Committee

Pastore, R.I.	Baker, Tenn.
Hart, Mich.	Cook, Ky.
Hartke, Ind.	Stevens, Alas.

House Administration

Hays, Ohio	Harvey, Mich.
Abbitt, Va.	Dickinson, Ala.
Gray, Ill.	

Senate Rules and Administration

Jordan, N.C.	Scott, Pa.
Cannon, Nev.	
Pell, R.I.	

House Commerce Committee conferees were restricted to negotiations on Titles I and II of the bill; House Administration conferees were responsible for the rest of the bill. Senate conferees were under no such restrictions. But whatever additional flexibility the Senate conferees enjoyed was probably offset by the special expertise that House conferees would bring to their sections of the bill.

The conferees met twice, on December 9 and 13—both times in H.328, a Committee on House Administration hearing room on the west front of the Capitol. Holding the conference committee meeting in one of Chairman Hays's House Administration Committee hearing rooms was an attempt to placate Hays, who had privately expressed little concern for the legislation.[6]

For a time it appeared that the conference might break down over the language dealing with Section 315(a). Senator Pastore, most of the Senate conferees, and the broadcasting industry all favored the Senate version. Minority Leader Scott circulated a note to his fellow Republicans during the conference indicating President Nixon's position on Section 315(a): repeal equal time for all candidates (an unacceptable position for the House) or for none at all. House conferees nonetheless

[6] The inner workings of the conference committee were admirably detailed by Don Oberdorfer, "Chronicle of Compromise," *The Washington Post,* December 26, 1971.

remained adamant in their opposition to total repeal. As Senator Pastore later related in his defense of the conference report on the Senate floor: "We were . . . given the ultimatum that if we insisted on the equal-time provision we could forget a bill." In the end, the House got its way.[7]

On the other hand, the Senate version prevailed on the issue of "lowest unit rate" on broadcast charges. Thus, during the forty-five days preceding a primary election and the sixty days preceding a general election, broadcasters may charge a candidate no more than the lowest rate charged to anyone else in the same time period—morning, afternoon, or prime time.

Both houses can live with the compromise spending limitation of ten cents per vote times the resident population, eighteen years and older. Although federal candidates at any level can spend no more than six cents per eligible voter on broadcast costs, they can choose to spend all of it on nonbroadcast media (newspapers, magazines, outdoor advertising, and paid telephone campaigns).

By and large, the reporting and disclosure provisions of the bill are a substantial improvement on the unrealistic and unenforceable provisions of the old Corrupt Practices Act of 1925. Instead of creating a new Federal Election Commission (Senate version) to oversee the new regulations, reports are to be filed with the Clerk of the House, the Secretary of the Senate, and the Comptroller General. Only contributions "in excess of $100.00" (House version) need be reported and identified by full name and mailing address. Thus, a standard fundraising device—$100-a-plate dinner—can continue unreported except for an over-all "total sum raised" quarterly report filed by the candidate or committee.

On the afternoon of December 14, 1971, as Senate debate on the conference report began, Senator Pastore told his Senate colleagues:

> The conference report the Senate considers today, in my judgment, substantially reflects the will of the Senate when it passed S.382 last August.
>
> To be sure, not everything we of the Senate wished remains, but the same is true for the House. And that is the essence of compromise.[8]

Senator Peter H. Dominick (R., Colo.) at first attempted to block quick action on the conference report. The final vote was taken only after Dominick was assured that the House would delay final passage until the second session. The Senate approved the conference report by a

---

[7] *Congressional Record* (daily edition), December 14, 1971, p. S.21633. Senator Pastore may attempt to introduce a separate measure, omitting coverage of House races, early in the second session of the 92d Congress. The potential Democratic Presidential nominee would, of course, welcome the opportunity to debate an incumbent President.

[8] *Congressional Record* (daily edition), December 14, 1971, p. S.21633.

voice vote, with Dominick voicing the only audible "nay." Dominick, as chairman of the National Republican Senatorial Committee, had recently announced a fund-raising dinner to be held in Washington in early March. Had the legislation been quickly enacted and, thus, effective by early March, the contributors to the $1,000-a-plate dinner would have lost their anonymity.

S.382, the Federal Election Campaign Act, was to undergo one final delay. At Speaker Albert's Monday noon press conference on December 13, a reporter had asked: "If the conferees finish campaign spending today, will you bring up the bill tomorrow?" The Speaker replied, "Yes, if they want me to bring it up."

For all practical purposes, "they" in this case was one man, Chairman Hays of the Committee on House Administration. The next afternoon, at almost the same time as the Senate was approving S.382, Hays explained why he did not intend to call up the conference report during that session.

> Mr. Speaker, I do not intend to call this conference report for the simple reason that it affects every Member of this body. I think every Member of this body ought to have a chance to read it and understand what it is before they are called upon to vote on it.[9]

Then Hays announced that he did plan to call up the report "the first week when we come back, and I would notify every Member that I expect to ask for a roll-call vote on it at that time." Three days later, Congress adjourned. S.382, the Conference Report on Federal Election Reform, became the second item on the program of the House for the week beginning January 18, 1972.[10]

PRESIDENTIAL CAMPAIGN FINANCING: THE TAX CHECKOFF PLAN

The struggle over the Political Broadcast Act of 1970 involved high stakes, both financial and political. Had the bill been passed in time to apply to the midterm election of 1970, the lowest unit cost provision alone would have saved some Senate candidates thousands of dollars. It is impossible to calculate the political benefits repeal of Section 315(a) would have brought about in the 1972 Presidential campaign: Even if President Nixon refused to confront his Democratic opponent (on, for example, grounds of national security),

---

[9] *Congressional Record* (daily edition), December 14, 1971, p. H.12476.
[10] "Democratic Whip Notice Information," December 17, 1971, p. 1.

the Democratic candidate and possibly third-party candidates might have gained considerable mileage out of that refusal.

Both the political and the financial stakes increased almost geometrically in the hard-fought battles over key provisions of the Federal Election Campaign Act of 1972. First, no longer was the bill dealing with broadcast media alone. As the bill evolved, it grew to include newspapers, magazines, outdoor advertising (billboards), and the use of organized telephone campaigns to get out the vote. Second, the political impact of the disclosure and reporting sections could be substantial. By limiting the contributions that a candidate and his family could make, the possibility of wealthy families "buying elections" becomes much more remote.

But even these two measures pale in comparison to the highly politicized impact of the proposed Presidential election-campaign fund amendment. Initially intended as a part of the campaign finance bill, this provision was eventually to be attached by Senate Democrats as a rider to President Nixon's tax-cut bill, which came before Congress in late November, 1971. Designed to stimulate a sluggish economy, The Revenue Act of 1971 (H.R.10947) had received the President's highest legislative priority. The campaign financing plan, proposed by Senator Pastore and strongly endorsed by all of the leading contenders for the Democratic Presidential nomination, would have created a campaign fund of up to $20.4 million for each major party. After a number of Republican delaying tactics, the amendment passed the Senate on November 22 by a near party-line vote of 52-to-47.

How would the original tax checkoff plan have worked? Beginning with income tax returns for the calendar year 1971, each individual filing a return could have arranged—by checking the appropriate box on the return—for $1 of his tax liability ($2 for joint returns) to be set aside in a Presidential Election Campaign Fund. He would have the option of not checking the box at all, but should he decide to participate, he could earmark the money for either major party, for a minor party, or for a nonpartisan fund. Minor parties and even new parties could qualify for the fund, providing they had received more than 5 per cent of the total popular vote cast for the office of the President in the immediate past election or, in the case of new parties, their candidates gained the same percentage in the current election. Their benefit from the fund would be proportionate to the amount their candidates received compared to the total vote cast for the office of President.[11]

---

[11] For example, under the checkoff plan, if George Wallace were to run again as the candidate of the American Independent Party, he would have been eligible to receive up to $6.3 million in earmarked funds. Thus, one important consequence of the legislation, had it passed, would have been to support and perpetuate the existence of strong third parties.

The upper limit for each major party in the Presidential Election Campaign Fund—its entitlement—was established by multiplying fifteen cents by the resident voting population, eighteen years or older, in the year preceding the election. In 1971, for example, fifteen cents times an approximate 138 million resident population of voting age would have yielded almost $20.4 million for each party.

Major "strings" were attached, however. If the candidates of a major political party elected *public* financing, they could not accept other contributions, unless there were insufficient money in the fund to meet their entitlement. A minor party or new party could accept contributions from private sources, providing it agreed not to spend more in the general election than the entitlement of the major parties for that year. Strict reporting provisions were set forth; a Presidential Election Campaign Fund Advisory Board was created to assist the Comptroller General of the United States in overseeing the fund.

For the Democratic Party, still $9 million in debt from the 1968 election, the checkoff scheme looked like the answer to many of its problems.[12] Democratic candidates for the Presidency were having enough difficulty raising money for the numerous spring primaries of 1972. Where would the money for the Democratic nominee come from after the July convention?

At the urging of Andrew Biemiller, chief lobbyist for the AFL-CIO, and Senator Russell Long, Larry O'Brien—the canny, experienced chairman of the Democratic National Committee—was quick to see the merits of a tax checkoff plan to underwrite the costs of a Presidential election.[13] Working closely with Long, Pastore, and the House and Senate leadership, O'Brien also got endorsements from his party's leading Presidential contenders at a July 14, 1971, dinner meeting. The key to successful passage of this measure, as is true with all tax legislation, lay with the approval of Wilbur Mills (D., Ark.), the influential chairman of the House Ways and Means Committee. Mills, himself a potential Presidential nominee, gave his approval to O'Brien.

In late July, the Democratic Congressional leaders agreed to separate out provisions dealing with campaign contributions from the rest of the electoral reform bill. It did not seem to be sound legislative strategy to endanger the bipartisan spirit developing around S.382.

---

[12] So severe was the Democratic Party's fiscal problem in 1971 that the American Telephone & Telegraph Company threatened to withhold telephone service from the 1972 Democratic National Convention. Only if back debts were paid and a bond posted to cover prospective telephone costs in Miami would AT&T install and operate the extensive telephone system.

[13] The full story of the checkoff battle would require, at the least, the space of a book to tell in all its detail. For a brilliant beginning, see Don Oberdorfer's two-part analysis: "Political Poker With a $1 Bill" and "Checkmating and the Checkoff," *The Washington Post,* December 13–14, 1971.

Later in the session a tax checkoff plan would be attached to another significant Nixon bill, one he would find extremely difficult to veto.

On August 15, 1971, President Nixon took to national television to announce his bold new economic program. An essential element in it called for legislation to bring about major reductions in individual and corporate taxes, including repeal of the 7 per cent auto excise tax and restoration of investment credits for business. From the viewpoint of Democratic leaders, it appeared to be the ideal vehicle for attaching their as yet unrevealed tax credit checkoff plan.

As H.R.10947, The Revenue Act of 1971, passed the House in early October, it would have reduced taxes by more than $15 billion over a three-year period. After the Senate had worked its will, cuts had multiplied to $28 billion. And, in the process of Senate action, Pastore and Long, with all but four of their Senate Democratic colleagues joining them,[14] had successfully attached their public campaign finance plan to the tax reduction bill.

It was now up to Mills and his fellow House conferees as to whether this provision would remain in the bill. And it was up to President Nixon, his Cabinet, and his Congressional liaison staff to bring all the pressure they could muster to bear on the conferees, either directly or indirectly, working through the business and financial groups supporting the bill.

Mills appeared to be irrevocably locked into supporting the checkoff plan. Nixon was thus on the horns of a dilemma: He was adamantly against public financing of the 1972 election, but he desperately needed the tax reduction to stimulate the economy. And he needed the tax bill immediately and not next January or February.

On Monday, November 29, President Nixon arrived at his decision. Through Clark MacGregor, his principal Congressional liaison man, he announced he would veto the tax bill if the checkoff plan in its present form were included. He also attacked the Senate version of the tax cuts for being too generous and indicated he wished to see most of its added reductions rescinded. That same morning, House-Senate conferees under the chairmanship of Wilbur Mills began their deliberations.

All that week, the conferees were under almost constant fire from affected business and financial interests. Among the most active lobbyists were the heads of major automobile companies. Plans had been formulated to have auto dealers contact recent purchasers telling them that the Democratic checkoff plan was seriously endangering the $200 automobile excise tax rebate contained in the Revenue Act.

No one except Mills himself knows quite what happened in conference. As late as Wednesday, December 1, 1971, Mills was still confi-

---

[14] The four defectors were among the most senior conservative southerners: Eastland (Miss.), Ervin (N.C.), McClellan (Ark.), and Stennis (Miss.).

dent he could keep the Senate checkoff provision. If need be, he felt he could beat back developing floor opposition. On Thursday morning, however, Mills received a call from Senator Pastore, floor leader for the checkoff plan in the Senate. Out of the mutual misgivings of the two men under the threat of the Presidential veto, a compromise of sorts emerged. The Senate language would stay in. *But the effective date of implementation was changed to January 1, 1973.* Thus, the tax checkoff would have no impact on the 1972 election.

Mills's turnabout could have been the result of his sense of responsibility for the country's economic well-being. In defending the conference report, Mills stressed the need for economic stimulation, which, he said, "commands the highest priority in decision-making. The Administration," he continued, "has made it perfectly clear that it is opposed to the checkoff procedure and is willing to jettison the entire tax bill if it cannot have its way on this matter."[15]

His critics see it otherwise. For one: "It was a failure of nerve." For another: "Mills lost ground all around here, over in the Senate, and especially with Larry O'Brien." (Apparently, the Democratic National Chairman did not hear about the abandonment of the checkoff plan until after the conferees had acted.) Still, confrontations and even personal disappointments have a short half-life on Capitol Hill. Mills is still the chairman of the Ways and Means Committee; and the issue of public financing of Presidential elections is not dead.

President Nixon, of course, is not satisfied with merely postponing the effective date. Unless the law is changed, a sizable fund could be raised between 1973 and 1976. On December 10, 1971, when he signed the Revenue Act of 1971 into law, President Nixon repeated his opposition to the tax checkoff: "I have signed this Act today because I am confident that, with the time now allowed for reconsideration, this provision . . . will not become operative. I urge outright repeal."[16]

CAMPAIGN FINANCE REFORM IN THE 1970's

The preceding pages chronicle campaign finance reform in the late 1960's and early 1970's. Focusing mainly upon the story of S.3637, the Political Broadcast Act of 1970, we have tried to show how the forces behind electoral reform escalated, leading to the passage of major federal election campaign reform and the near pas-

[15] *Congressional Record* (daily edition), December 9, 1971, p. H.12117.
[16] Carroll Kilpatrick, "Nixon Signs Tax Relief Bill, Asks Checkoff Plan Change," *The Washington Post*, December 11, 1971.

sage of a tax-credit checkoff plan that might have drastically altered the outcome of the 1972 Presidential election.

How will S.382, the Federal Elections Campaign Act of 1972, affect candidates for public office in the 1970's? For Presidential, Senate, and House contests, the constraints appear to be broad and important: television broadcasting limits prohibiting a party from spending more than $8.4 million in 1972; limits on all other media, less than ten cents per resident voter in a given constituency; stronger reporting and disclosure provisions.

Of course, no legislation of this magnitude, especially legislation aimed at the very heart of the democratic electoral process, could hope to be perfect. Loopholes still exist, most notably the "in excess of $100 provision." And, in the main, this legislation—like S.3637 before it—is an "incumbent's" bill. Familiarity with the incumbent's name has largely been secured; it is he and not his opponent, who in the main reaps the benefit of the "bona-fide news broadcast" clause of Section 315 of the Communications Act of 1934.

Ironically, one of the core provisions of the 1970 act, the repeal of the "equal opportunities" provision of Section 315(a) for Presidential elections, was a victim in the struggle over S.382. The Senate voted to extend this repeal to House and Senate races as well as to Presidential contests. House members, more apprehensive of the discretion allowed any single broadcaster in their districts, refused to endorse the Senate provision. Although House Commerce Committee Democrats attempted to maintain the final language of S.3637, applicable only to Presidential races, they ran into too much floor opposition and had to scrap the provision. Nonetheless, Senate and House Democratic leaders might yet attempt to push through a "great debate" bill in the second session of the 92d Congress, if only in an effort to embarrass President Nixon.

In 1971, as in 1969–70, the National Committee for an Effective Congress played an instrumental role in bringing about campaign finance reform; however, as the stakes increased and many more forces became involved, their over-all impact inevitably lessened. Russell Hemenway and Susan King spent most of their time monitoring the ongoing legislation, serving as a communications clearinghouse, and goading the press to action and reaction. NCEC paid only marginal attention to the tax checkoff plan; the Democratic National Committee was the driving force behind that effort. At the height of the overlapping battles on the tax checkoff plan and the campaign reform bill in late November and early December, 1971, nearly the entire Washington community—the President, Cabinet, Congressional liaison staff, Congress, lobbyists, and journalists—was involved in trying to shape the final outcomes.

Undoubtedly, the overwhelming number of candidates running for federal office will try to conform to the new law. Almost as certain, some candidates, or perhaps a media owner, will try to bring litigation against one or more provisions of the law. The November, 1972, elections will provide evidence as to the viability and fairness of the new law, and, at the opening of the 93d Congress (1973–74), we can expect new or modified legislation directed at shortcomings of the act and/or problems as yet uncovered—for example, limitations on individual contributions.

In the ebb and flow of the legislative cycle, as in life, there is "a time to sow and a time to reap." Most Congressmen who had been mobilized to productivity in 1969 and 1970 found themselves reaping the harvest of campaign finance reform in 1971 and early 1972. Some would shift their interests and legislative drive to other fields. Still, campaign finance reform is a never-fulfilled endeavor. That there is "nothing new under the sun" seldom applies here.

APPENDIX

COMPARISON OF MAJOR POLITICAL BROADCAST BILLS, 91st CONGRESS (1969–70)

	S.2876/H.R.13721 Original NCEC Proposal	S.3637 Political Broadcast Act of 1970 as Passed by Senate	H.R.18434 Political Broadcast Act of 1970 as Passed by House
EFFECT ON EQUAL-TIME REQUIREMENT:	NONE		REPEAL OF EQUAL-TIME REQUIREMENT FOR CANDIDATES FOR PRESIDENT AND VICE-PRESIDENT*
EFFECT ON CANDIDATE SPENDING:	70–80 PER CENT DISCOUNTS FOR TV TIME		LOWEST UNIT CHARGE FOR TV TIME*
ELECTIONS TO WHICH APPLICABLE:	GENERAL ELECTIONS	GENERAL ELECTIONS	PRIMARY AND GENERAL ELECTIONS, EXCEPT PRESIDENTIAL PRIMARIES
APPLICABLE TO CANDIDATES FOR:	U.S. SENATOR U.S. REPRESENTATIVE	PRESIDENT VICE-PRESIDENT U.S. SENATOR U.S. REPRESENTATIVE	PRESIDENT VICE-PRESIDENT U.S. SENATOR U.S. REPRESENTATIVE GOVERNOR LIEUTENANT GOVERNOR
SPENDING LIMIT:	NONE	SEVEN-CENTS-PER-VOTE LIMIT FOR GENERAL ELECTIONS	SEVEN CENTS PER VOTE FOR GENERAL ELECTIONS. FOR PRIMARIES: ONE-HALF OF GENERAL ELECTION LIMIT

CANDIDATES' RIGHT TO PURCHASE TV TIME:	SENATE CANDIDATES: 120 one-minute spots at 70% discount, 30 minutes of program-length broadcast time at 80% discount HOUSE CANDIDATES: 60 one-minute spots at 70% discount, 30 minutes of program-length broadcast time at 80% discount STATIONS MUST MAKE PRIME TIME AVAILABLE TO CANDIDATES	STATIONS MUST MAKE PRIME TIME AVAILABLE TO CANDIDATES	NOT SPECIFIED
EFFECTIVE DATE:	180 DAYS FOLLOWING ENACTMENT	30 DAYS FOLLOWING ENACTMENT	JANUARY 1, 1971

* Senator Pastore's measure, as it was reported out of committee, incorporated only these provisions.

Index